Business Travel and Tourism

Business Travel and Tourism

John Swarbrooke and Susan Horner

Routledge
Taylor & Francis Group

LONDON AND NEW YORK

First published in 2001 by Butterworth-Heinemann

This edition Published 2011 by Routledge
2 Park Square, Milton Park, Abingdon, Oxfordshire OX14 4RN
711 Third Avenue, New York, NY 10017

First issued in hardback 2016

Routledge is an imprint of the Taylor and Francis Group, an informa business

© John Swarbrooke and Susan Horner 2001

British Library Cataloguing in Publication Data
Swarbrooke, John
    Business travel and tourism
    1. Tourist trade
    I. Title   II. Horner, Susan
    338.4′791

ISBN 13: 978-1-138-14272-5 (hbk)
ISBN 13: 978-0-7506-4392-4 (pbk)

Composition by Genesis Typesetting, Laser Quay, Rochester, Kent

Contents

Exhibits

Figures

Tables

Preface

This is a book which is nothing if not ambitious.

First, it attempts to offer a comprehensive overview of the diverse and fragmented world of business travel and tourism. It endeavours to do this at a time when there is still relatively little literature on any aspect of this subject. However, the authors believe that there is a need for a text which, albeit tentatively, tries to offer a holistic view of business travel and tourism given that most of its elements are interrelated. We cannot separate the time spent at a conference from the journey that took delegates there or the leisure activities they indulge in when the working day is over. Likewise, both practitioners and students need to have an understanding of both the design and development of convention centres and their marketing. The authors also believe it is important that the text covers both the supply and the demand side of business tourism, for both are clearly interdependent.

The second way in which this book is ambitious is in its commitment to cover both:

- the theoretical dimension of business travel and tourism, and a consideration of its social, economic and environmental consequences, *and*
- the practical dimension, in other words, how business tourism events are organized and what constitutes good practice in their management.

Thus, it is hoped that both students and practitioners will find something of value in this book. Students will gain a greater appreciation of what business tourism means in the real world. At the same time, practitioners will be given an opportunity to think about some of the wider issues involved in this exciting, relatively new and rapidly growing field of tourism.

The authors hope that this book can help overcome the 'them and us' barrier that too often exists between academics and industry. This barrier is a tragedy, for both have much to learn from each other.

For this reason, great efforts have been made by the authors to involve industry in this book in a variety of ways. It is to their great credit, that in spite of being busy people, everyone we have approached has been very co-operative, generous with their time, and enthusiastic about the book.

The book is also ambitious in another way, in that it endeavours to provide a learning resource for tutors by providing them not only with a text, but also with case studies, problems, exercises and discussion points. Hopefully these will also appeal to practitioners.

No one seems to deny that there is a need for a book about business travel and tourism. After all:

- this form of tourism involves, in general, a higher level of per head spending than any other type of tourism
- the business traveller is the core market for most airlines and hotel chains
- business tourism and the business tourist are serviced by their own infrastructure of specialist suppliers and marketing intermediaries which operate in parallel to that which supports leisure tourism
- business tourism is the major form of tourism in many urban destinations
- business tourism has its own unique physical facilities such as convention and exhibition centres.

Although relatively recent in origin, there is clear evidence that business travel and tourism is coming of age, both as a field of study and as an area requiring specialist management. In the last few years a number of business tourism courses and modules have been established, while a number of professional bodies now exist in the area of business tourism. Hopefully this book will be another small step towards business tourism gaining the recognition it deserves.

The book has been structured in, what we hope the reader will agree, is a logical manner.

In Part One, the authors define business travel and tourism and talk a little about its historical development. They identify the different types of business travel and tourism, from the individual business trip to major conventions and exhibitions to incentive travel packages, training courses to product launches. Chapters 3 and 4 then focus on the demand and supply side of the industry, respectively, while Chapter 5 looks at the role of the destination in business travel and tourism. Part One ends with two chapters on the macro-environment of business travel and tourism and its economic, social and environmental impacts.

Part Two concentrates on the development and management of business travel and tourism in terms of its physical and the human infrastructure, as well as the marketing of the business travel and tourism product.

The book then changes to the practical side of business travel and tourism, in Part Three. Chapter 11 looks at the key issues involved in the organization of business tourism events, with Chapter 12 offering examples of good practice. The final chapter in Part Three offers seven detailed interactive exercises to provide an opportunity for the reader to think about what is involved in organizing business tourism events, designing business tourism facilities or marketing business travel and tourism destinations. The aim throughout Part Three is to encourage good practice and professionalism.

Part Four looks at a range of challenges that the authors believe will face business travel and tourism in the future.

The penultimate part, Part Five, features a variety of detailed case studies, designed to illustrate points and issues covered in the text.

Part Six consists of a glossary of terms – a valuable explanation of some of the jargon used in this specialist field of tourism.

A full bibliography, provides a wide variety of relevant references for the reader who wishes to look deeper into issues raised in this book.

Throughout the book, copious use is made of examples drawn from around the world. Furthermore, each chapter concludes with discussion points and exercises to help readers deepen their understanding of the subject.

This book is aimed at both students and practitioners. The authors hope it is written in a style which will make it accessible and attractive to both audiences. It should be particularly useful for students on undergraduate and diploma courses in tourism.

However, it will, hopefully, also be of interest to professional conference organizers, incentive travel executives, destination marketers, and those involved in the planning of new conference and exhibition venues.

The book's appeal should be to those interested in business tourism wherever in the world they are based, from Brighton to Bangkok, Brisbane to Barcelona, Bogota to Bethlehem, Boston to Beirut, or Barbados to Bali.

We hope you enjoy reading this book and that you find it useful in some way. If it helps raise the profile of this largely undervalued and under-recognized sector of tourism, then writing it will have been time well spent.

John Swarbrooke and Susan Horner

Acknowledgements

The authors would like to thank all those who have helped with the writing of this book.

First, there are those kind people who helped us write the case studies in Part Five. Each of them is acknowledged individually at the end of each case study. We would also like to thank all those people who have provided useful information and encouragement with the writing of this book.

We also owe a great debt to Judy Mitchell, who deciphered our writing and typed the manuscript, as efficiently and cheerfully as ever.

We greatly appreciate all the support we have received from our parents, Pauline and Norman Horner, and Maureen and John Swarbrooke.

Finally, we must say 'thank you' to our son, John, who helped us to see that writing books is less important than collecting Pokémon cards, watching *Fawlty Towers* videos, playing football in the yard, collecting anything and everything, and going on holidays.

This book is dedicated to John.

Part One
The Context

These seven chapters set the scene for the later chapters and give the reader an overview, from a global perspective, of the world of business travel and tourism.

We begin by endeavouring to define business travel and tourism and recognize that it is an umbrella term that covers a variety of very different forms of business-related tourism.

In Chapter 2 we look at the historical development of business travel and tourism, noting that it has a long history but, also, that it has probably grown more in the last century than in the rest of recorded history.

The third chapter examines the market for business travel and tourism in terms of segmentation and the geographical pattern of demand, for example.

The supply side of business travel and tourism is considered next in terms both of producers and intermediaries, as well as professional bodies and the trade media.

Chapter 5 looks at the role of destinations and attempts to develop a typology of destinations from the point of view of business travel and tourism.

The penultimate chapter in this part of the book explains the macro-environment in which business travel and tourism organizations operate.

Chapter 7 describes the economic, social, and environmental impacts of business travel and tourism, distinguishing between those that are positive and those that are negative.

1 Introduction

As you are reading these words, tens of thousands of business travellers worldwide are beginning or ending their trips. At the same time, thousands of major conferences and exhibitions are taking place globally, while hundreds of incentive travel programmes are being enjoyed in your country.

In other words, business travel and tourism is big business. It employs millions of people around the world and is the core of the tourism market for many leading destinations.

Yet, this massive phenomenon of our age has, to date, received scant attention from governments, academics and researchers. Perhaps this apparent lack of attention is because business travel and tourism is notoriously very difficult to define and place within clearly identified boundaries.

What is business travel and tourism?

Rob Davidson, in his ground-breaking book on business tourism in 1994, attempted to define business tourism as follows:

> *Business tourism is concerned with people travelling for purposes which are related to their work. As such it represents one of the oldest forms of tourism, man having travelled for this purpose of trade since very early times. (Davidson, 1994)*

The terms 'business travel' and 'business tourism' are often used almost interchangeably but the authors feel there is a qualitative difference between them.

Business tourism is the broader term which encompasses all aspects of the experience of the business traveller. Furthermore, using the standard interpretation of the term 'tourism' or 'tourist' this term seems to focus on those business people who are true tourists, in other words, those who stay away from home for at least one night.

Business travel on the other hand seems to focus particularly on the movement of business travellers from place 'A' to place 'B'. It also seems to include those who make day trips for business purposes, and are therefore not true 'tourists' in the conventional meaning of the term.

However, it is clear that there is great overlap between these terms.

In this book the authors will tend to use what they see as the broadest term of 'business tourism' where space limitations prevent the use of 'business travel and tourism'.

A typology of business travel and tourism

The broad definition of business travel and tourism on page 3 is simple but it embraces a variety of different forms of business travel and tourism, some of which are illustrated in Figure 1.1. The typology in Figure 1.1 does not claim to be exhaustive, but it does cover most of the major forms of business travel and tourism.

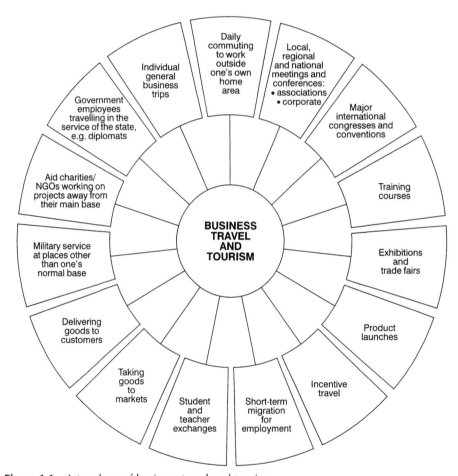

Figure 1.1   A typology of business travel and tourism

Each of the fifteen categories in Figure 1.1 has a number of subdivisions. For example, an individual general business trip could involve:

● a salesperson trying to sell his or her company's food product to a new customer
● a computer consultant visiting a client to sort out the client's problem
● the senior manager of a major multinational corporation visiting a branch factory
● a business person visiting a government department to apply for an export licence.

It is clear, therefore, that business travel and tourism is a diverse, complex field.

However, this book will focus on the main areas of meetings, conferences, conventions, exhibitions, training courses, product launches and incentive travel. We will therefore, now, define these terms, to ensure that we all understand what we are talking about.

Meetings, conferences and conventions

According to Davidson, a meeting is:

> *an organised event which brings people together to discuss a topic of shared interest. [It may] be commercial or non-commercial ... may be attended by 6, or many hundreds ... it may last from a few hours to a week ... [What makes] a meeting qualify as part of business tourism is that it engages some of the services of the tourism industry, and (is usually) held away from the premises of the organisation running it. (Davidson, 1994)*

The terms used to describe meetings tend to vary depending on the size of the event and where it is held. A small gathering is a meeting but a large meeting is usually called a conference in the UK, a convention in the USA and a congress in much of mainland Europe.

Exhibitions

Davidson defines exhibitions as:

> *presentations of products or services to an invited audience with the object of inducing a sale or informing the visitor ... Exhibitions are considered part of the business tourism industry because they stimulate travel (for both exhibitors and visitors). [They also] create a high level of demand for travel services, catering, and accommodation. (Davidson, 1994)*

Exhibitions may also be called trade fairs or expositions in different parts of the world.

Training courses

These are events where participants gather together at a specific time and place to receive information or to be helped to develop their skills. These can be 'internal' training courses where all the participants are employed by a single organization, or 'open' events where the training organization offers a programme which is available to all those who feel it might benefit them.

Product launches

These are the high-profile special events which many organizations now use to attract publicity for new products and services they are launching. They usually have a range of audiences including the media, retailers and consumers. They often take place over a short time period – as little as a few minutes – but often involve a very large budget.

Incentive travel

The key professional body, the Society of Incentive Travel Executives (SITE) defines this form of business tourism as follows:

> *Incentive Travel is a global* management tool that uses an *exceptional* travel experience to *motivate* and/or recognize participants for increased levels of *performance* in support of the organizational goals. (SITE, 1998)

The italic words are those identified by SITE as being elements of the definition.

Interestingly, incentive travel uses leisure tourism as a reward for good performance at work. It therefore bridges the divide between leisure tourism and business tourism. We will return to this distinction between the two types of tourism later in the chapter.

```
(i)    Frequency of travel:
                  Daily …….. Weekly …….. Monthly …….. Annually
                  Less than once a year …….. Once in a career ……..

(ii)   Distance of travel:
                  Local …….. Regional …….. National …….. International

(iii)  Mode of travel:        Public vs private transport
                  :           Single mode vs multimode, i.e. car-air-taxi

(iv)   Duration of trip or event:
                  Hours …….. Days …….. Weeks …….. Months ……..

(v)    Lead-in time to plan trip or event:
                  Hours …….. Days …….. Weeks …….. Months …….. Years

(vi)   Degree of compulsion on business traveller to take a trip:
                  No choice - obliged     Some choice of        Choice of whether
                  to travel whether       date but trip must be or not to take the
                  want to or not          taken at some time    trip at all

(vii)  Business travel as an element of one's occupation:
                  Business travel is an   Business travel as    Little or no
                  essential part of role, a reward for good     business travel
                  regardless of           performance           involved in the job
                  performance

(viii) Who makes the decision on the travel destination?
                  Individual    Employer  Client         Committee      Wholly
                  traveller               organization,  or association external
                                          e.g. company   with which     organization
                                          to whom one    traveller is   e.g. exhibition
                                          sells goods    associated     organizer

(ix)   Individual vs group travel

(x)    Travel to undertake a task vs travel to attend an event
```

Figure 1.2   Alternative typologies of business travel and tourism

Further typologies of business travel and tourism

In addition to the typology featured in Figure 1.1, there are other ways of looking at, and subdividing, business travel and tourism, based on various criteria. These would result in alternative typologies reflecting different factors. Some of these typologies are illustrated in Figure 1.2 and are just ten of the many other ways in which we could endeavour to subdivide business travel and tourism.

The structure of business travel and tourism

Figure 1.3 represents an attempt to model the structure of the types of business travel and tourism which are the core concern of this book. Of course, the reality is much more complex than this simple diagram suggests. For example, transport operators include:

● air, rail, ferry, cruise liner, taxi, bus, coach and rail operators
● transport operators offering transport to the destination
● transport operators operating transport networks within the destination.

It is also clear that there is a high degree of interdependency between the various players involved in business travel and tourism. For example, incentive travel agencies rely on the

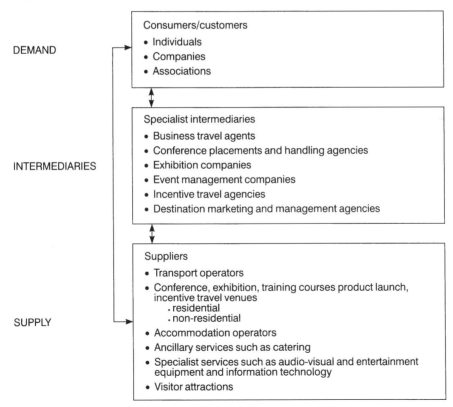

Figure 1.3   The structure of business travel and tourism
Source: after Horner and Swarbrooke (1996).

services of airlines, entertainment providers, hotels, restaurants and visitor attractions so that they can meet the needs of their clients.

The scale of business travel and tourism

By anyone's standards, work-related travel and tourism is big business. A few figures will serve to illustrate the global scale of business travel and tourism:

1 The *WorldWide Guide to Conference and Incentive Travel Facilities, 1999–2000* guide listed more than 6000 major venues worldwide. This was a clear underestimate as this guide focuses disproportionately on the UK.
2 It is estimated that in the late 1990s, business tourism contributed around £12 billion to the UK economy alone (Rogers, 1998).
3 In the mid-1990s, the German conference market amounted to DM43 billion (approximately £16 billion) at 1996 prices. This represented more than 1 per cent of the German gross national product (German Convention Bureaux, 1996).
4 Deloitte and Touche estimated that in 1996 the meetings, convention, exhibition and incentive travel market in the USA was worth around $83 billion (around £55 billion) at 1996 prices (Rogers, 1998).
5 A survey of international convention delegates in Australia in 1996 found that they spent an average of over £2000 each on their visit to the city (Sydney Convention and Visitors Bureau, 1997).
6 A single political party conference in the UK injects over £10 million to the destination economy over a period of just three or four days (Rogers, 1998).
7 The global incentive travel market is already worth more than $20 billion even though it is a relatively recent development (SITE, 1998).
8 The average cost of running an association conference in the USA was $130 000 (£85 000 approximately) in 1997–8, while convention and exhibition delegates spent an average of $696 (around £460) attending events which involved a three-night stay in 1997–8 (International Association of Convention and Visitor Bureaux, 1998).
9 The 1998 Association of British Travel Agents Conference in Marbella cost a total of £1.5 million to organize (*Conference and Incentive Travel*, 1998).
10 Over a seven-day period the launch of the Peugeot 206 car in Birmingham, UK, cost the company £1.6 million (*Conference and Incentive Travel*, 1998).
11 In France, towards the end of the 1990s, 750 million francs were spent expanding the Palais de Congrés in Paris (*Conference and Incentive Travel*, 1998).
12 Over 7300 organizations exhibited at the International Confex exhibition which took place in London in March 1999 (*Conference and Incentive Travel*, 1999).

It is clear therefore that business travel and tourism is a major economic phenomenon, around the world.

The benefits of business travel and tourism for destinations

Given the expenditure levels of business travellers noted in the previous section, it is not surprising that many destinations are keen to attract all forms of business tourism. Figure 1.4 summarizes the main benefits of business tourism for destinations.

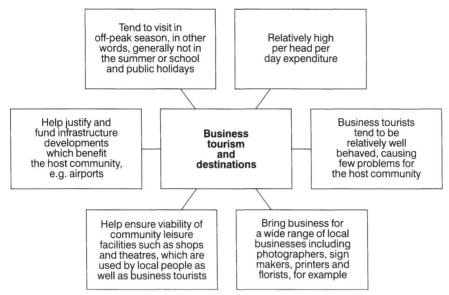

Figure 1.4   The main benefits of business tourism for destinations

There is also a belief that business tourism can lead to increased inward investment. While there is little empirical evidence to support this idea, the suggestion is that the business tourist who is an owner of an enterprise visits the destination as a business tourist, likes what he or she sees and decides to set up a new business or transfer their existing business to the destination.

It is not surprising therefore that business tourism has been used as a key point of the strategy of both:

● industrial cities, seeking to diversify and modernize their economies, such as Birmingham in the UK
● traditional coastal resorts which are keen to extend their season and attract higher spending business tourists, such as Brighton and Bournemouth in the UK.

Of course, business tourism can also bring problems for destinations in terms of congestion and the attraction of criminals who see the business tourists as easy, lucrative targets.

Serving the demanding business traveller can also force destinations to make large investments in infrastructure such as airports and convention centres, with no guarantee these will repay the investment.

Nevertheless, overall it appears that business tourism is a positive phenomenon, as far as destinations are concerned.

The relationship between business tourism and leisure tourism

There are numerous links between business tourism and leisure tourism in terms of both the supply side and the demand side.

As we can see from Figure 1.5, business tourism makes use of a lot of the same supply-side elements as leisure tourism, although it also needs additional services that a leisure tourist does not require.

Of course, business tourists often use the elements they share with leisure tourism in different ways to leisure tourists. For example, while leisure tourists visit a museum during normal opening hours, conference delegates probably visit in the evening for a private visit and reception with drinks and canapés.

```
┌─────────────────────────────────────────────────────────────────────┐
│  Business tourism                                                     │
│  ┌────────────────────────────────────────────────────────────────┐ │
│  │  Leisure tourism:                                                │ │
│  │  • Accommodation                                                 │ │
│  │  • Bars, cafés and restaurants                                   │ │
│  │  • Transport                                                     │ │
│  │  • Retail outlets                                                │ │
│  │  • Entertainment venues                                          │ │
│  │  • Visitor attractions                                           │ │
│  │  • Tourism information offices                                   │ │
│  │  • Bureaux de change                                             │ │
│  └────────────────────────────────────────────────────────────────┘ │
│  Leisure tourism +:                                                   │
│  • Convention and exhibition venues                                   │
│  • Audio-visual specialists and information technology facilities     │
│  • Secretarial services                                               │
└─────────────────────────────────────────────────────────────────────┘
```

Figure 1.5   The supply side: business tourism and leisure tourism

Business tourists also often pay more for the use of the same hotels at airports as used by the leisure traveller, because business travellers often need, or at least demand, better quality services or extra specialist facilities, compared to the leisure tourist.

However, in terms of the demand side, there are four ways in which the world of business tourism and leisure tourism overlap, as follows:

1 The business traveller usually becomes a leisure traveller once the working day is over.
2 Conferences often include a programme of leisure activities in between conference sessions for delegates.
3 Incentive travel, as we saw earlier, involves offering leisure travel as a reward for good performance at work.
4 Many business travellers are accompanied by their partners and/or children. These accompanying persons are to all intents and purposes leisure travellers for all or most of the duration of their trip.

On the other hand, there are real differences between leisure tourism and business tourism on the demand side. Some of these were identified in 1994 by Davidson, and a modified version of his model is illustrated in Table 1.1.

Table 1.1   Leisure tourism and business tourism

	Leisure tourism	*Business tourism*	*But . . .*
Who pays?	The tourist	Not the traveller but employer or association	self-employed business travellers pay for their own trips
Who decides on the destination?	The tourist	The organizer of the meeting/incentive trip/conference/ exhibition	organizers will often take into account delegates' wishes
When do trips take place?	During classic holiday periods and at weekends	All year round, Monday to Friday	July and August are avoided for major events
Lead time (period of time between booking and going on the trip)	Holidays usually booked a few months in advance: short breaks a few days	Some business trips must be made at very short notice	major conferences are booked many years in advance, and some holidays are now also booked a few hours before
Who travels?	Anyone with the necessary spare time and money	Those whose work requires them to travel, or who are members of associations	some people on business trips are accompanied by partners who are not on business
What kind of destinations are used?	All kinds – coastal, city, mountain and countryside sectors	Largely centred on towns and cities in industrialized countries	some meetings and training courses take place in remote rural locations and incentive destinations are much the same as for upmarket holidays

Source: adapted from Davidson (1994).

Problems of studying business travel and tourism

For those wishing to study this dynamic sector of tourism, there are two real problems. First, there is the lack of literature and reliable up-to-date statistics. Often what data there is has been collected on different bases in different countries, which makes comparison very difficult.

Second, there is the problem of terminology. There are national and cultural differences in the terms used within the business tourism industry. We hope that you will find our Glossary of Terms contained in Part Six of this book, useful.

Conclusion

We have seen that business travel and tourism is a complex sector of the modern tourism industry. It is clearly distinct from leisure tourism yet in a number of ways there are links between them. We have noted that because business tourism is a high-spending activity it is an attractive prospect for destinations. However, as we will see later in the book, it is also an activity which is difficult to manage and can bring costs as well as benefits.

Discussion points and essay questions

1 Select two of the types of business travel and tourism illustrated in Figure 1.1. Discuss the similarities and differences between these, as forms of business travel and tourism.
2 Evaluate the extent to which business travel and tourism is different from leisure tourism.
3 Critically evaluate the role that business tourism can play in the economy of industrial cities like Birmingham, UK.

Exercise

You should individually, or in a group, carry out a literature search of the business tourism field. Then try to answer the following questions:

1 How many texts and articles could you find?
2 Which sectors of business travel and tourism – as defined in Figure 1.1 – did they concentrate upon?
3 Which topics and subjects did they cover?
4 In what ways, if any, were you surprised by the results of your search?

2 The historical development of business travel and tourism

Business travel and tourism is certainly not a new phenomenon. People have been travelling because of their work for many centuries. However, some forms of business tourism, such as incentive travel, are modern inventions.

The problem with writing about the historical development of business travel and tourism is that it is a subject that has attracted very little attention from academics. There are, therefore, few sources to draw upon other than archive material relating to specific forms of business travel such as the Silk Route or the medieval trade fairs of Europe.

Nevertheless, understanding current business travel and tourism requires an appreciation of its origins and history, for some forms of business tourism today are simply the latest manifestations of age-old phenomena.

In Figure 2.1 we have attempted to offer a comprehensive, if highly generalized, view of the historical growth of business travel and tourism. This is clearly not based on hard data but is instead a generalized impression. Nevertheless, it makes the important point that business travel and tourism has grown more in the twentieth century than in all previous centuries, for a variety of reasons we will look at later in the chapter.

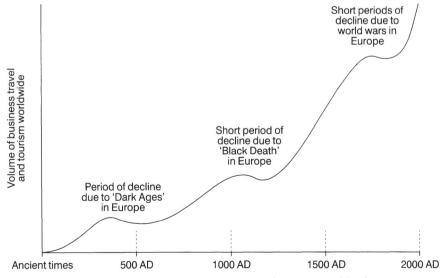

Figure 2.1 The historical growth of business travel and tourism worldwide

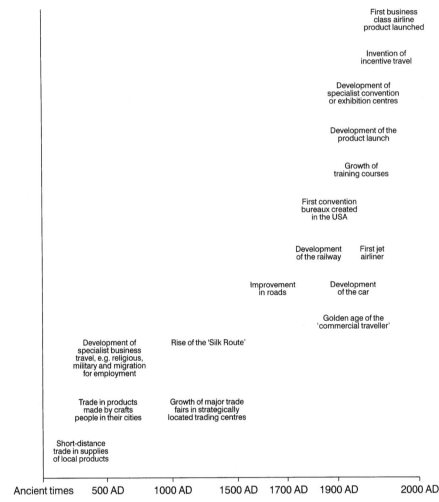

Figure 2.2   Major developments in the history of business travel and tourism

Figure 2.2 looks at some important developments in the historic development of business travel and tourism. We can also see that there have been some fluctuations in the volume of business travel during periods of war, instability or widespread disease.

While endeavouring to be a truly global picture, it is likely that Figure 2.2 reflects the situation in Europe and North America, more accurately than that in Africa and Asia, for example. Figure 2.2 suggests that business travel and tourism changed dramatically in the latter half of the twentieth century as new forms of business tourism developed and the supply side responded with new products and services.

The origins of business travel and tourism

Business travel and tourism originated with trade between communities. Once agriculture developed beyond the subsistence level in areas of Africa, Asia and Europe, thousands of years before Christ was born, communities began to trade agricultural products. This led to the growth of markets, and producers travelled sometimes hundreds of kilometres to take their produce to market.

Then urban settlements began to grow and develop. These were home to artisans producing a range of products including clothes, tools and decorative arts. These were traded with the surrounding countryside for foodstuffs. However, they were also marketed further afield, particularly if they were of high quality or were made of materials not available in other countries. Archaeological evidence shows us that this trading often took goods thousands of kilometres from where they were made.

The earliest business travellers were, therefore, artisans and small-scale traders.

The great empires of Egypt, Persia, Greece and Rome

The rise of great empires including those of Egypt, Persia, Greece and Rome, among others, further stimulated this growth of trade-based business travel.

For example, in the Roman Empire, well-established trade routes developed across the empire, transporting goods in all directions. The museums of Europe, the Middle East and North Africa are full of evidence of this fact. A local museum of the Roman period in the UK, for example, could well contain pottery made in Italy, olive stones from Spain, wine jars from Greece and precious stones from Asia and the Middle East.

However, once these empires fell, there was often a period of economic and political instability, and as ever such instability was seen as undesirable and tended to temporarily reduce the volume of business travel and tourism.

The medieval trade fairs

By the medieval period business travel for trade was well established and its infrastructure included a number of massive trade fairs in strategically located towns and cities. These were vital days in the calendar for medieval merchants. The fairs might last for several weeks during which time great use was made of local accommodation, eating and entertainment facilities. One of the most famous of these fairs was the Beaucaire trade fair on the Rhône river in Southern France, which attracted tens of thousands of visitors.

The Silk Route

In the Middle Ages, perhaps the greatest business travel route of all time, the Silk Route, reached its peak. Although named after one commodity, this route was a conduit for the transportation of a wide variety of goods from Asia to Europe and vice versa. And while the term Silk Route implies a single route, the fact is that there were a number of routes, starting and ending in different places.

The Silk Route was very important in two main ways:

1 It stimulated the growth of a sophisticated set of support systems for business travellers including accommodation and restaurants – the 'Caravanserai' – transport services such as camel traders and guides.

2 The route was also the way in which scientific inventions and ideas, as well as goods, moved from Asia to Europe and vice versa. It is this route which brought phenomena as diverse as gunpowder, new religions, knowledge of astronomy and advances in medicine to Europe and the Middle East, from Asia.

The Silk Route also created a network of major stopping points on the route which have tended to remain major trading cities ever since. For example, the role of Istanbul, a great trading centre, linking Asia and Europe, was established partly due to the Silk Route.

Other early forms of specialist business travel

Throughout history, there have been three highly specialist but important forms of specialist business travel, notably:

1 Priests of all religions, who have often had to travel with their employment, making pilgrimages to shrines.
2 Soldiers, particularly mercenaries, travelling to take part in battles or moving into newly occupied territory. Even more often they simply moved because they were ordered to move to a different garrison.
3 Workers migrating temporarily in connection with their trade. In many rural communities in France, for example, there was until recently a tradition of crafts people moving to cities to practise their trade for a few months every year when there was little demand for their services at home on the farms at certain times of the year.

Interestingly, while very ancient in origin, all three forms of business travel survive in many parts of the world.

The industrial age and business travel

Business travel and tourism in Europe grew dramatically between 1750 and 1900, for three main reasons:

1 The Industrial Revolution, which began in the UK, steadily spread to many other European countries. This movement increased the scale of production of industrial goods which then had to be marketed and transported. This stimulated a growth in business travel and tourism, particularly with the rise of the on-the-road salesperson, the commercial traveller.
2 Many European countries developed empires in Africa, the Middle East and Asia, and these colonies created a demand for business travel. Industrialists needed the raw materials from these countries while their populations also provided a market for the finished goods. Furthermore, administering the colonies created a demand for business travel for the 'army' of colonial administrators from the home country to the colony, and within the colony.

3 This period saw the improvement of roads in general in Europe which made business travel easier. However, more importantly, the railway was born. Rail travel was faster than road transport and allowed business travellers to make business trips to more distant cities without it costing too much in terms of time or money.

Because of these factors, in Europe at least, the late nineteenth century in particular was a major period of growth for international business travel and tourism.

The early twentieth century

As the twentieth century dawned, the next major development in business travel and tourism was taking place in the USA. Meetings have gone on since time immemorial, but the concept of the conference or convention was developed, at this time, in the USA.

Trade and scientific associations, together with the political parties, began to organize large-scale gatherings in the late nineteenth century. This activity gathered pace in the early decades of the twentieth century. Cities soon realized that hosting such events brought great economic benefits and convention bureaux began to appear to market cities as convention destinations. As Rogers (1998) notes, the first was established in Detroit in 1896, followed soon after by Cleveland (1904), Atlantic City (1908), Denver and St Louis (1909) and Louisville and Los Angeles (1910). The phenomenon of the convention bureau is now well established around the world.

The development of the private car in the first half of the twentieth century further stimulated the growth of domestic business travel, primarily in Europe and North America.

The explosion of business travel and tourism since 1950

While there is little hard data, it is clear that business travel and tourism has grown dramatically worldwide, since around 1950.

There are two types of reason for this growth:

- factors leading to a growth in demand
- positive changes on the supply side which have facilitated the growth of business travel and tourism.

We can also distinguish between the reasons for the growth of business travel and tourism as a whole, and the reasons why particular sectors of business tourism have grown.

Let us now look at these issues in a little more detail.

The growth of business travel and tourism as a whole

Business travel and tourism overall, has grown worldwide because of a number of factors relating to both the demand and supply sides.

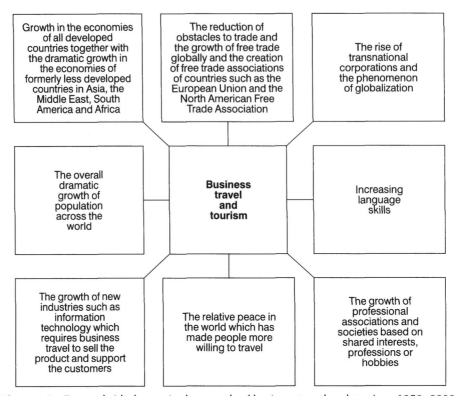

Figure 2.3 Demand-side factors in the growth of business travel and tourism, 1950–2000

Demand-related factors

Figure 2.3 illustrates the demand-side factors which stimulated the growth of business travel and tourism worldwide in the second half of the twentieth century.

Supply-related factors

Supply-side factors

The increase in business travel and tourism has only been possible because of developments on the supply side. These are illustrated in Figure 2.4.

Factors relating to the growth of particular types of business travel and tourism

Table 2.1 lists the factors that have stimulated the growth of some particular types of business tourism.

The changing geography of business travel and tourism

Over the ages, the geography of business travel and tourism has changed in a variety of ways. Having started in Asia, Africa and the Middle East in ancient times, the focus of

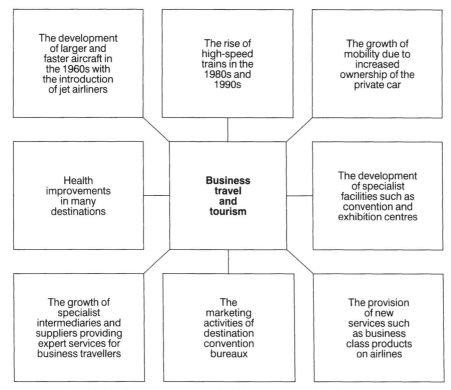

Figure 2.4 Supply-side factors in the growth of business travel and tourism, 1900–2000

Table 2.1 Factors stimulating the growth of selected types of business tourism

Type of business	Factor
Incentive travel	• Introduction of human resource management theories and practices based on stimulating performance at work by offering non-monetary rewards and tangible recognition of the contribution of key individuals • The rise of specialist incentive travel agencies which offer tailor-made incentive travel packages
Training courses	• The growth of new technologies which require staff to be trained • The emphasis on quality and service which requires training
Product launches	• The growing globalization of markets and the need to market products to more than one country • The growth of competition and the need for high-profile launches to raise awareness of new products very quickly
Education-related travel	• The growth of transnational co-operation in education • The increase in student exchanges • The growth of field visits in education at all levels

development between 1000 BC and AD 1900 was generally Europe. Then the USA increasingly began to make its impact felt, but in the late twentieth century the 'tiger economies' of South East Asia and the oil-rich states of the Middle East dominated developments in terms of both demand and supply. In spite of the economic problems in Asia in the late 1990s, Japanese and Taiwanese business travellers are now a major element in the global market, and Asian cities and hotel chains are widely regarded as the leaders in terms of quality and service. Will the future reinforce this trend, will Europe and the USA regain their previous dominance or will the future belong to the newly developed countries of South America or Africa?

The future of business travel and tourism

While we are debating which part of the world will lead the way in developing business travel and tourism in the future, some commentators are suggesting the future for business travel and tourism may be much less buoyant than in the recent past. They argue that after several decades of rapid growth business travel will be badly affected by the threat of substitution, that is, the replacement of business travel by the use of new information and communication technologies, such as video- and computer-conferencing as well as virtual reality. These, it is suggested, will reduce the overall demand for general business travel. Others dispute this, suggesting that the social and personal contact dimension of business travel will reduce this impact. Only time will tell who is right.

Conclusion

We have seen that business travel and tourism is a very old phenomenon but that it has grown, probably, more in the last fifty years than in all the previous centuries put together. It has also been seen that it is now a truly global industry, and that new special forms of business tourism have developed in the last few decades of the twentieth century. However, at the end of the chapter, we have noted that there are some doubts over the future of business travel and tourism.

Discussion points and essay questions

1 Discuss what you consider to be the three most important factors in the growth of business travel and tourism since 1950.
2 Discuss and explain the current geography of business travel and tourism demand.
3 What lessons can we learn from the history of business travel and tourism that might help accurately to predict its future?

Exercise

Select one of the following forms of business travel and tourism:

● conferences or conventions
● trade fairs and exhibitions
● individual business trips.

Produce a brief history of your chosen subject from its beginnings to the present day, highlighting changes in its nature and geography. You should note any problems you have in obtaining relevant information.

3 The demand side of business travel and tourism

Given the complexity of business travel and tourism, any attempt to seek to measure its volume is almost certainly doomed to failure. Data is collected on different bases in different countries and it can be a considerable time between the collection of data and its publication. Furthermore, much data is collected for commercial purposes and is never published.

There is also considerably more data available on conferences and meetings than on incentive travel or exhibitions, for example. This chapter, therefore, has a bias towards conferences and meetings, although it does endeavour to consider all types of business travel and tourism.

However, before we begin to look at the demand for business travel and tourism, in statistical terms, we need to say a few words about the nature of demand, in this field, in general.

First, we need to recognize that demand in business travel and tourism has two dimensions, namely, the customer and the consumer.

Customers and consumers

A major difference between business travel and leisure travel is the fact that in the former, there is often a clear distinction between the customer and the consumer. This phenomenon is illustrated in Table 3.1.

Table 3.1 The distinction between the customer and the consumer in business travel and tourism

Customer	Consumer
• Employers or sponsoring organizations who make decisions that employees will travel, or give permission for employees to travel	• Employees who actually travel and consume business travel and tourism services
• Employers or sponsoring organizations who usually pay the bill for the travel undertaken by employees or representatives	• Employees and representatives who travel but do not usually pay the bills themselves

While this is clearly a gross simplification of the situation it is still valid and helps explain one of the key perceived characteristics of the business travel and tourism market, namely the idea that business travel is less price elastic than leisure travel because, often, the business traveller him or herself is not paying the bill. However, this generalization does not apply to the self-employed, who constitute a significant proportion of the business travel and tourism market.

At the same time the customer and consumer can often be one and the same person or body. For example, the scientific committee of an international association conference will be both customer and consumer. They decide on the conference venue, pay to attend the event, and then attend and consume a range of travel and tourism services in so doing.

Motivators

The motivators for business travel will be different for the customers and consumers and perhaps in relation to different types of business travel. Let us look at some hypothetical examples to illustrate this point.

The managing director of a UK-based food company books a stand for the company at a trade fair in France. He wants to raise the profile of the company and increase sales in France, as cheaply as possible. He selects Mr 'A' to represent the company at this event because he speaks good French. Mr 'A' also has a taste for French food and wine and sees this as an ideal opportunity to indulge in both at the company's expense! He also sees it as an ideal opportunity to make contact with French companies to help him get a job in France. He spends lots of money but devotes little time to selling his own company's products.

Playtime Inc., a young computer games company decides to take staff on an incentive travel trip to help with team-building and to encourage staff to work harder in the future. The company does not explain this to the staff, who therefore think the trip is a reward for past efforts which, to be honest, have not been that great. The staff see this trip as a 'freebie', a perk, some fun at the company's expense. Not surprisingly, the trip is not a great success.

The head of the Philosophy School at Newton University gives permission for Dr Socrates to attend the International Symposium on German philosophers and their work, in Acapulco. This conference is part of Dr Socrates' staff development and is designed to help her keep up to date with developments in her field. It is also intended to give her an opportunity to network and raise the profile of the university's new MA in the Philosophical Aspects of Mobile Phone Use. Dr Socrates has other ideas, however, and prefers to spend most of the conference discussing the philosophy of coastal tourism, on the beach, with an attractive male philosopher from the University of Nether Hampton!

All three scenarios illustrate the potential for a gap in the motivators of customers and consumers in the different areas of business travel and tourism.

Those interested in motivators should note that there is also a section on this subject in Chapter 10.

The structure of demand

Business travel and tourism demand has a number of dimensions. Clearly, in its simplest sense it is the number of people travelling for business purposes in a particular region, country or worldwide.

However, this total demand can be subdivided in a number of ways, as can be seen from Figure 3.1.

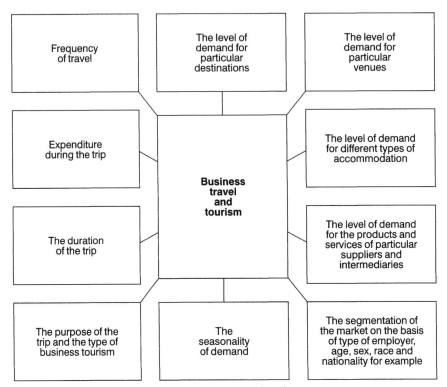

Figure 3.1   Dimensions of demand in business travel and tourism

The factors which influence business travel and tourism demand

Business travel and tourism demand is influenced by a broad range of factors found in both the generating region and the destination. These are summarized in Figure 3.2.

The factors outlined in Figure 3.2 tend to focus on the forces that will influence demand between a specific generating region and a particular destination. It also gives an indication of the factors that will influence demand overall in any particular generating region.

However, this is a highly generalized picture and specific factors will influence the demand for particular forms of business tourism such as incentive travel and training courses. Let us now look at how the market can be subdivided and segmented.

Segmentation

It is possible to segment the business travel market in many ways, as can be seen from Figure 3.3.

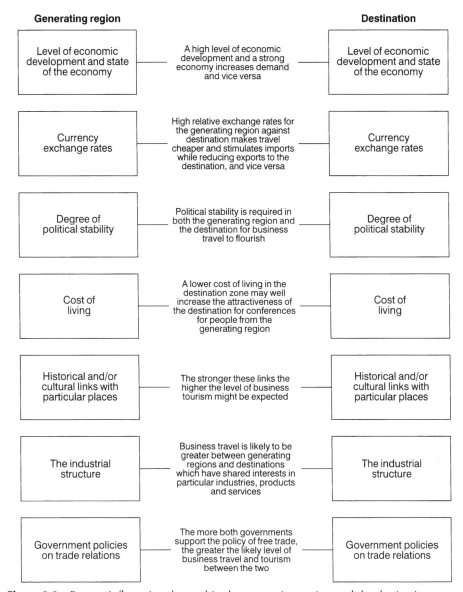

Generating region   **Destination**

| Level of economic development and state of the economy | A high level of economic development and a strong economy increases demand and vice versa | Level of economic development and state of the economy |

| Currency exchange rates | High relative exchange rates for the generating region against destination makes travel cheaper and stimulates imports while reducing exports to the destination, and vice versa | Currency exchange rates |

| Degree of political stability | Political stability is required in both the generating region and the destination for business travel to flourish | Degree of political stability |

| Cost of living | A lower cost of living in the destination zone may well increase the attractiveness of the destination for conferences for people from the generating region | Cost of living |

| Historical and/or cultural links with particular places | The stronger these links the higher the level of business tourism might be expected | Historical and/or cultural links with particular places |

| The industrial structure | Business travel is likely to be greater between generating regions and destinations which have shared interests in particular industries, products and services | The industrial structure |

| Government policies on trade relations | The more both governments support the policy of free trade, the greater the likely level of business travel and tourism between the two | Government policies on trade relations |

Figure 3.2   Factors influencing demand in the generating region and the destination

The growing segments in the market appear to be:

- business travellers from newly industrialized countries such as South Korea or Taiwan
- business travellers from Eastern Europe where political change has led to growth of business tourism
- female business travellers
- people taking incentive travel packages
- frequent travellers
- long-haul business travellers.

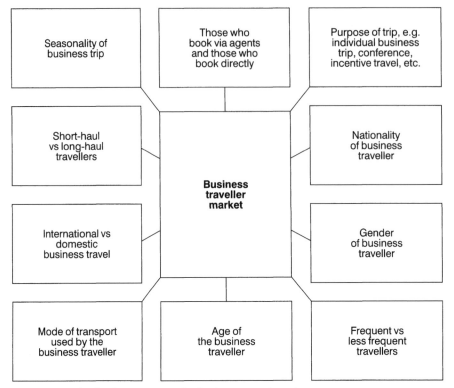

Seasonality of business trip	Those who book via agents and those who book directly	Purpose of trip, e.g. individual business trip, conference, incentive travel, etc.
Short-haul vs long-haul travellers	**Business traveller market**	Nationality of business traveller
International vs domestic business travel		Gender of business traveller
Mode of transport used by the business traveller	Age of the business traveller	Frequent vs less frequent travellers

Figure 3.3   Methods of segmenting the business travel market

The situation is constantly changing and the ways of segmenting the business travel market are likely to change, too, over time. Segmentation is also briefly discussed in Chapter 10.

There are three other issues we would like to consider at this stage:

● the nature of demand for different types of business travel and tourism
● the levels of business travel and tourism and different industries
● the question of seasonality of demand.

The nature of demand and different types of business travel and tourism

The nature of demand obviously differs between types of business tourism. While much of the data in this chapter relates to the meetings market, other types of business travel and tourism have very different market characteristics. This can be seen if we look, for example, at the exhibition market in Europe.

The exhibition market

In spring 2000 *Travel and Tourism Analyst* published a report on the European Exhibition and Trade Fair Market, based on data obtained from its markets by the European Major Exhibition Centres Association. These are the main findings of this survey:

1 It was suggested that Europe hosts more than 3000 major exhibitions and trade fairs every year.
2 In 1996 it was estimated that 50 million people visited exhibitions and trade fairs in Europe.
3 Expenditure by exhibitors and visitors to trade fairs was thought to be worth between £6 billion and £15 billion to the European economy.
4 The average size of a major exhibition in 1996 was 14 900 square metres compared with 18 000 square metres in 1990.
5 Most exhibitions lasted from three to nine days, with an average duration of from three days in London to nearly six in Hanover, in 1998.
6 More than 5 million visitors attended exhibitions and trade fairs in Paris in 1998.
7 Individual exhibition centres hosted events with an economic impact of nearly £1 billion.

Levels of business tourism demand and different industries

The level of demand for business travel varies dramatically between different industries. This is illustrated in Figure 3.4 in relation to the market for the services of conference and incentive travel agencies in the UK.

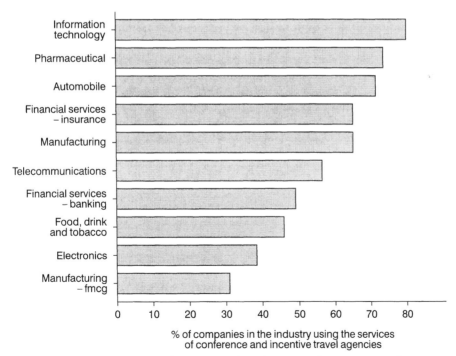

Figure 3.4 Level of demand for the services of conference and incentive travel agencies in the UK, between different industries
Source: Conference and Incentive Travel (February 2000).

Seasonality

It is often said that one of the advantages of business travel and tourism is that it is less seasonal than leisure tourism. While the season is longer and less pronounced than leisure tourism, business travel still does have an element of seasonality. In general it is an activity which takes place outside the summer holiday months, in the Northern Hemisphere at least, and is predominantly a Monday to Friday activity.

It is now time for us to move on to look at the geographical pattern of demand for business travel and tourism.

The geography of demand

By definition, business travel and tourism involves the movement of people so its pattern of demand will clearly have a strong geographical dimension. This is manifested in two ways:

1 A distinction, as with leisure travel, between domestic, inbound and outbound travel. The balance of these three types of demand will vary significantly between destinations.
2 Geographical differences, in terms of countries or regions of the world, from which a destination attracts the majority of its business travellers.

The global picture

It has been estimated that the value of the global business travel market in 1995 was approximately US$398 billion of which 47 per cent came from Europe and 30 per cent from the USA (WEFA/WITC, 1998).

The International Convention and Congress Association estimated that, in 1999, 56 per cent of international meetings took place in Europe, 15 per cent in Asia, 11 per cent in North America, 10 per cent in Australasia/Pacific, 6 per cent in Central/South America and 2 per cent in Africa (Spiller and Ladkin, 2000).

Within the world, there are, however, great variations in levels of demand for business travel and tourism. We will now look at these at three different levels:

- regions of the world, focusing on Europe and Asia
- different countries of the world
- different cities of the world.

Regions of the world

Here we will concentrate on the issue of demand in what are probably the two leading business tourism areas of the world, namely, Europe and Asia.

The European business travel market

O'Brien, in 1998, published an interesting paper on the situation in the European business travel market in 1997 and 1998, using a variety of sources. The main conclusions of his work were as follows:

1 Europe, in 1998 accounted for an estimated 47 per cent of all business trips (international and domestic) throughout the world.

2 The split of revenues from business travel in Europe in 1998 were estimated to be: Western Europe $180.2 billion; Eastern Europe $5.8 billion.

3 The top four business travel markets in Europe in terms of expenditure in 1998 were, in descending order of importance: France; Italy; Germany and the UK. France had a 17 per cent share of all European expenditure on business travel in 1998.

4 Business travel expenditure as a percentage of all travel expenditure varied from 13 per cent in Germany to 37 per cent in Turkey.

5 The highest proportion of outbound business travel in 1998 came from the UK market.

6 The market share in national outbound markets of the five leading agencies in business travel in European countries ranged from 15 per cent in Italy to 80 per cent in Norway.

7 European business travellers accounted for approximately 17 per cent of international business trips but contributed more than 80 per cent of the total revenues for major European airlines.

8 European business travellers accounted for 43 per cent of the bed nights in hotels worldwide.

9 Fewer than 15 per cent of European business travellers were under 35 years of age.

10 Less than 15 per cent of European business travellers worked for organizations with more than 550 employees.

11 Approximately 62 per cent of European business travellers made their reservations via a travel agent.

12 Only 24 per cent of those questioned had ever accessed the Internet for travel information.

13 Twenty per cent of UK companies were unable to estimate how much they spent on travel.

14 There was a growing interest amongst European business travellers in new forms of longer-stay accommodation such as serviced apartments.

15 It was generally agreed that business travel costs have risen significantly in recent years, particularly in terms of business class air fares.

These figures show that Europe is a major force in global business travel demand and that there are significant differences between the business travel market in different European countries.

The conference, meetings and incentives market in Asia

Until the late 1990s the booming 'tiger economies' of Asia were recording impressive increases in business travel – inbound, outbound and domestic – year on year.

Research reported in 1997 by Muqbil estimated that 10 000–20 000 meetings, incentive events, conferences and exhibitions (MICE) were taking place in Asia each year, involving as many as 14 million participants. Of these people it was thought around 80 per cent were attending exhibitions and trade shows. This flourishing MICE market was being fuelled by annual economic growth rates of up to 8 per cent per annum on average.

The leading destinations in the mid-1990s for hosting MICE events were, in order of importance:

1 Singapore.
2 Japan.
3 Thailand.
4 Hong Kong.
5 China.

The region was particularly successful at attracting both international events and incentive travel events.

Because of this growth, investment in new facilities and infrastructure took place all over the region. For example, in the late 1990s Hong Kong opened its new airport and unveiled its new conference and exhibition centre which offers over 25 000 square metres of exhibition space.

Confidence was high in the mid-1990s. The number of exhibitions held in Bangkok was expected to rise by 17 per cent between 1996 and 1999, for instance, and the Putra World Trade Centre in Malaysia targeted a 30 per cent increase in business between 1996 and 1997.

Muqbil, in *Travel and Tourism Analyst* in 1997, boldly predicted that: 'The confluence of economic progress, booming trade centres . . . as well as increased tourism are going to lead to sustained growth in the region's MICE industry' (Muqbil, 1997).

Then everything changed and the picture became more negative between 1997 and 1999, due to several factors, including:

● a severe economic crisis in most of the countries of South East Asia
● a serious reduction in the value of the currencies of many Asian countries such as Thailand and Malaysia
● political instability in Indonesia
● the 'smog' which affected large areas of the region in 1998
● the uncertainty surrounding the implications of the return of Hong Kong to China in 1997.

While one or two countries such as Singapore weathered the storm quite well, the economic crisis dealt a serious blow to most countries in the region. We can illustrate this point by looking at Indonesia.

While it is impossible in the statistics to separate leisure travel from business travel, it seems reasonable to assume that the fall in business travel to Indonesia from different markets fell at least as much as the general figures, between 1997 and 1998, illustrate in Table 3.2.

Demand for travel relating to business between the countries in the region, as well as with the rest of the world, fell. Airlines and hotels reduced their prices as the problems mounted. However, paradoxically, the weak currencies made Asia an attractive destination for incentive travel groups from other regions of the world.

Now that the economies of Asia are recovering we may well see them re-establish their strong position in the global business travel market.

Table 3.2 Falls in inbound tourism arrivals to Indonesia from selected countries, 1997–8

Country	Arrivals 1997	Arrivals 1998	Percentage change
Japan	706 942	469 409	−34
Australia	539 156	394 543	−27
Taiwan	404 929	281 959	−30
Netherlands	144 622	81 507	−44
USA	171 707	150 042	−13
Hong Kong	103 450	53 500	−48
Germany	185 976	141 314	−24

Source: *Travel and Tourism Intelligence Country Reports*, no. 1 (2000).

Differences in levels of inbound business tourism between countries

We noted earlier in this chapter that the volume of demand for business travel and tourism in any destination is influenced by a wide variety of factors, in both the destination itself and the generating countries. It is not surprising, therefore, that the demand for business travel to different countries varies dramatically in terms of:

● the number of inbound business travellers
● the balance between business travel demand and other forms of tourism.

These differences are illustrated in Table 3.3 which relates as far as possible to 1998, the latest year for which data was available at the time of writing (summer 2000).

Table 3.3 National differences in inbound business travel markets, 1998

Country	Number of inbound business travellers	Percentage share of all inbound tourism
Australia	430 300	10.3
Baltic States (Estonia, Latvia, Lithuania)	N/A	24.0
Botswana	112 273	14.7
Brazil	N/A	22.7
Canada	2 360 000	N/A
Chile[1]	173 000	9.5
Dominican Republic	69 192	3.2
Egypt	N/A	8.9
Germany	10 500 000	35.0
Israel	N/A	13.0
Hungary	N/A	10.0
Jamaica	58 000	7.3
Mexico[1]	711 000	4.6
Myanmar[1]	38 686	22.0
New Zealand	173 600	12.0
Uruguay	149 000	11.5

Note: [1] 1997 data.
Source: *Travel and Tourism Intelligence Country Reports* (1999 and 2000).

The geographical pattern of demand for different countries

Two examples will show the way in which there can be great variations in the geographical pattern of demand for business travel and tourism trips to different countries.

1 *The USA.* In 1998, 43 per cent of French visitors to the USA went on business compared with 37 per cent of Mexican visitors, 28 per cent of UK visitors, but only 16 per cent of Japanese visitors. The proportion of different national markets that were visiting the USA specifically to attend conventions ranged from 5 per cent from the UK to 15 per cent from Mexico and 19 per cent from Brazil (*Travel and Tourism Intelligence Country Reports*, no. 3, 1999).
2 *South Africa.* The percentage of tourists from different regions of the world visiting South Africa specifically for business purposes was, in 1997, as follows: The Middle East, 19.2 per cent; North America, 18.1 per cent; Asia, 6.7 per cent; Australasia, 12.9 per cent; Europe, 12.1 per cent; the rest of Africa, 11.3 per cent; Latin America, 8.7 per cent (*Travel and Tourism Intelligence Country Reports*, no. 2, 1999).

The conference market in an individual country: Great Britain

Let us continue this geographical survey of the world business travel and tourism market by looking in detail at one country, namely, Great Britain.

It is indicative of the paucity of data in this field that the latest figures available for the UK conference market, in summer 2000, relate primarily to 1998. They were published in January 2000 by Tom Costley in an *Insights* article based on the 1998 British Conference Market Trends Survey. The results of this survey are summarized in Table 3.4.

Table 3.4 Key findings from the British Conference Market Trends Survey, 1998

Number of conferences which took place in Great Britain in 1998	Estimated 685 900
Percentage change in number of conferences 1997–1998	+ 2%
Percentage of conferences taking place in urban hotels, 1998	60%
Percentage of conferences which were residential in 1998	26%
Average duration of residential conferences	2.37 days
Type of conferences	Corporate 73% Associations 14% Public sector 12% Others 1%
Average number of conferences held by each venue	160
Percentage of conferences booked via an agency	20%
Average revenue per delegate	£66
Revenue earned by British conference venues 1998	£2000 million
Percentage of conferences with more than 700 delegates 1998	8%
Percentage change in number of delegates per conference 1997–8	−17%
Economic impact of the largest conference held in Great Britain	£30 million

Source: Costley (2000).

The data in Table 3.4 show that the typical conference in Great Britain is actually small, non-residential and with a predominantly local, regional or perhaps national market. This is at odds with the common stereotype of people flying around the world to mega-conferences.

Individual cities and business travel and tourism

There are large differences between individual cities in terms of the proportion of their inbound tourism which is based upon business travel and tourism specifically. These differences are illustrated in Table 3.5.

Table 3.5   Differences between cities: proportion of all inbound tourism which is business travel and tourism, 1998

City	Percentage of all inbound tourist trips which are business travel and tourism related
Barcelona	35 (international visitors only)
Chicago	43 (international visitors only)
Copenhagen	39 (international visitors only)
Delhi	22 (international visitors only)
Geneva	70 (international visitors only)
Glasgow	18 (international visitors)
	27 (domestic visitors)
Hong Kong	32 (international visitors only)
London	21 (international visitors only)
Melbourne[1]	14 (international visitors only)
Montreal	17 (international visitors only)
Paris	18 (international visitors only)
Rome	11 (international visitors)
	31 (domestic visitors)
Singapore	16 (international visitors only)
Sydney	12 (international visitors only)
Toronto	21 (international visitors only)

Note: [1] 1997 data.
Source: *Travel and Tourism Intelligence Country Reports* (1999 and 2000).

The scale of convention business in different cities

Several thumbnail sketches of different cities will illustrate the variations between cities in terms of the scale of their convention business. All data is from *Travel and Tourism Intelligence Country Reports* in 1999 and 2000.

1 In 1998, New York welcomed more than 1 700 000 convention delegates.
2 Convention delegates generated 361 000 bed nights in Sydney in 1997.
3 In 1998, Barcelona welcomed 7002 meetings with a total of nearly 264 000 delegates. This represents an increase of over 250 per cent since 1990.

4 Toronto welcomed 898 000 delegates to conventions and trade shows in 1997.
5 In summer 2000 Toronto hosted one convention that alone attracted more than 50 000 delegates
6 The Acropolis Convention Centre in Nice attracted 340 000 visitors in 1999.
7 In 1999, Copenhagen hosted 94 major conventions.
8 In 1998, the Budapest Tour Centre was the venue for more than thirty events.
9 The Singapore International Exhibition and Convention Centre held a total of 706 events in 1996.
10 Around 2000 trade fairs and conventions are held each year in Paris generating an estimated £700 million in 1997.

Future projections of demand

As we saw from the example of Asia, forecasting future demand in business travel and tourism is fraught with problems and made very difficult by unforeseen circumstances. Nevertheless, attempts are always being made to forecast the future of demand in this sector.

O'Brien (1998) estimated that the European business travel market would grow, annually, by 3.7 per cent in real terms from US$186 billion in 1998 to US$380 billion by 2010. Whether this becomes reality will depend upon the way the European economy develops and the success or otherwise of the single European currency, the Euro. It will also depend on how the political and economic situation evolves in Eastern Europe.

Conclusion

In this chapter, we have been able to note that:

1 The business travel market is a complex and fragmented market which is constantly changing.
2 Europe currently dominates the global business travel market.
3 There are significant national differences in the nature of the business travel market.
4 Predicting the future of demand in business travel is difficulty and risky.

Nevertheless, overall, it seems that business travel and tourism is a buoyant, growing market across the world.

In the next chapter we will look at the supply side of business travel and tourism.

Discussion points and essay questions

1 Discuss the implications of the distinction between customers and consumers for business tourism organizations.
2 Evaluate the reasons which you think explain why Europe dominates the global business travel market.
3 Discuss the factors that will influence the future size and nature of business travel and tourism demand in Asia.

Exercise

Select one country of the world and produce a report concerning its domestic, inbound and outbound business travel markets. In your report you should note any difficulties you experience in obtaining suitable data.

4 The supply side of business travel and tourism

The supply side of business travel and tourism is a complex phenomenon because of the different types of business tourism, each with their own specific supply chain.

However, we can produce a generalized clarification that can divide the supply side into four overall categories, which are illustrated in Figure 4.1. We will look at each of the categories in a little more detail later in this chapter.

However, there are other ways of classifying the supply side. For example, we can divide the supply side into those organizations which operate in the destination zone, those which work principally within the generating region or market, and those found in the transit zone between these two, notably the transport industry.

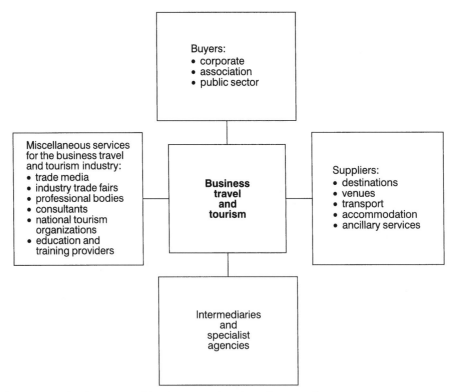

Figure 4.1 The four types of business travel and tourism supplier

We can also split the supply side into:

● compulsory supplies, those services which are required for all business travel, namely transport
● sectoral supplies, those services which are specific to particular business tourism sectors, such as exhibition venues for the exhibition sector
● optional supplies, services which may be used to enhance the product or experience but which are not an essential part of it such as bars and entertainment.

Let us now look at how the supply side varies between different types of business tourism.

The supply side and different types of business travel and tourism

Each type of business travel and tourism has its own specific supply network. This point is illustrated in Figures 4.2, 4.3, 4.4 and 4.5 which model the supply side in relation to four different types of business tourism.

Every business travel and tourism trip or event has a destination but the role of these destinations varies between types of business tourism. This issue will be explored further in Chapter 5.

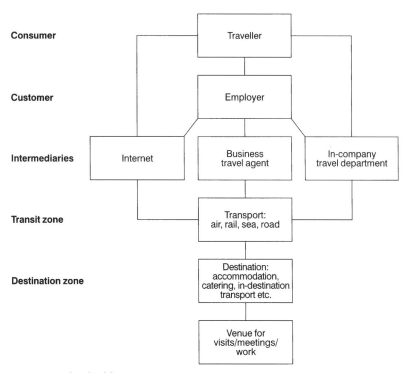

Figure 4.2   An individual business trip

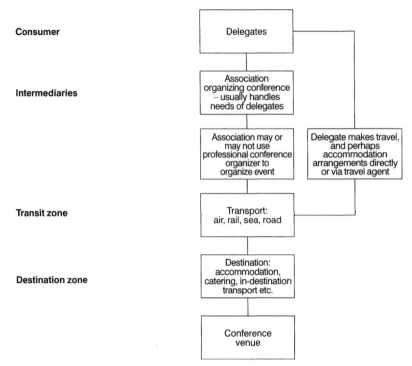

Figure 4.3   Delegates attending a professional association conference

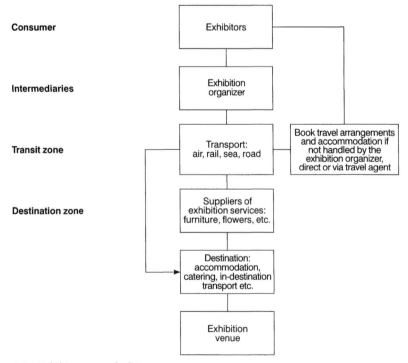

Figure 4.4   Exhibitor at trade fair

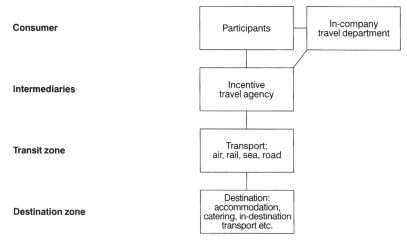

Figure 4.5 Participants in incentive travel trip

Buyers

As we saw in Figure 4.1 there are three types of buyer, namely corporate, association and public sector.

The *corporate buyer* is someone employed by a private sector enterprise. Buying business travel services can be the main or total role for an employee, or it may be an occasional task within a much broader job description.

The main industries which organize business tourism events include energy, medical, computing, engineering and financial services for example.

Research has shown that people involved in purchasing in the corporate sector can have a wide variety of different job titles and may have received little or no formal training in business travel and tourism.

It is clear that personal assistants and secretaries play a major role in buying business travel services in the corporate sector. Sales and marketing staff are also heavily involved in this activity.

In 1998 Rogers published the results of research carried out as part of the UK Conference Market Survey which throws further light on the corporate buyer in the UK.

Rogers noted that corporate buyers were particularly involved in organizing board meetings, annual general meetings, corporate hospitality, exhibitions, incentive travel, product launches, sales conferences, team-building activities and training courses.

This research covered organizations ranging from enterprises with less than ten staff to those with over 5000. Clearly, the way business travel is bought is likely to vary between small and large organizations.

The research quoted by Rogers also highlighted several other characteristics of corporate buyers:

1 The lead-in, or planning, time for many corporate events is measured in days and weeks rather than months or years.
2 Seventy-one per cent of corporate buyers would return to a venue if they were happy with it.

3 Fifty-five per cent of buyers said they would like to see a classification or grading system for venues.
4 More than 80 per cent of buyers were satisfied with the venue they had used most recently.
5 Corporate buyers made relatively little use of trade fairs and publications to obtain information.

Association buyers is a term that covers a multitude of different types of association. Rogers (1998) identifies six types:

- professional and trade associations whose members join because of their employment
- voluntary associations and societies whose members join to further an interest, belief, or hobby
- charities
- religious organizations
- political parties
- trade unions.

Most of these organizations are non-profit making but they normally have to cover their costs. They usually, therefore, have very clear budgets for business tourism events which they must not exceed.

Association buyers organize some of the largest conferences and these may have over 10 000 delegates attending, in the case of international annual conventions. Associations often employ someone specifically to organize events but they may also utilize volunteers. Decisions are often made by a committee.

When setting up conventions, associations have to take into account the needs of all their members. Many will endeavour to move their annual convention to different destinations each year to appeal to members who live in different areas.

Table 4.1   Characteristics of corporate and association buyers

Corporate buyers	Association buyers
Work for 'for profit' organizations	Usually employed by 'not for profit' organizations
Event decision-making process is often straightforward and rapid	Event decision-making process is complex and prolonged
Events have a relatively short lead-in time	Events often have a relatively long lead-in time
Buyers may organize a wide variety of events	Buyers often organize a limited number of events
Events often have fewer than a hundred delegates	Events often have hundreds, if not thousands, of delegates
Per head costs are usually relatively high as the company is paying	Per head costs are usually relatively low as delegates are often paying themselves
Events are organized year round	Most events take place in spring and autumn
Most events last two days or less	Major events last three or four days
Delegates' partners rarely attend	Delegates' partners frequently attend

Rogers distinguished between corporate and association buyers as can be seen from Table 4.1.

Public sector buyers – central and local government, and statutory agencies – are often operating on very tight budgets. The health and education sectors are two important public sector activities which are heavily involved in organizing business tourism events.

In general, public sector buyers are employees for whom buying business tourism services is only a minor part of their job.

Most events are organized by buyers but, increasingly, private companies, associations and public sector bodies, are using specialist intermediaries to plan and manage their event.

Intermediaries and specialist agencies

There are a number of types of specialist intermediary performing different roles in different sectors of business travel and tourism. These are listed in Table 4.2.

Table 4.2   Types of intermediaries in business travel and tourism

Type of agency	Role	Types of business tourism
Professional conference organizer	Organizing a whole meeting/ conference or aspects of it such as venue funding, financial arrangements or social programme organization	Conferences and meetings training courses
Venue-finding service	Finding rooms for conferences and meetings	Conferences, meetings, training courses, product launches
Conference production service	Specialize in actual staging of the event including lighting, special effects, sound systems	Conferences, meetings, training courses, exhibitions, product launches
Incentive travel agency	Organizing incentive travel packages for clients	Incentive travel
Destination management company	Specialist ground handlers who handle practical arrangements in destinations	Conferences, meetings, incentive travel, exhibitions, product launches
Corporate hospitality company	Focus on organizing corporate hospitality and entertainment events either as stand-alone events or as part of other events	Conferences, meetings, exhibitions, product launches, incentive travel
Business travel agency	Providing travel agency services for business travellers including transport bookings and accommodation services	Individual business trips
Exhibition organizer	Organizing exhibitions/ reservations	Exhibitions

Source: adapted from Rogers (1998).

A few further words will help clarify some issues relating to the content of Table 4.2. Most intermediaries receive a commission from the client on whose behalf they are operating. Otherwise, they receive a fixed fee. Some business travel agencies are located within large organizations, working exclusively for them. These are described as 'implants'.

Let us now look at two of these intermediaries in more detail – professional conference organizers and incentive travel and event management agencies.

The professional conference or congress organizer

Many organizations are making increasing use of professional conference/congress organizers to manage their business tourism events.

The International Association of Professional Congress Organizers (IAPCO), in one of its brochures promoting the use of professional conference organizers (PCOs) outlines the reasons for using a PCO in the form of answers to hypothetical questions from potential clients. These are outlined in Exhibit 4.1.

The brochure also details the services that a PCO can provide. These are set out in Exhibit 4.2.

Exhibit 4.1 The role of professional conference/congress organizer

Q What can a PCO do that my staff can't

A PCOs do not have supernatural powers but they do cast a kind of magic on a conference! They have human resources, technical resources and contacts built up over many years. They have the experience and skills to produce professional results even on a shoestring budget. Undertaking your project from scratch would demand a great deal of your staff's valuable time. A PCO will save them the headache.

Q What is the difference between a PCO and a travel agency, destination management company, tour company, convention bureau, hotel, caterer, public relations consultancy, production house, conference centre?

A Not such a silly question because you may find all those establishments offering some conference-management services. An independent PCO company has no other conflicting interests. It is the only one specializing in every aspect of conference organization and co-ordination, taking full responsibility for budget control and liaising whenever necessary with all other suppliers, including those listed above.

Q Would the PCO take over completely?

A Don't worry! You and your colleagues retain complete control of your conference, with none of the day-to-day logistical hassle. At the outset of a project, the PCO sits down with the client to discuss the aims and objectives. Many decisions need to be made and the PCO can help identify those critical for success and offer advice on how to achieve them. The client is still responsible for the content of the programme, but the PCO can give full administrative and technical support in managing it.

   A PCO is a consultant, an administrator, a creator, an extension of your organization

Q What will it cost?

A There are various ways of charging for a PCO's services. It could be either as a percentage of the budget or on a fee basis. Such fees cover a PCO's staff and time costs. The actual costs of the conference, including expenses such as mailing, telephones etc. are usually charged separately. All costs, including fees, will be incorporated into the conference budget. Whatever the arrangements the client and PCO must agree what the fee covers so there are no surprises. A written contract between the two parties, client (principal) and PCO (agent), is essential. Most PCOs will also offer delegates an accommodation booking service, costs of which in some countries are covered by commissions from hotels.

At first sight employing the services of a PCO might look expensive but you have to count the many man-hours [*sic*] involved. In the long run the PCO's expertise means the client avoids wasting money – a bonus for low-budget conferences – and there is less chance the event will make a loss. Indeed, in many cases where events are intended to be money-making, profits are actually increased. The PCO can also suggest sources of finance or pre-finance and, given sufficient lead time, assist in identifying potential sponsors.

In the end what you are paying for is professionalism.

The final result will be a congress which meets international standards of event organization.

Source: IAPCO literature.

Exhibit 4.2 The services of a professional conference/congress organizer

Assistance with conference bids.
Help in defining objectives.
Advice on congress taxation liabilities.
Preliminary outline plan.
Draft income and expenditure budget.
Finance consultancy – pre-finance, sponsorship, exhibitions, loans, registration fees
Book-keeping.
Control of bank accounts, income and expenditure ledgers.
Venue negotiation.
Organizational structure.
Meetings with organizing committees.
Liaison with production companies.
Secretariat and office facilities, including mailing address.
Registration processing systems.
Scientific or technical programme support.
Exhibition and poster sessions.
Speaker liaison.
Marketing and public relations.
Press office.
Staffing on site.
Social events.
Liaison with airlines.
Delegate transportation.
Closure of conference accounts.
Post-event evaluation.

The PCO will commission or bring in:
Design and print (congress image).
Gifts and conferences accessories.
Insurance cover.
Food and beverage.
Decor and staging.
On-site services – electronic message systems, signs, security.
Audiovisual equipment.
Simultaneous interpretation.
Conference recording.
Translation of conference documentation.
Video-conferencing.

Additional services offered:
Accommodation bookings.
Tour programmes.

Source: IAPCO literature.

Incentive travel and event management agencies

These organizations specialize in organizing:

● incentive travel packages
● corporate hospitality and entertainment
● conferences and meetings, particularly those with a major partners and/or a social programme.

As these sectors of business tourism continue to grow such agencies are flourishing. This fact is clearly illustrated by the results of the 1999 Annual Conference and Incentive Travel Survey which was published in February 2000. This survey covers UK-based agencies only and shows a picture of growth and optimization.

Table 4.3 provides data on the top twenty-seven UK-based agencies in terms of their turnover. Table 4.4 offers information on twenty-two agencies in the UK covering their number of groups handled and the number of employees.

The survey contained some clear useful information about the agencies in this field, some of which are highlighted below:

1 Around 30 per cent of agencies had a turnover in excess of £5 million per annum.
2 Nearly a quarter of all agencies made less than £100 000 profit.
3 Fifty per cent of agencies employed less than twenty staff.
4 Eighty per cent of all agencies believed the incentive travel market was in a healthy or very healthy state.

As we have seen in this section, intermediaries are playing an increasing role in the interface between buyers and suppliers. It is now time for us to turn our attention to the latter group.

Table 4.3 UK agencies ranked by incentive travel (IT) turnover, 1999

Rank 1999	Rank 1998	Company	IT turnover 1999 (£m)	IT turnover 1998 (£m)	Total turnover 1999 (£)m	Total turnover 1998 (£m)	IT as % total turnover 1999	IT as % total turnover 1998	Pretax profit 1999 (£)	Pretax profit 1998 (£)
1	1	Maritz	20.0	20.0	91.0	8.0	22	24	n/a	n/a
2	2	The Marketing Organization[1]	16.0	14.0	25.0	22.0	62	59	700 000	770 854
3	3	World Event Management[2]	12.0	11.0	16.0	13.0	73	70	600 000	200 000
4	–	Universal Conference & Incentive Travel	11.8	9.0	11.8	9.0	100	100	438 881	641 789
5	5	Global Event Solutions[3]	10.0	12.8	52.6	46.0	19	28	n/a	n/a
6	4	P&MM[4]	8.7	9.4	23.0	22.0	38	43	900 000	327 000
7	6	Purchase point[5]	8.0	7.0	17.0	17.0	47	41	650 000	450 000
8	–	Thomas Hannah & Associates	6.0	5.0	20.7m	12.5	29%	40	802 000m	740 000
9	13	Corporate Innovations Company	5.3	3.3	10.0	6.5	53%	52	1 200 000	805 000
10	16	Talking Point	4.8	4.2	8.9	7.8	53%	53	180 000	104 000
11	9=	Conference & Motivation Management[6]	4.7	3.6	5.0	4.0	95%	90	n/a	n/a
12	14=	Peltours	4.0	4.0	33.0	37.0	12%	11	n/a	n/a
13	–	Capital Incentives	3.2	0.6	36.0	38.0	9%	2	2 000 000	2 000 000
14	17	Incentive & Conference Centre	2.5	2.9	3.0	3.5	85	85	n/a	n/a
15	14=	Grass Roots Group[7]	2.0	1.6	49.0	41.0	4	4	n/a	1 900 000
16	23	Archer Young Marketing	1.8	1.3	5.1	3.8	35	35	n/a	n/a

17	19=	Travel Impact	1.7	1.8	2.3	2.6	73	70	80 000	109 000
18	21	Convention Travel Company	1.6	1.3	2.0	1.6	80	80	n/a	n/a
19	25=	Travel for Industry	1.5	1.2	4.6	4.0	30	3	160 000	137 000
20	22=	Travel Talk II	1.4	1.4m	1.5	1.7	90	85	n/a	n/a
21	25=	McGarvey Russell	1.2	1.2m	2.3	2.0	55	60	50 000	43 000
22	28	Eyas	1.1	0.6	1.9	1.4	60	45	60 000	35 000
23	29	Pinacle[8]	0.4	0.4	1.2	0.9	35	46	n/a	n/a
24	30	Genesis	0.1	0.1	3.4	2.8	3	4	100 000	41 818
25=	–	Martlet	n/a	n/a	5.0	5.8	n/a	n/a	452 000	470 000
25=	11=	Motivation Travel Management	n/a	2.7	3.0	3.0	n/a	85	n/a	n/a
25=	–	Teamwork Travel Management	n/a	n/a	n/a	n/a	70	80	n/a	n/a

Notes: 1 The Travel Organization is the conference and incentive travel division of The Marketing Organization.
2 World Event Management was formed by the merger of World Meetings and LMG International.
3 Global Event Solutions replaced Hogg Robinson's Group Travel Division.
4 P&MM was formed by the merger between Page and Moy Marketing and sister company Brevis in January 2000.
5 Purchasepoint and Motivforce have merged and the new agency is trading under both names at the time of going to press.
6 Conference & Motivation Management is WGT's incentive department.
7 Travel Awards is the city division of the Grass Roots Group.
8 Pinacle was formerly Elegant Incentives.

Source: Conference and Incentive Travel (February 2000).

Table 4.4 UK agencies ranked by number of delegates, 1999

Rank	Company/contact	No. of participants 1999	No. of participants 1998	No. of groups 1999	No. of groups 1998	No. of employees 1999	No. of employees 1998	Employee increase (%)
1	Maritz (01628 895264)	32 800	27 600	183	160	600	580	3.5
2	The Marketing Organization (01908 214700)	21 000	25 999	115	130	124	115	8.0
3	Travel for Industry[1] (0171 233 5644)	17 600	13 050	37	23	30	27	11.0
4	World Event Management (01274 854100)	9 000	n/a	140	n/a	4 4	n/a	n/a
5	Universal Conference & Incentive Travel (01753 632000)	13 500	–	124	–	36	–	n/a
6	P&MM (01908 608000)	6 500	6 500	85	90	135	150	–10.0
7	The Grass Roots Group (01442 829400)	6 400	5 900	80	78	210	196	7.0
8	Capital Incentives (0181 847 5824)	4 500	–	50	–	65	–	n/a
9	Conference & Motivation Management (01943 882800)	4 000	–	70	70	15	15	0
10	Thomas Hannah & Associates Group (0116 269 0500)	2 900	–	35	–	92	–	n/a
11	The Incentive & Conference Centre (01424 772255)	2 600	2 400	26	37	5	8	–37.0
12	Travel Talk II (01299 400754)	2 047	2 400	38	43	10	8	25.0

13=	Motivation Travel Management (01344 872699)	2 000	–	50	–	10	–	n/a
13=	The Corporate Innovations Company (01295 272747)	2 000	1 200	61	45	26	22	18.0
15=	Archer Young Marketing (01442 877177)	1 500	1 100	52	42	29	24	21.0
15=	Talking Point (01628 776303)	1 500	n/a	n/a	n/a	60	n/a	n/a
17	Eyas	1 200	1 400	24	26	6	5	20.0
18	McGarvey Russell (0115 982 6767)	1 200	1 400	20	20	16	16	0
19	Convention Travel Company (01483 304184)	875	n/a	16	n/a	18	n/a	n/a
20	Travel Impact (0181 940 7888)	720	n/a	20	n/a	6	n/a	n/a
21	Genesis Motivation (01444 476110)	148	292	3	5	7	8	12.5
22	Pinacle[2] (01342 316426)	137	5	194	5	8	4	100.0

Notes: 1 TFI has included long-term contract staff in its numbers.
2 Pinacle was formerly Elegant Incentives.
Agencies which did not supply information on delegates have not been included.
n/a = not available

Source: *Conference and Incentive Travel* (February 2000).

Suppliers

As we saw in Table 4.1, suppliers can be divided into five types: destinations, venues, transport, accommodation and ancillary services.

Destinations are dealt with in detail in Chapter 5 so here we will simply make just a few comments on their role in the supply side of business tourism.

Rogers (1998) states:

> *Conference organisers attach greater importance to 'location' than to any other single criterion when selecting their sites. Location may be expressed in terms of 'town', 'city', 'region', or 'country'. The widely accepted term to describe each of these is destination ... A destination ... is usually a discrete area with identifiable boundaries. Each ... destination must contain a range of venues, facilities, attractions, supply services, and infrastructure.*

Destinations are usually marketed by public sector bodies or joint public–private partnership agencies but most of the elements of the destination are in private ownership.

Venues are the places where business tourism events actually take place, whether they are conferences, meetings, exhibitions, training courses, incentive travel packages or product launch sites.

Venues can be classified in a number of ways, as can be seen from Figure 4.6.

Hotels are perhaps the best known venues for meetings, and conferences in particular, but there are different types of hotel venue, including:

- city centre hotels
- 'motels' located on major roads
- coastal resort hotels
- 'country house' hotels in rural locations.

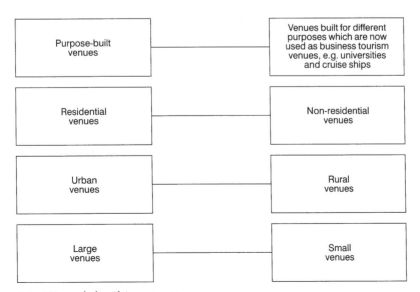

Figure 4.6   Ways of classifying venues

Organizers are increasingly looking for more unusual venues to make their events special. These may include the following:

- sporting venues, e.g. golf courses, football grounds, and racecourses which offer high profile venues
- historic buildings, e.g. castles and stately homes
- theme parks
- transport venues, e.g. cruise ships, ferries and trains
- museums.

In 1999 Leask and Hood published a survey of such venues in the UK. They found that:

1 Unusual venues had only recently started to provide facilities for business tourism events, with 37 per cent of them only providing such facilities for less than five years.
2 Forty-three per cent of such venues entered the market because of demand, in other words, people wanting to use them, and approaching them.
3 Corporate clients were more important clients for the venues than association clients.

Leask and Hood (1999) identified the following strengths and weaknesses of these unusual venues. The main weaknesses in the provision of unusual venues were as follows:

- the size and range of facilities available
- the lack of accommodation on site
- limited technical and audiovisual equipment
- poor industry knowledge and trained staff
- accessibility and suitability of buildings
- offering a unique experience, once experienced not required again.

On a more positive note, the strengths identified were that unusual venues:

- offer a unique, memorable experience
- are competitively priced
- offer facilities particularly suitable for small meetings
- meet the needs of buyers demanding 'something different' in a venue
- provide a quality and friendly service.

The growth of business tourism has encouraged the public and private sectors to invest in new purpose-built exhibition and conference venues. The 1999–2000 'venue' guide, for example, identified around 6000 venues, many of which were recently developed facilities.

The *Conference and Incentive Travel* preview of the International Confex 2000 exhibition gave details of the opening or refurbishment of more than fifty major purpose-built venues worldwide.

These purpose-built venues are designed for both conferences and exhibitions with multipurpose spaces. The Lille Grand Palais, for instance, has an auditorium which seats 5000 together with 22 000 square metres of exhibition space.

Transport clearly is vital to business tourism in that it moves the business traveller to their desired destination, and then moves them around the destination.

All forms of transport are used in business tourism industry:

- air transport – scheduled and charter flights, private aircraft, air taxis, chartered helicopters
- rail transport – scheduled railways, steam railways
- road transport – private cars, scheduled buses, chartered coaches, car hire, taxis
- water transport – ferries, cruise ships.

We can see from this list that transport is not only a way of moving from A to B in business travel and tourism. It can also be:

- a venue, such as the trains with meeting rooms offered by SNCF, the state railway operator, in France
- a core element of social programmes as when delegates' social programmes involve horse-drawn carriage 'taxis' in Central Park, New York and Killarney, Ireland.

Airlines have certainly realized the importance of business tourism to their operations and have invested heavily in facilities for business travellers including dedicated lounges and on-board computer access.

A recent survey conducted by *Conference and Incentive Travel* showed that airlines have tried to improve services, particularly for conference organizers. For example, 32 per cent of airlines allow name changes for group travel passengers within three days of travel, and some 60 per cent of airlines questioned now have a department dedicated to conference and incentive travel.

Table 4.5 illustrates some aspects of the relationship between airlines and conference and incentive travel.

Accommodation is clearly required for all residential business tourism. Most of that used is commercial accommodation although some business travellers stay with friends and relatives.

There are several aspects of the link between accommodation and business tourism, including the following:

1 Accommodation establishments can be both venues and places to sleep and delegates can meet in one hotel but sleep in another.
2 Organizers can meet the needs of different delegates by offering different types of accommodation at varying price levels.
3 Some accommodation establishments can encourage people to attend conferences, because of their fame and high-quality reputation, if they are the conference venue.
4 Accommodation does not just mean hotels. It can also include:
  (a) timeshare developments
  (b) self-catering complexes
  (c) university halls of residence
  (d) youth hostels
  (e) cruise ships
  (f) novel forms of accommodation such as an ice-hotel in Sweden, 'Rorbus' in the Lofoten Islands, Norway, and horse-drawn carriages in Ireland.
5 On wilderness based training courses or incentive travel packages, no formal accommodation may be provided as participants will be expected to 'survive'. Alternatively they may simply be accommodated in tents.

Table 4.5 Airlines and conference and incentive travel business

Airline	Number of c&i passengers/ percentage of c&i passengers[1]	Best-selling destinations[1]	Dedicated group check-in in advance of travel	Reservations one year in advance
Air Canada	1800 passengers	Western Canada, Calgary, Vancouver	Yes	Yes
Air China	n/a	n/a	Yes	Yes
Air Malta	n/a	Malta	Yes	Yes
Air New Zealand	n/a	Los Angeles, South Pacific, New Zealand	Yes	Yes
American Airlines	25% of total	New York, Miami, Los Angeles	Yes	Yes
Ansett Australia	n/a	Cairns, Sydney, Ayer's Rock	Yes	Yes
Austrian Airlines[3]	n/a	n/a	Yes	Yes
Bahamasair	n/a	Nassau	Yes	Yes
British Airways	150 000 passengers	Madrid, Malaga, Barbados, Bangkok, Nice	Yes	Yes
British Midland	2.2% of total	Dublin, Belfast, Amsterdam	Yes	Yes
Canada Airlines	n/a	n/a	Yes	Yes
Cathay Pacific	n/a	Australia, Hong Kong	Yes	Yes
City Flyer[2]	n/a	Dublin, Nice	Yes	Yes
Continental Airlines	n/a	New Zealand, San Antonio, New Orleans	Yes	Yes
Delta Airlines	n/a	New Orleans, Atlanta, Florida, New York, Las Vegas	Under review	Under review
Egyptair	n/a	Cairo, Luxor, Sharm-El-Sheikh	Yes	Yes
KLM[3]	50 groups	Amsterdam	Yes	Yes

Airline	Number of c&i passengers/ percentage of c&i passengers[1]	Best-selling destinations[1]	Dedicated group check-in in advance of travel	Reservations one year in advance
Lufthansa	n/a	Germany	Yes	Yes
Middle East Airlines	n/a	Beirut, Dubai	Yes	Yes
Qantas[3]	20 groups	Sydney, Melbourne, Singapore, Bali, Cairns	Yes	Yes
South African Airways	n/a	Cape Town	Yes	Yes
Singapore Airlines	n/a	Singapore, Bali	Yes	Yes
Swissair	50% of total	Zurich, Geneva	Yes	Yes
TAP Air Portugal	n/a	Lisbon	Yes	Yes
Thai Airlines	2.5% of total	Phuket, Chiang Mai	Yes	Yes
Virgin Atlantic	40% of total	New York, Las Vegas, Cape Town, Johannesburg	Yes	Yes

Notes: 1 Number of conference and incentive (c&i) groups carried between May 1999 and April 2000.
      2 Subsidiary of British Airways.
      3 Figures from CIT 1998 survey; no results for 1999 available at time of going to press.

Source: Conference and Incentive Travel (May 2000).

Accommodation, together with travel, is usually the largest element in the budget for a conference delegate.

Accommodation providers, notably hotel chains, have provided an increasing variety of facilities to attract the business tourist from in-room computer access, to business centres, to a wide variety of meeting rooms. For many hotels, business tourism, of all types, is the source of the majority of their revenue.

Finally, business travel and tourism requires a range of other *ancillary services* including:

- audio-visual equipment suppliers
- badge-makers
- caterers
- computer hire
- couriers
- designers
- direct marketing agencies
- entertainment
- exhibition constructors
- exhibition display-makers
- fireworks suppliers
- florists
- freight forwarders
- furniture hire
- gift and souvenir suppliers
- graphic artists
- insurance services

- Internet developers
- interpreters and translators
- lighting specialists
- marquee hire
- mobile toilets
- photographers
- public relations consultants
- recruitment agencies and event personnel providers
- research organizations
- security
- sign-makers
- speaker groups
- ticket agencies
- training specialists
- video-conferencing specialists

Sometimes the existence in a destination of particular ancillary services may influence an organizer's decision about destinations for business tourism events. For example, a company arranging a high-tech product launch may choose a destination which has expert information technology and audiovisual companies located there.

While we have divided these suppliers into five categories, it is important to recognize that there is a great interdependence between all five elements. The business tourism product and experience utilizes all five of these and there is also interdependency between these suppliers, the intermediaries and the buyers.

It is now time for us to look at the final category, those who provide other services to the business tourism industry as a whole.

Miscellaneous services for the business travel and tourism industry

This category includes six types of organization or phenomena which provide diverse services to the business travel and tourism industry, those which were set out in Figure 4.1.

The business travel and tourism sector has its own *trade media* read by suppliers, buyers and intermediaries. Rogers (1998) identified twenty-four leading international conference industry trade journals. Of these, fifteen were based in the UK, four in the USA, two in Italy, one in France, one in Spain and one in Germany. This Anglocentric list probably excludes a number of non-UK journals. In 1999, the European Meetings Industry Liaison

Group (EMILG) produced a list of twenty-seven trade journals which included five from the UK, five from the USA, four from Spain, four from Germany and two from Belgium. Both lists excluded titles known to the author, notably *Synedrio* from Greece. In spring 2000 it was announced that a new journal was to be launched for Asia. Finally, there are also specialist journals for the exhibition sector.

There are a number of industry *trade fairs* which serve the industry and provide an interface between producers, intermediaries and customers, including EIBTM and International Confex. A case study of these two events is to be found in Part Five of this book.

In recent years there has been a growth of *professional bodies* in this field. Rogers (1998) identified seven UK associations and seven leading international professional bodies. These latter included:

● Association Internationale des Palais de Congrés (AIPC)
● European Federation of Conference Towns (EFCT)
● International Association of Convention and Visitor Bureaux (IACVB)
● International Association of Professional Congress Organizers (IAPCO)
● International Conference and Convention Association (ICCA)
● Meeting Professionals International (MPI)
● Society of Incentive Travel Executives (SITE).

Some of these organizations, such as SITE, relate to one sector only while others have a broader remit. At the same time, some focus on Europe while others are truly global.

Meeting Professionals International was founded in 1972, has 18 000 members and is run from its headquarters in Dallas, USA, and its European bureau in Brussels, Belgium. Its members are divided evenly between planners and suppliers. It has developed a highly recognized education programme for members including its Certificate in Meetings Management. It provides a resource database for members and produces a monthly journal. It seeks greater recognition of the meetings industry.

In 1999, MPI's European membership comprised:

● professional congress organizers, 28 per cent
● corporate buyers, 18 per cent
● hotels, 15 per cent
● congress centres, 9 per cent
● associations, 7 per cent
● destination management companies, 7 per cent
● convention and visitor bureaux, 6 per cent
● others, 10 per cent.

The International Association of Professional Congress Organizers was founded in 1968 to:

● gain further recognition of the professional congress organizer's role
● maintain a high professional standard
● carry out research on industry problems
● offer a forum for sharing experiences
● liaise with other, relevant bodies.

It organizes a major annual seminar and produces a range of publications.

The Society of Incentive Travel Executives, founded in 1973, has sought to raise the profile of incentive travel and increase standards of professionalism. It funds relevant research and provides teaching materials for tutors.

It is clear from these three examples that one major aim of professional bodies in this field is to gain recognition for business tourism, or at least for their sector of it However, the fragmentation of these bodies is, perhaps, an obstacle to the 'industry' gaining greater recognition from policy-makers in government.

Business travel and tourism makes use of a variety of *consultants* including:

- design consultants for new conference and exhibition facilities
- marketing advice for destinations and businesses
- carrying cost feasibility studies for new facilities
- human resource specialists advising on human resource management strategies and incentive travel packages
- training consultants to advise on training courses.

Most countries now have a *national tourism organization* (NTO), usually publicly funded, and many of these now have specialist business tourism departments. *Conference and Incentive Travel* reported in June 2000 that thirty-one out of fifty leading NTOs had a dedicated conference and incentive travel department. Their role is usually to attract new business tourism events to the country through the provision of advice, brochures, advertising, research and useful contacts. The role of these organizations will be discussed further in Chapter 10.

Educational institutions are also playing an increasing role in business tourism, including:

- offering modules and courses in business tourism and conference or exhibition management
- undertaking research and consultancy for the industry
- providing students to work with industry organizations on placement.

However, there is still scope for greater co-operation between education and industry in the business travel and tourism field.

Key issues

There are two issues that need to be noted before we conclude this chapter:

1 *The geography of supply.* The supply side in business travel and tourism is not consistent around the world. In some countries it is highly developed reflecting a well-established domestic and/or inbound and/or outbound business tourism market. These countries include the USA, Canada, Australasia, Hong Kong, Singapore and many European countries. In other countries there may be pockets of well-developed supply in resorts where business tourism is well established but where levels of business tourism covered in the country are low. Supply also crosses national boundaries with intermediaries in country 'A' working with venues and accommodation operators in country 'B'. This is particularly evident between so-called developed and less developed countries.

2 *The link between business and leisure.* Business tourism, as we have seen, has its own distinct supply side. However, just as leisure and business overlap in terms of how business tourists spend their time, there is also a link between them in terms of supply. For example:

(a) Visitor attractions aimed at leisure tourists also provide services, such as corporate hospitality, for business tourism events.

(b) Hotels and airlines serving the needs of business and leisure travellers alongside each other.

(c) The transport infrastructure used by leisure and business travellers is generally the same, such as airports and roads.

Conclusion

We have seen that the supply side in business travel and tourism is highly complex and varies between types of business tourism events. At the same time, we have noted that there are clear links and interdependencies between buyers and intermediaries and intermediaries and suppliers. The whole industry is supported by a range of other supply-side organizations, including trade media and professional bodies.

Many of the issues raised in this chapter will be taken up in detail in later chapters.

Discussion points and essay questions

1 Discuss the main advantages for organizations of employing a professional congress organizer or incentive travel agency to organize their conference or incentive travel package.

2 Discuss the reasons why there has been a growing interest in unusual venues for conferences and meetings.

3 Devise a simple model which graphically represents the relationship between buyers, suppliers and intermediaries.

Exercise

Select a business tourism destination with which you are familiar or for which you can obtain information. Produce an inventory of suppliers in the destination who are involved in business travel and tourism, and list their strengths and weaknesses, and their links with buyers and intermediaries outside the destination.

5 The role of destinations in business travel and tourism

Every single business travel trip has one or more destinations. However, as we will see, the destination can play a number of roles in business tourism.

In this chapter we will explore the following issues:

- the definition of a destination
- the distinction between destinations and venues
- the history of business tourism destinations
- the destination product
- a typology of destinations
- types of business tourism in destinations
- conference and convention destinations
- incentive travel destinations
- the links with leisure tourism
- destination management.

The definition of a destination

The destination is a place where the main focus of the business travel trip will be, whether a conference, a sales mission or an incentive travel package. Destinations can be viewed on a number of different geographical levels, from whole countries, through regions, to a rural area, an individual city or a single coastal resort. Destinations have different types of boundaries; they can be seen in terms of central government or local government boundaries, geographical features or even the perceptions of the client. Indeed it could be that the latter is the most important, for it is those perceptions which determine customer purchasing behaviour. Many destinations are branded to increase their appeal, such as the 'Big Apple' for New York. While having little meaning in geographical terms these brands can be powerful marketing tools. Names such as the French Riviera have great power to attract business tourists. Destinations, however they are branded, are discrete areas which supply all or most of the attractions and services required by the business traveller, whatever the purpose of their trip.

The distinction between destinations and venues

Traditionally there has been a clear distinction between destinations and venues. The former were areas while the latter were individual units within these areas. Venues are supposed to provide one or some of the services needed by the traveller, while destinations overall are meant to provide virtually every service the traveller needs. However, the distinction has become blurred as major attractions and resort complexes have sought to become destinations in their own right, providing all the services required by the business tourist. Such examples include Center Parcs, Club Med and Disneyland Paris, which have all sought to become 'destinations' for conferences and incentive travel packages.

The history of business tourism destinations

The business tourism 'destination', as we saw in Chapter 2, dates back to pre-history. Individual business trips linked to trading have been taking place for, literally, thousands of years. In the Middle Ages we saw the rise of trade fairs in Europe, with their own infrastructure of services.

However, it is only in the last hundred years that we have seen the rise of convention tourism, beginning in the USA. This was an innovation because business tourism was no longer simply trade-related. In this case the destination was central to the trip rather than just being a 'backdrop' for the business activities.

During the 1980s and 1990s we have seen the rise of incentive travel where the destination is the principal attraction and focus of the trip.

Destinations have realized that business tourism brings great benefits and every year new destinations try to attract convention, exhibition and incentive travel business. The reasons for this are not hard to identify, for business tourism has a number of advantages over leisure tourism. As they are usually not paying the bill, business tourists tend to spend two or three times as much money per day as leisure tourists. However, they are more likely to spend their money with transnational companies so that a higher proportion of their expenditure may be lost to the local community. Business tourists demand a high level of personal service, so accommodating them is a labour-intensive activity which creates more jobs than leisure tourism. Business tourism spreads its benefits widely around local enterprises because of its demand for everything from florists to secretarial services, photographers to security people. Business tourism tends to be less seasonal than leisure tourism, and it is complementary to leisure tourism in that it:

● is in full swing in the months which are the off-peak season for leisure tourism
● fills hotels on weekdays but leaves them empty for the leisure tourist at the weekends.

The destination product

The business tourism destination product is not really a product; it is more an amalgamation of individual products at the disposal of the business traveller. These individual products can be divided into a number of groups as we can see in Figure 5.1.

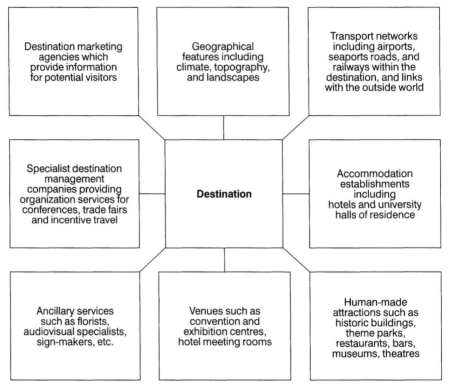

Figure 5.1   The elements of the destination product

The destination is like a do-it-yourself kit, from which the business tourist constructs his or her own product or experience.

There are clearly a myriad of possible permutations of all these elements and each business tourism event or individual business traveller will use the destination in a different way.

The destination, like all tourism products, is a mixture of tangible and intangible elements. The intangible elements are vital to the success or otherwise of a destination, but they are often highly subjective and are subject to customers' perceptions. These perceptions include issues such as:

● whether or not the destination is seen as safe, secure and stable
● the perceived ambience and atmosphere
● the degree to which the destination is seen to be friendly or not
● the perceived efficiency and reliability of services within the destination.

As yet, relatively little research has been conducted concerning business tourists' perceptions of destinations. However, we cannot overestimate these perceptions as determinants to decision-making in the conference, exhibition and incentive travel sectors.

The last important point to recognize about the business tourism destination product is the high level of interdependence between the various elements. If one element fails the whole product collapses. For example, an excellent conference venue and a superb range of social programme attractions will not produce a successful conference experience for delegates if the coaches booked to take delegates to the attractions fail to appear!

A typology of destinations

Figure 5.2 offers a typology to illustrate the different roles which destinations can play in business travel and tourism. This is clearly a highly generalized picture but it does indicate the breadth of types of business tourism destinations and their roles.

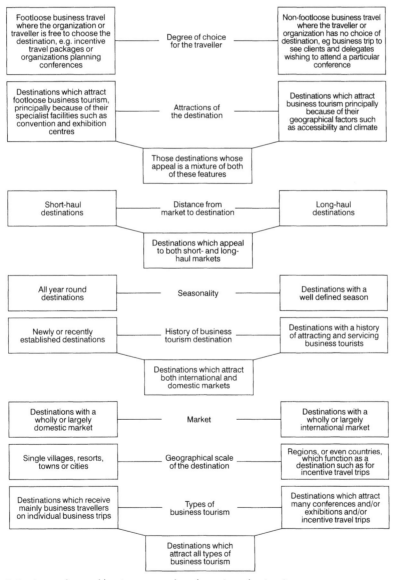

Figure 5.2   A typology of business travel and tourism destinations

The types of business tourism in destinations

Most destinations receive and service a wide variety of types of business tourism simultaneously.

Leong and Chaplin, for example, have looked at the activities of business tourists in Macau. The results of their work are illustrated in Table 5.1. This table shows the diversity of reasons travellers have for visiting particular business tourism destination. In the case of Macau, the vast majority of business visitors are engaged in individual business trips or attending exhibitions or trade fairs.

Table 5.1   Types of business tourism in Macau

Types of business tourist	Percentage
Attending exhibitions of my company's products	60
Marketing and promotional activities	58
Negotiating with clients and customers	50
Consultation, information seeking and networking	33
Attending exhibitions of other companies' products	30
Managing the operation of a business in Macau, entertaining colleagues, clients, customers	27
Meeting with government officials	25
Attending company meetings	25
Incentive trip	15
Others	15
Supervising the management of the operations of a business in Macau	5
In transit to China or Hong Kong	3

Note: Multiple responses account for the fact that percentages do not add up to 100 per cent.

Source: Leong and Chaplin, in Leong and Leong (1999).

Conference and convention destinations

Rogers (1998) recognized the importance of destinations in the conference – or congress or convention – sector when he stated: 'Conference organizers attach greater importance to 'location' (destination) than any other single criterion when selecting their sites.'

However, the destination will only be acceptable if it offers the right range of services and facilities, including individual venues. Thus, there is a strong link between destinations and venues.

Most conferences take place in large urban areas or coastal resorts. The destination has to offer:

- a suitable venue for the meeting or meetings
- sufficient accommodation if the venue is non-residential
- attractions for successful social and/or partner programmes
- good accessibility to the generating market(s)
- efficient transport systems within the destination.

A destination also has to be seen to offer an acceptable level of safety and security for delegates, and to offer all these features at a price which is perceived to offer value for money.

The most popular destinations for international conventions in the 1990s have included:

- *Europe*: Barcelona, Dublin, Copenhagen, Vienna, Budapest, Paris, Stockholm, Amsterdam
- *North America*: San Francisco, Atlanta, Washington, New York, Orlando, Vancouver
- *South America*: Rio de Janeiro
- *Asia*: Hong Kong, Seoul, Singapore, Beijing, Manila, Kuala Lumpur
- *Australasia*: Melbourne, Sydney
- *Africa*: no destination in the top seventy in 1996 (Rogers, 1998).

Incentive travel destinations

This form of business tourism is interesting as it is leisure tourism for business purposes. Incentive travel destinations must first and foremost have status, be out of the ordinary and offer something special and unusual.

The destinations are usually sophisticated cities, although increasingly remote, wild regions, off the 'beaten track' are becoming more popular.

A survey in *Conference and Incentive Travel* suggested that the most popular destinations for incentives were as shown in Table 5.2.

Table 5.2   The ten most popular international incentive travel destinations for UK delegates 2000–2001

Rank	Country	City/resort
1	Dubai	1 = Cape Town
2	South Africa	1 = New York
3	France	1 = Harare
4	Spain	4 Barcelona
5	USA	5 Dublin
6	Hong Kong	6 Cannes
7	Italy	7 = Boston
8	Singapore	7 = Hong Kong
9	Portugal	7 = Paris
10	Turkey	10 Algarve

Source: *Conference and Incentive Travel* (March 2001).

The relative price inelasticity of incentive travel is illustrated by the fact that New York is in equal first place in Table 5.2, yet it is perhaps the most expensive city in the world.

In the same issue of *Conference and Incentive Travel* it was suggested that new destinations were emerging rapidly, often due to:

- investments in the accommodation sector, made by international hotel chains
- the influence of good quality destination management companies in these regions
- the falling real costs of long-haul travel.

The survey conducted by this journal showed that the top ten emerging destinations for incentives were, in 2000–2001 in order:

1 Ecuador and the Galapagos Islands.
2 Peru.
3 Chile.
4 Yukon/Canada.
5 China.
6 New Zealand.
7 Brazil.
8 Oman.
9 Tanzania.
10 Mozambique.

The links with leisure tourism

Many decisions concerning the selection of conference destinations are heavily influenced by the recognition that delegates will often decide to attend if they perceive the destination to be attractive for leisure activities.

There are three links between business tourism and leisure travel that have implications for destinations:

1 Business travellers become leisure travellers when the working day is over, whatever time of the day this may be.
2 Many conferences have social programmes of leisure activities for delegates. These may take place in the evenings or even in the daytime. Alternatively, or additionally, they can also feature post-conference tours which take place once the conference has ended.
3 Partners often accompany business tourists on their trips, and while the business tourist is working, the partner is free to act as a leisure tourist. Once the working day is over they will usually become a leisure couple.

Furthermore, in addition to incentive travel, there are other forms of business tourism which explicitly and directly link business and leisure tourism. For example, some training courses take the form of team-building exercises involving sailing and mountain sports, for example.

Destinations which seek to attract business tourism must recognize the importance of the existence of leisure attractions to the decisions made by the business traveller.

Destination management

Destinations require effective management if they are to satisfactorily meet the needs of business tourists. This management takes several forms, as can be seen from Figure 5.3.

However, these responsibilities are not often exercised by just one organization. While local government is usually responsible for many management roles in destinations, the issues mentioned in Figure 5.3 could also involve:

● central government agencies
● regional government agencies

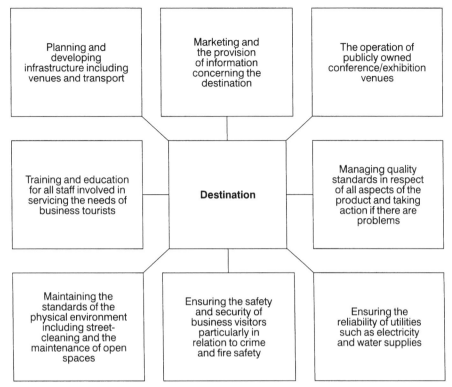

Figure 5.3   The scope of business tourism destination management

- joint public–private sector partnership organizations
- private companies
- universities and colleges.

This fragmentation can lead to a lack of consistency and co-ordination in the delivery of services to business tourists.

Conclusion

In this chapter we have seen the important role which destinations play in business travel and tourism. However, it has also been noted that the destination is a complex product or set of products, and that there is a complex variety of types of business tourism destinations.

It is clear that some destinations specialize in one particular type of business tourism but that many others serve simultaneously the needs of different types of business tourism. We have recognized that there is a strong link between leisure tourism and business tourism. Finally, we have seen that destination management is, in general, an activity where the responsibility is fragmented between different organizations.

Discussion points and essay questions

1 Critically evaluate the typology of business travel and tourism destinations that is presented in Figure 5.2.
2 Discuss the factors which you think determine whether or not a destination will be viewed, by conference delegates, as an attractive destination.
3 Discuss the extent to which the distinction between venues and destinations is becoming increasingly blurred.

Exercise

Select a business tourism destination. Investigate each of the issues relating to destination management which are covered in Figure 5.3.

Then identify which organization(s) is (are) responsible for each of these issues.

You should conclude by suggesting the extent to which the existing situation is likely to lead to effective destination management or not.

6 The macro-environment of business travel and tourism

Every business travel and tourism organization has a so-called 'business environment'. This is another term for the factors which affect the organization and its market. Some of these factors – the micro-environment – are 'close' to the organization, physically and/or organizationally speaking, such as suppliers and intermediaries. These factors can be influenced or even controlled by the organization.

However, the business environment also includes the macro-environment; this comprises wider, more remote factors which have great influence, but over which the organization has no control and practically little or no influence. These factors exist at a national or even global level, and are therefore well outside the physical or organizational field of influence of any individual business travel and tourism organization.

These macro-environment factors are very influential in business tourism, and organizations therefore must seek to try to anticipate them and proactively prepare for them.

In this chapter we will explore some of the complex issues involved in the macro-environment in business travel and tourism. First, however, we need to identify the main elements of the macro-environment, using the well known PEST Analysis technique.

PEST analysis

Political, economic, technological, social (PEST) Analysis is the technique used to analyse an organization's macro-environment. It involves looking at four types of factors, namely, political, economic, social and technological. Figure 6.1 outlines the scope of PEST analysis.

All of these factors clearly have implications for business travel and tourism organizations, as of course they have for organizations in all other industries.

The geography of the macro-environment

Clearly, the PEST factors obviously exist at different geographical levels, in different ways. Figure 6.2 attempts to illustrate this point.

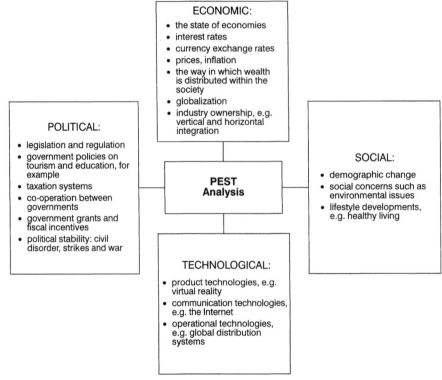

Figure 6.1   PEST Analysis factors

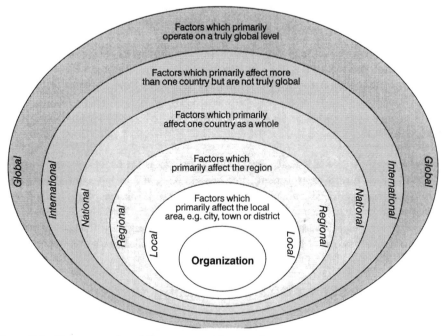

Figure 6.2   The geography of the macro-environment

These five geographical levels of the macro-environment can be illustrated as follows:

- Global – the Internet, a technology that knows no national boundaries.
- International – the 'Single Market' which covers the fifteen countries of the European Union.
- National – national laws on employment.
- Regional– regional government funding of tourism infrastructure.
- Local – local government regulation of restaurant hygiene standards.

The impact of the macro-environment on business travel and tourism organizations

The political, economic, social and technological factors in the macro-environment affect every aspect of the life of business travel and tourism organizations, as can be seen from Figure 6.3.

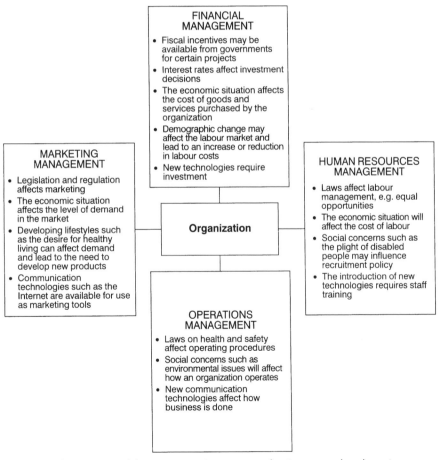

Figure 6.3 The impacts of the macro-environment on business travel and tourism organizations

Figure 6.3 is clearly a highly generalized and stylized picture but it does illustrate the fact that different factors affect different aspects of management within an organization.

Many business travel and tourism organizations do not just have to think about one macro-environment but, rather, three different ones. These three macro-environments are identified in Figure 6.4 in relation to a convention centre, for example.

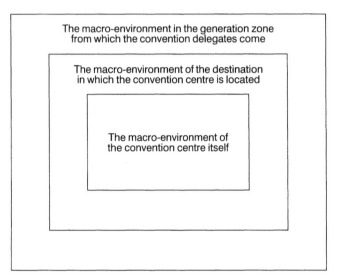

The macro-environment in the generation zone
from which the convention delegates come

The macro-environment of the destination
in which the convention centre is located

The macro-environment of
the convention centre itself

Figure 6.4   The three macro-environments of a convention centre

The real picture is more complex in several ways:

1 The 'generation zone' for a convention centre, may include several different countries, each with their own distinct national macro-environment.
2 There is also a 'transition zone' between the generation zone and the destination, which is the one delegates to conventions travel through or over to reach the destination. These too have their own macro-environments which can affect the traveller. For example, a British delegate travelling to a convention in Athens can be affected by a 'political event' such as a strike of air traffic controllers against their government employers, in France. Hence a convention centre in Athens will be affected by events in the 'transition zone' macro-environment, namely France.
3 There are clear overlaps between the convention centre's macro-environment and that of the destination in which it is located, but they are nevertheless different.

We also need to recognize that the scale of impact of different factors in the macro-environment will vary from organization to organization for reasons which will be explored in the next section of the chapter. It is important that any PEST factors are therefore allocated a weighting for each organization, reflecting the scale of impact each factor is likely to have.

It is now time for us to look at how the macro-environment varies between different types of organizations.

Different types of organizations and different macro-environments

Every business travel and tourism organization has its own unique macro-environment. Figure 6.5 illustrates some of the ways of classifying business travel and tourism organizations which will mean that they have different macro-environments.

We also need to recognize that business travel and tourism is a diverse industry, with different sectors, as can be seen from Figure 6.6.

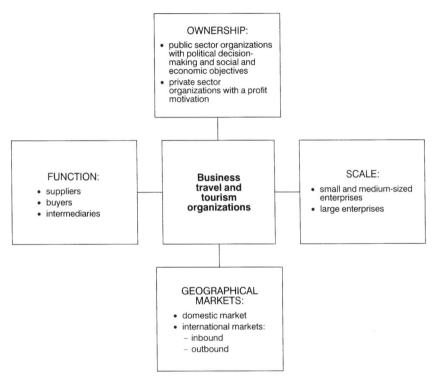

Figure 6.5   Different types of organizations, different macro-environments

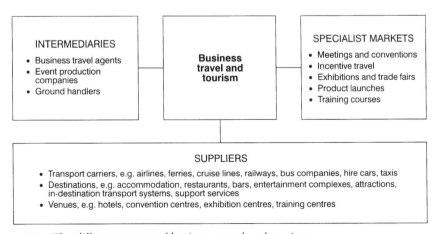

Figure 6.6   The different sectors of business travel and tourism

There are clearly strong links and interrelationships between these different sectors.

If we consider the points made in Figures 6.5 and 6.6 then we will appreciate that the macro-environment of organizations will differ dramatically between different organizations involved in business travel and tourism. The authors have tried to illustrate this in Table 6.1, where they have sought to, rather subjectively, identify the most important factors in the macro-environment of different types of organization.

Table 6.1   The most important factors in the macro-environment of different types of organization

Type of organization	The most important factors in the macro-environment
1. Airlines	
State-owned airline	• Political decisions on the level of public sector financial support that will be given to the airline • Political decisions on the ownership structure of the airline, e.g. selling off shares to private investors or full privatization • State of the economy in key markets
Privately-owned airline	• State of the economy in key markets • Legislation on environmental performance and other operational matters • Ownership trends and the growth of strategic alliances
2. Hotels	
Transnational hotel chains	• State of the economy in key national markets and in the destinations where the chain owns hotels • Cultural differences in consumer behaviour between different national markets • Different national legal systems in terms of everything from employment law to taxation to systems of ownership • Developments in Global Distribution Systems
Small independent hotels	• State of the economy in key target markets which are likely to be within the country where the hotel is located • National legislation on everything from employment to food and hygiene • The price of goods and services, and the level of inflation • National interest rates and their effects on investment decisions
3. Specialist intermediaries	
Incentive travel agency	• State of the economy in the generation zone • Developments in thinking in human resource management • Political stability in the destination • Taxation policy towards incentive travel
Product launch organizers	• The state of the economy in the generation zone • New communication and entertainment technologies that can be used in launches • Political stability in the destination

As we can see from Table 6.1 there are clear differences, as well as similarities, in the weighting of individual factors within the macro-environment of different types of organizations in business travel and tourism, even in the same sector.

It is also important to note that most business travel and tourism organizations identify political and economic factors as the most important in their macro-environment, generally. This is because they are easy to recognize and are constant. However, in the longer term, social and technological factors may have a greater impact. Furthermore, these may be more difficult for organizations to manage because their effects are rather less visual and tend to develop and grow over time. This brings us to the vitally important subject of time.

Time and the macro-environment

It is important to understand that analysing the macro-environment is a matter of recognizing *today* which factors will affect us *tomorrow* and how we should prepare for them.

However, it is not always easy to define, 'tomorrow'. For example:

1 When will tomorrow start?
2 How long will it last before we enter the 'day after tomorrow', a different world, that we cannot even visualize today?

Some factors are already being seen and will continue to develop steadily in the future. Others have only just been recognized but will be incredibly important within a year or two.

Predicting the future is notoriously difficult but that is what PEST Analysis and scanning the business environment is all about.

Conclusion

Every business travel and tourism organization has a macro-environment, and each is unique to the organization. The key factors in these macro-environments will greatly influence the future of the organization. The successful organizations are those which most accurately predict what will happen in their macro-environment in the future and plan most effectively in anticipation of these changes. This is clearly a continuous process which cannot be stopped. The macro-environment provides the context in which all management within business travel and tourism organizations takes place.

Discussion points and essay questions

1 Critically evaluate the suggestion that political factors are the most important factors in the macro-environment of business travel and tourism organizations.
2 Discuss the idea that the macro-environment of transnational hotel chains is more complex than that of a small independent hotel.
3 Discuss the ways in which managers in business travel and tourism organizations could become better informed about their macro-environment.

Exercise

Select a business travel and tourism organization for which you can obtain information. For your chosen organization, you should attempt to model its current macro-environment and what you think will be its macro-environment in ten years time.

You should then seek to identify and explain differences and similarities between the two models.

7 The impacts of business travel and tourism

As with leisure tourism, business travel and tourism has economic, environmental and social impacts – both positive and negative. In this chapter, we will endeavour to produce a balanced picture of these impacts.

Following conventional practice we will identify and briefly discuss the economic, environmental and social impacts separately, although in reality they are highly inter-dependent. We will then look at how the impacts vary between different types of business tourism, different sectors of the business tourism industry and different kinds of destinations.

The authors will try to produce a generalized 'balance sheet' to see if the benefits of business travel and tourism outweigh its costs. Finally, at the end of the chapter, we will look at how we might develop more sustainable forms of business travel and tourism.

Let us now start to look at the three types of impact in a little detail, starting with perhaps the most obvious one, the economic impact.

The economic impact of business travel and tourism

More and more countries, regions, cities and resorts have been trying to attract all kinds of business tourism because it is seen to be the most economically beneficial form of tourism. Surveys all over the world tend to show business tourists, and particularly conference delegates, spending between two and four times as much money as tourists as a whole.

However, the picture is much more complex than this fact might suggest. Figure 7.1 attempts to provide a realistic picture of the economic impact of business travel and tourism. As you can see the situation appears to be that, in general, the economic impacts outweigh the economic costs in relation to business travel and tourism.

There is no doubt that business tourism can bring substantial economic benefits to destinations and suppliers. It is estimated that in 1998, conferences held in the UK alone generated £5 billion for the national economy (UK Conference Market Survey, 1999), while in the same year business travellers to Canada spent some C$1.7 billion (*Travel and Tourism Analyst*, 1999).

Congress and trade show visitors in the USA spent an average of US$696 each on their trip in 1998 (IACVB, 1998).

Sadly, economic impact data is not collected frequently enough to allow the authors to provide an up-to-date picture. However, some older data, which is now a significant

Positive

Negative

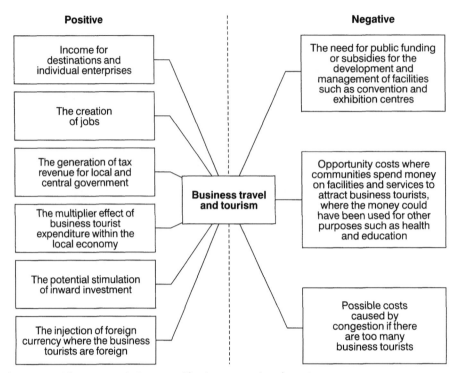

Income for destinations and individual enterprises

The creation of jobs

The generation of tax revenue for local and central government

The multiplier effect of business tourist expenditure within the local economy

The potential stimulation of inward investment

The injection of foreign currency where the business tourists are foreign

Business travel and tourism

The need for public funding or subsidies for the development and management of facilities such as convention and exhibition centres

Opportunity costs where communities spend money on facilities and services to attract business tourists, where the money could have been used for other purposes such as health and education

Possible costs caused by congestion if there are too many business tourists

Figure 7.1   The economic impact of business travel and tourism

underestimate will give some idea of the scale of these impacts (*Travel and Tourism Analyst*, 1999).

1 In 1994 it was estimated that the meetings industry in the USA generated US$82.8 billion in direct spending (Convention Liaison Council, 1994).
2 It was estimated that in the same year the same sector generated a third of all hotel revenue and 22 per cent of airline operating income in the USA, as well as generating over US$12 billion in sales and income taxes (Convention Liaison Council).
3 Between September 1992 and August 1993, it was estimated that the International Convention Centre, National Indoor Arena, Symphony Hall and National Exhibition Centre in Birmingham, UK, had the following impacts:
    (a) Generated US$438 million in expenditure in the region.
    (b) Supported directly 5800 jobs (KPMG Peat Marwick, NEC Group Ltd, 1993).
    Furthermore when Bournemouth UK hosted a major political conference in 1996, it brought £10 million spending to the region in just a few days.

However, we need to recognize that the picture is not always as positive as it may at first appear. For example:

1 Most of the expenditure goes to hotels and transport operations, many of whom may not be locally owned, within the destination.

2 Local taxpayers who are not employed in the business tourism sectors, may be net losers for they will receive no tangible income from business tourist but their taxes may, for example, be used to fund a new convention centre.

3 Business tourists often do not pay the full cost of their trip, for when they attend conferences or exhibitions at publicly owned venues, the venue may not even charge for the use of its facilities. On the other hand, tax income from business tourists can be used to support community projects.

Nevertheless, it is generally accepted that the economic benefits of business tourism are positive in most places.

The environmental impacts of business travel and tourism

Business travel and tourism, like leisure tourism, has a great impact on the physical environment. In Figure 7.2 the authors endeavour to present a balanced view of these impacts. This is a highly generalized picture and issues like building design are largely subjective matters. However, it appears that, in general, business travel and tourism is negative in terms of its environmental impacts.

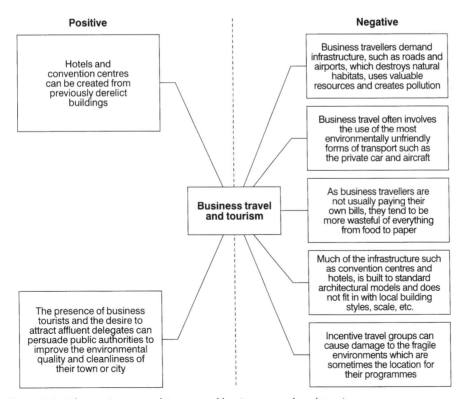

Figure 7.2   The environmental impacts of business travel and tourism

The business tourism industry has yet really to address this issue. In the very good text, by Rogers (1998), *Conferences: A Twenty-First Century Industry*, it is interesting that there are only two brief references to environmental issues.

On the other hand some suppliers such as airlines and hotels have been tackling these issues in recent years. For example, British Airways has pursued a proactive policy on all environmental aspects of its operations and we have seen hotel industry initiatives such as the International Hotels Environmental Initiative. As many clients of these organizations are business tourists these initiatives are clearly helping to reduce – a little – the negative environmental impacts of business travel and tourism.

However, normally, such initiatives seem not to be about tackling the impacts of business tourists fundamentally but, rather, about budget savings for the companies.

In Chapter 8 we will look in some detail at the issue of the design of business tourism physical infrastructure, particularly convention centres. At same time we will also look at the environmental aspect of these designs.

However, we can say, at this stage, that several trends are making the future look rather bleak in terms of reducing the negative environmental impacts of the transportation of business tourists. For example:

1 The lowering of air fares, in real terms, which is encouraging organizations to organize conferences and incentive travel packages thousands of kilometres from their clients' home areas, thus causing more pollution, over a wider area.
2 Business people are still often given a car as part of their remuneration package, which encourages them to travel by car. This is made worse by the fact that a business person's status is often judged by the size of their car and bigger cars usually do more harm.

Finally, business tourists could be seen as being even worse than leisure travellers in terms of negative environmental impacts, because they travel more frequently.

The social impacts of business travel and tourism

Social impacts are perhaps less visible or tangible than economic or environmental impacts, yet they are still very important.

Figure 7.3 seeks to identify the main social impacts of business travel and tourism. The picture is a mixed one with both significant negative and positive impacts.

Interestingly, in this section, we will also consider business travellers themselves, for whom business travel can be both a negative and a positive experience from a social or psychological point of view.

Summary

There is no doubt that business travel has the potential to cause social, economic and environmental problems, often through ignorance or insensitivity. The hypothetical situation shown in Exhibit 7.1, while extreme, does raise some real questions about the behaviour of many business tourists around the world. Imagine, Mr A. is a North European business executive visiting business clients in an African, Asian or South American country, for example.

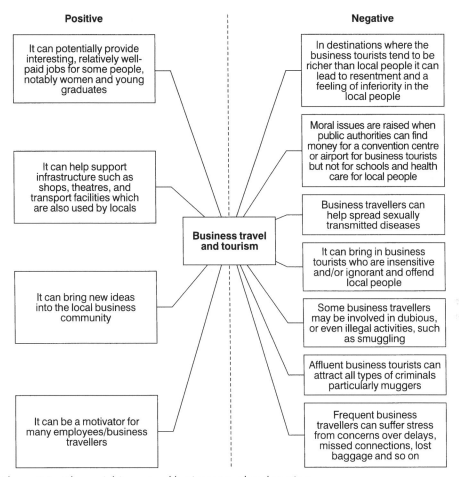

Figure 7.3 The social impacts of business travel and tourism

Exhibit 7.1 Ethical issues case study: a day in the life of the business tourist

- 07.10: Mr A wakes up and complains that the alarm call he ordered did not materialize.
- 07.30: Mr A showers using the complimentary toiletries provided in plastic, disposable containers by the hotel. He puts other bottles of the rather nice shampoo in his case to take home for his daughter, a keen vegetarian and animal rights campaigner, unaware of the fact that it was tested on animals.
- 08.00: Mr A goes down to breakfast. He rejects fresh local fruit in favour of imported yoghurts and marmalade, all packed in plastic, disposable portion packs.
- 09.00: Mr A leaves for his appointment with a client in a large luxury car that guzzles petrol as it sweeps past the poor local people waiting in the bus queue.
- 12.00: Mr A spends a large amount of money on an expensive business lunch with his clients in a luxurious international-style hotel restaurant.

- 14.00: Mr A finishes his business and goes to the shopping area by taxi to buy gifts for his wife and daughter. Ignoring the local traders he spends several hundred pounds at the local branch of a well-known international clothes chain.
- 16.00: Mr A then spends a further £100 buying a very old piece of pottery that has been stolen from an archaeological excavation elsewhere in the country.
- 17.30: Mr A returns to his hotel room by taxi, switches on the air conditioning and then he leaves the room.
- 18.30: Mr A goes to McDonald's for a snack.
- 19.00: Mr A starts drinking in a nearby hotel bar in a country where alcohol is not drunk by local people because of their religion.
- 21.00: Mr A goes to a well-known local massage parlour where he spends some of his expenses on some rather unusual 'extras'. The masseuse is about the same age as his daughter.
- 02.30: Mr A goes to a casino and spends the last of the expenses given him by his company on a little gambling.
- 00.30: Mr A returns to his hotel, and realizes that he has been robbed of his credit cards. Mr A is surprised that all the people who smiled at him and obeyed his requests when he had money no longer seem interested in him.

Source: Swarbrooke (1999).

Towards a cost-benefit analysis of business travel and tourism

At this stage the authors would like to have been able to present the reader with a 'cost-benefit' analysis of business travel and tourism which could say whether, overall, it has positive or negative impacts.

Interestingly, this is not possible for two main reasons, notably:

1 Little reliable empirical research has been published on the impact of business travel and tourism. The industry produces data on the economic impact which it feels shows it in a positive light. However, it does not seem to try to collect information on social and environmental impacts which it may fear could be less positive. Academic researchers have devoted little effort, as yet, to studying the impacts of business tourism, whereas they have carried out a huge volume of research on the impacts of leisure tourism. In any event, given the complexity of the sector it would be very difficult to measure the impacts fairly.
2 Not everyone is affected equally by business travel and tourism. There are big winners such as hotels and the owners of successful conference production companies and smaller winners such as the low-paid operational staff in the service delivery side of the industry. There may even be overall losers, such as the residents in a coastal resort, not employed in business tourism, where local councils have invested millions of pounds of taxpayers' money in a new convention centre.

Nevertheless, overall, the general belief appears to be that business travel and tourism has the following impacts:

- *Economic* – positive.
- *Environmental* – negative.
- *Social* – mixed. Generally positive for the business traveller; more negative for the local community in the destination.

However, as we will now see, the question of whether business travel and tourism has negative or positive impacts is difficult to judge because the nature and scale of the impacts varies between:

● different types of business travel and tourism
● different sectors of the business tourism industry
● different types of business tourism destinations.

Impacts and different types of business travel and tourism

The nature of impacts varies between different types of business travel and tourism. Some of these differences are outlined in Table 7.1 although it must be noted that this is based on opinion rather than empirical evidence.

Impacts on different sectors in business travel and tourism

As we can see in Table 7.2 the impacts of business travel and tourism also vary depending on the sector of the industry we are considering. Again, this table is based on opinion rather than empirical research.

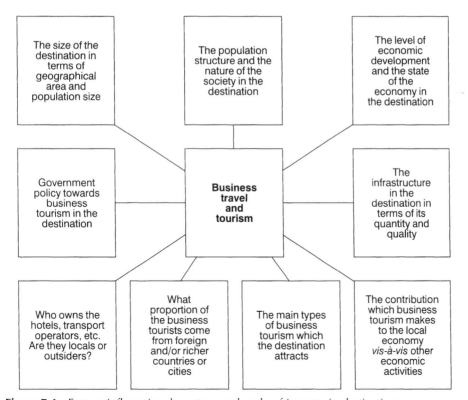

Figure 7.4 Factors influencing the nature and scale of impacts in destinations

Table 7.1 The impacts of different types of business travel and tourism

Type of business travel and tourism	Economic impact	Environmental impact	Social impact
Individual business trip	Higher than leisure tourism, but very little for an individual traveller. However, can be considerable in cities which attract a lot of individual business trips	Very limited for the individual traveller. In major destinations for individual business trips the volume of travellers can have great transport-related environmental impacts	Very limited for the individual traveller. Can be substantial in destinations which receive a considerable number of individual business trips
Conferences and meetings	Significant positive impact due to relatively high-spending by delegates. Individual conferences can generate millions of pounds of expenditure over a short period. Creates more economic impact if it is a residential conference. Creates income for individual smaller specialist suppliers such as audiovisual companies, photographers, etc. as well as venues	Apart from transport impacts there is the impact caused by the construction of new conference facilities, particularly large-scale convention centres	Depends on the volume of conferences in a particular destination. High in major convention destinations
Exhibitions	Considerable as they are often major events using the services of a wide range of suppliers. However, often suppliers are not locally based so that the expenditure 'leaks' from the local economy	Apart from transport, there are also impacts caused by new exhibition centre construction	Limited unless destinations attract large numbers of exhibition visitors
Incentive travel	Limited as groups tend to be relatively small. However, spending per head is usually high	Depends on the location of the package. Problems may arise with packages where the core activity includes visits to fragile environments or wild-life watching	Very limited unless the volume of incentive travel in a particular destination is particularly high
Product launches	High spending but usually over very short time periods	Limited unless using the environment as the venue for the launch	Very limited due to it being a short-duration, infrequent activity
Training courses	Considerable if destination/venue attracts many such courses. Can be long in duration which also increases economic impact	Limited unless it involves 'survival' type adventure training in fragile environments for example	Very limited

Table 7.2 The impacts of business travel and tourism on different sectors of the industry

Sector	Economic impact	Environmental impact	Social impact
Air transport	Business travel contributes the majority of the revenue for most airlines which employ tens of thousands of people in many countries	The demand by business travellers for air travel causes significant environmental problems such as emissions, noise pollution, use of non-renewable resources, waste, etc.	Very limited
Road transport	Business travel is a major source of revenue for taxis and car hire. The use of cars for business is a major source of income for many car dealers. The use of cars causes congestion which is often not costed	Major impact in terms of pollution and the use of non-renewable energy services	Limited
Hotels	Business tourism is a major source of income for most hotels. It supports a large proportion of the considerable number of jobs in this sector	Problems range from poor design and operation in terms of the use of inappropriate architectural designs that do not fit well with the surroundings, to waste and high energy consumption	Very limited
Agencies and intermediaries	Business tourism supports thousands of jobs in specialist intermediaries and agencies. Many of these jobs are relatively well paid for the tourism industry	Very limited, directly	Very limited, directly
Convention and exhibition centres	Can attract substantial income to a destination. However, their capital costs are high and often they are publicly owned and require a revenue subsidy	Can be very negative if poorly planned and/or designed and/or operated	Can be considerable if they attract a lot of events to the destination
Destinations	Provides income for a range of local enterprises together with tax income for local and central government. However, it depends on the type of business tourism and the local infrastructure. If the latter is poorly developed, many services may be provided by outside companies which results in leakages from the local economy	Depends on the volume and type of business tourism	Depends on the volume and type of business tourism

Impacts and different types of destinations

Clearly, the impact of business travel and tourism is not the same in every destination. Figure 7.4 seeks to identify some of the factors that will affect the scale of impacts in a destination.

Not only do these factors influence the scale of impacts. They also determine if the impacts are likely to be more positive or more negative. Figure 7.5 endeavours to illustrate this point with two hypothetical, extremely polarized examples.

DESTINATION A

A large successful city with a booming economy in a developed country

Most hotels and conference centres are primarily owned by local entrepreneurs and most staff are locals

The season is all year round as the city enjoys a good climate in every season

DESTINATION B

A small destination backed by mountains with a largely poor resident population, in a developing country

The government has spent $100 million dollars on a new convention centre. Poor education levels mean that new staff in the convention centre are in-migrants

The convention centre brings in conference delegates from rich countries looking for luxury at a low price

The season is very short because for six months each year the climate is very bad

Very positive impact —————————————————————————— **Very negative impact**

Most business tourists coming to the destination are from other cities in the same country and speak the same language

The business tourists make great use of local attractions and facilities during their stay

Most tax income from business tourism is a sales tax and hotel tax which goes directly to the local government

The city is located on a flat plain and is expanding on a planned basis, within strict environmental protection laws

Most business travellers are richer than the locals and are ignorant of the local language

The public utilities are already overwhelmed by demand before the business tourists arrive

Most business tourists rarely leave the convention centre or hotel during their stay

The tax income from the business travellers largely goes to the central government in the national capital

Tourists arrive on foreign airlines

Because the site of the resort is geographically constrained by the mountains, the hotels are high rise and the airport is very close to a poor residential district

Figure 7.5   Impacts and different types of destination

Towards more sustainable forms of business travel and tourism

We have seen that along with its positive side, business travel and tourism has a number of significant negative impacts.

In recent years some progress has been made in the air transport field. Airlines have introduced quieter, more fuel efficient aircraft in the wake of tighter international regulations and many now have comprehensive environmental management systems covering their ground operations. Hotels too, inspired by the desire to reduce costs, have also taken action to reduce the negative effects of their operations on the environment.

However, what we may describe as the 'mainstream' business tourism industry – conference and exhibition centres and incentive travel, for example, – have shown little apparent interest in environmental issues. At the same time little attention has been paid to the social impacts of business travel and tourism by any sector. Likewise no real concern has been expressed over the economic costs of business tourism. Instead, there has been a concentration on its economic benefits.

If the industry does not prove it can regulate itself and adopt a more responsible attitude towards its impacts, then some form of regulation may be required. The industry cannot simply rely on the actions of its 'suppliers' such as airlines and hotels, it must take responsibility itself for its effects.

We need to recognize that some of the negative impacts of business tourism, while they can be reduced, will not be eliminated. They are the inevitable result of the mere act of travelling. Aircraft, for example, will truly never be neutral in terms of their environmental impacts, and rich business travellers will always cause resentment among some poorer people in their destinations.

If we want to make business travel and tourism more sustainable, we have to recognize that there are characteristics of business tourism which make it particularly problematic in relation to the concept of sustainable tourism. First, most business tourists take more trips in a year than the average leisure tourist, thus making more demands on transport infrastructure and destination services. Business tourists tend to be very demanding and want high-quality facilities, even in towns and cities in developing countries. While both of these are difficult to reconcile with the concept of sustainable tourism, the positive side of business tourism is the fact that business travellers tend to be higher spending than leisure tourists (Swarbrooke, 1999).

Therefore, we have to endeavour to minimize the costs, and maximize the benefits, of business travel and tourism through better management in the transport sector and in the destination.

There is a need to:

- persuade the business tourist to use public, rather than private, transport whenever possible
- educate business travellers about the social problems caused in destinations by prostitution and about the risks to their own health involved in having sex with prostitutes
- make business travellers aware of the need to spend their money with local enterprises rather than with externally based multinational corporations, wherever possible
- encourage business tourists to welcome local cultural differences rather than searching for familiar but 'foreign' products and services (Swarbrooke, 1999).

There is a more radical approach, namely, trying to reduce the overall volume of business travel and tourism. This may sound very unlikely in the face of the growth of business tourism in recent years. However, some commentators argue that the rise of new technologies will reduce or at least slow down the demand for business travel.

It could be argued that the growth of satellite, video-conferencing and computer-conferencing should reduce the demand for business travel. Likewise Virtual Reality technologies are also allowing people to train to do everything from fighting fires to carrying out surgical operations, without the need to travel to a training centre or another hospital for example.

This should appeal to employers, who stand to save money if use of these technologies becomes more common. Conversely, the business traveller may resent these developments. They will reduce the number of trips business travellers take to interesting places, when they might often take a partner along, mixing business with pleasure. This could reduce their job satisfaction and their status. At the same time, fewer trips will mean fewer points for the consumer from frequent flyer programmes which may also cause resentment amongst business travellers. (Swarbrooke, 1999)

On the other hand there is the fact that much business travel is to facilitate face-to-face contact between conference delegates and salespeople and their clients, for example. It may be difficult to replace this by the use of communication technologies.

Nevertheless technology may dampen or even reduce demand for business travel and tourism in the years to come. While this would be good in terms of reducing the negative impacts of business tourism, it would also reduce the economic benefits of business tourism for destinations, airlines and hotels.

Conclusions

In this chapter, we have seen that business travel and tourism has many different impacts, both positive and negative. It has also been noted that the nature of the impact varies between different types of business tourism, different sectors of the industry and different types of destinations. We have suggested that, to date, the business tourism industry does not seem to have been very concerned about its impacts. Finally, we have looked at some ways in which business travel and tourism could be made more sustainable, including the role of new technologies in reducing the demand for business travel and tourism overall.

Discussion points and essay questions

1 Discuss the ways in which a destination could try to maximize the economic benefits of business travel and tourism while minimizing its economic costs.
2 Critically evaluate the idea that business travel and tourism is less harmful than leisure tourism in terms of its impacts.
3 Using examples, discuss the ways in which airlines and hotels have sought to become more environmentally friendly in recent years.

Exercise

Select *one* conference venue *or* convention centre *or* exhibition centre and *one* business travel agency *or* incentive travel agency. Interview a representative from your *two* chosen organizations and ask them to outline for you what they consider to be the main impacts, both positive and negative, of business travel and tourism, or at least their relevant sector of it.

Conclusions to Part One

In Part One we have set the scene for the rest of the book, by looking at a number of aspects of business travel and tourism.

We have seen that business travel and tourism is not new; it has a long history. It was recognized in Chapters 3 and 4 that business travel and tourism is complex, in terms of both the market and the supply side. We have noted that destinations play a unique role in business travel and tourism. In the penultimate chapter we saw that business travel and tourism organizations live within a complex, multifaceted macro-environment. Finally, in Chapter 7, we noted that business travel and tourism, like leisure tourism, has economic, environmental and social impacts, both positive and negative.

It is now time for us to turn our attention to the development and management of business travel and tourism in terms of its physical infrastructure, human resources, and marketing.

Part Two
The Development and Management of Business Travel and Tourism

Part Two of the book examines three major aspects of the development and management of business travel and tourism.

Chapter 8 looks at an often ignored topic, namely, the physical infrastructure and how it is designed and constructed, including convention centres, hotels and airports. It focuses upon a range of key design issues including user friendliness and environmental quality.

The next chapter considers the rise of the human resource infrastructure, in other words, the people who deliver the service to all business travellers. It looks at how they are treated and rewarded, as well as examining their training and education.

The final chapter in this part of the book concentrates upon the marketing of business travel and tourism. This includes the application of the marketing mix, or 4 Ps, to business travel and tourism, as well as other marketing concepts such as brand loyalty, segmentation, and relationship marketing. This chapter also examines the issues of quality and customer satisfaction in business travel and tourism.

8 The physical infrastructure of business travel and tourism

Business travel and tourism relies on a complex, multifaceted physical infrastructure. In this chapter we will look at a range of issues relating to this physical infrastructure, notably:

- a typology of the physical infrastructure of business travel and tourism
- design matters, including user friendliness, environmental concerns and multipurpose use
- operational issues relating to the physical infrastructure
- costs and funding issues.

A typology of business travel and tourism physical infrastructure

Figure 8.1 illustrates the nature of physical infrastructure in business travel and tourism. It does not aim to be comprehensive but simply to illustrate the diversity of the physical infrastructure.

Figure 8.1 clearly illustrates that, in general, business travel and tourism uses infrastructure which may also be used regularly or occasionally by other groups for different purposes. However, the key issue is that while others may use these facilities, they have to be designed in a way that meets the specific needs of the business traveller or

Physical infrastructure used exclusively by the business traveller or tourist	Physical infrastructure primarily used for business travel and tourism but which can be used by others	Physical infrastructure which is shared with leisure tourists and travellers
Specialist training centres	Convention and exhibition centres which may also be used for concerts and shows to which the public are invited Function rooms in hotels which are used for private leisure parties	Hotels Airports Railway stations Roads Port installations

Figure 8.1 The physical infrastructure of business travel and tourism

Hotels	Purpose-built convention centres
• Large city centre hotels • Budget motels on road junctions or motorway locations • Self-contained resort complexes • Hotels linked to attractions such as theme parks	• Large-scale or small-scale centres • Centres with one major auditorium vs those which also have small 'break-out' rooms • Centres with facilities just for conventions vs those centres which also have facilities for exhibitions

Figure 8.2   Sub-classification of hotels and purpose-built convention centres

tourist. This is a very broad typology. Each of these categories could be further subdivided, as we can see in Figure 8.2, in relation to hotels and purpose-built convention centres, for example.

Design matters

The scope of design

Not only are there different types of infrastructure, but we must also remember that an infrastructure development requires the design of a whole range of elements including, in relation to a convention centre, for example:

- main buildings and structures – location, scale and materials
- internal fittings and fixtures including catering facilities, retail outlets and toilets
- landscaping around the buildings and structures
- the layout of the site, as a whole
- support services such as car parks
- signing

A holistic approach has to be taken to ensure that the entire final design works for users.

Design issues

When we design anything we are always trying to meet a number of design objectives. Figure 8.3 identifies some of the key design objectives in relation to the physical infrastructure of business travel and tourism. We will look at three of these in detail in this chapter, namely user friendliness, environmental friendliness and multipurpose use. However the others are all also important.

User friendliness

Clearly, everyone agrees that any physical structure should be user friendly. However, first we need to decide who the users will be. As a spokesperson for the Right Solution Limited says:

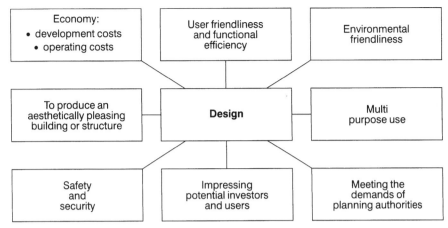

Figure 8.3   Design objectives

When designing a convention centre one has to consider first and most importantly, who will be using the facilities and for what purpose? The target markets and the likely occupants of the facilities are crucial to their viability and must be considered separately at each stage of the design. In other words, form must follow function, not the other way round, which is too often the case. (The Right Solution Limited, quoted in Rogers, 1998)

There are a number of different groups of users who have special needs, that need to be recognized by designers. Some of these are outlined in Figure 8.4.

We will now use hypothetical examples to illustrate good and bad practice in the design of physical infrastructure.

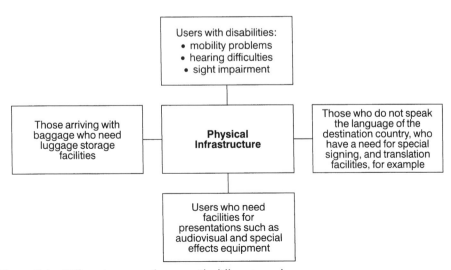

Figure 8.4   Different groups of users with different needs

A hypothetical example of good practice: the Sunnyville Convention Centre

This purpose-built convention centre is located on a formerly derelict site, surrounded by a nicely landscaped area, near to the town centre. A railway station is next door and there is a secure car park adjacent to the centre. The centre is clearly signposted from every direction. The entrance to the auditorium is clearly marked, and is accessed via a ramp with a very low gradient, ideal for those using a wheelchair.

The doors are automatic, ideal for delegates carrying heavy bags. The information centre is right by the entrance, next to the cloakroom, and there is clear signposting to every part of the complex. Symbols are used for the benefits of foreign guests and there are Braille signs for those with sight difficulties.

The building has been designed to allow large numbers of people to pass through quickly and the food and drink outlets have been designed to allow quick throughput.

At the back of the exhibition hall, on a service road, is a large entrance for those bringing equipment for the exhibitions, which support many conferences. Vehicles can even gain access via this entrance, if necessary.

There is a large auditorium with tiered seating which can also be used for concerts and shows. It has many emergency exits in the event of fire alarms and other emergencies.

There are a number of flat-floored spaces which can be effectively subdivided to meet the needs of groups of different sizes, for 'break-out' sessions.

Each meeting space, together with the auditorium is fitted with an Induction Loop system for hard of hearing delegates, together with spaces for wheelchairs.

Lifts are available to all floors and each floor has facilities for wheelchair-based delegates. In many countries such provision is now obligatory, including the UK.

No meeting space or room is more than sixty seconds walk from a toilet or a catering outlet.

Plentiful offices are available for event organizers and the press, for example.

The meeting rooms are almost wholly lit by natural light which is less expensive for the venue and is kinder to delegates' eyes. Floors have been designed to cope with heavy loads of equipment.

The decor is light and airy and there is plenty of space for safe storage of materials. All meeting rooms are away from the food production areas to reduce noise and smells.

There are plenty of power points and computer access points around the room.

The centre is already proving profitable because it was designed in consultation with the industry and is meeting the needs of its different groups of clients admirably.

A hypothetical example of bad practice: Newtown airport

Newtown airport is over forty years old. It was opened in 1960 and enlarged in a piecemeal fashion in 1969 and 1988. Then, in 1995, a new terminal was opened on the other side of the airfield. It seems that the airport has always been too small to meet demand comfortably.

The train station is 2 kilometres away, and passengers have to take a shuttle bus from there to Terminals 1A, 1B, 1C and 2. A shuttle bus also operates between terminals 1A, 1B, 1C and 2. The transfer from the station to the airport takes between 5 minutes and 30 minutes depending on the time of day and traffic volume.

Once inside the terminals, passengers are immediately struck by the low ceilings and the lack of air conditioning which makes the building feel oppressive. Signposting is inconsistent in that signage for a particular place suddenly stops before that place is reached.

The main toilets are in the lower ground floor to which there are stairs but no lifts.

The check-ins are cramped and too small. Once passengers have checked-in there is a café in a dark corner without a 'no-smoking area'.

The business traveller lounge is too small and is on the sixth floor so that passengers have to take the overcrowded lift, up five floors. There are not enough passport control points, so queues develop at busy times.

The airside of the departure section has no catering facilities, just a big duty free shop. There are too few seats and, again, there are no dedicated no-smoking areas.

No announcements are made about flights and there are no information panels in Braille.

At the departure gate the temperatures mount and there is no air conditioning.

Because of the design, aircraft cannot be connected to the gate with covered walkways. Instead passengers have to be bussed out to the aircraft. Passengers who use wheelchairs, therefore, have to be physically carried on to the aircraft, not a very dignified experience.

In the arrivals area passengers have to walk 500 metres to collect their baggage. They often have to wait because there are not enough baggage carousels. Quite often bags get mixed up, and sometimes they are lost.

The car parks are dark, dingy and not very secure. Furthermore the dedicated disabled parking is on the far side of the car park, furthest away from the entrance.

The major airline based at Newtown airport has experienced a fall in passengers through this airport, its major hub. At the same time its main competitor, which is based at an airport in another country, has noticed an increase in passengers through its hub since it built its new state-of-the-art terminal.

Having looked at this hypothetical example, let us now look at some real airports in terms of their business class lounges, and whether or not they meet the needs of business travellers through their design.

Airline Business Class lounges

In recent years airlines have done much to provide business traveller lounges at airports as part of their attempt to woo such passengers. In February 2000, *Business Traveller* magazine published a survey of six such lounges to evaluate them. This specialist 'consumer' magazine was impressed by the following lounges:

1 The large (4200 square metres) Cathay Pacific 'The Wing' lounge at the new Hong Kong airport, together with the cabins with their massage showers, and the rippling water feature. They also noted the quiet reading room. However, the author warned readers that a 20-minute walk and a train trip is required to reach the furthest gates
2 The British Airways 'The Terraces' lounge at Manchester airport, which has been zoned and designed for different activities, such as dozing or reading with sunloungers, fax and computer facilities, and smoking. It notes with approval that the children's area is well away from the working area. They mention the 'Country Kitchen' in the food area and the '1930s style' cocktail bar.

3 The Virgin Atlantic 'Clubhouse' at Gatwick and the fact that drinks are served under an aircraft wing-shaped canopy. It says there is a soundproof cinema for viewing videos, films and CDs. There is a video games room, and meeting facilities.
4 The British Airways Concorde lounge at Heathrow lacks business facilities but is artistically decorated with drawings, sculptures and glass panels. Designer furniture completes the effect.
5 The Singapore Airlines 'Kris' lounge at Singapore Changi airport seats 600 and is decorated with national materials. The author liked the development of five self-service food and drink service points. High-quality furnishings and aquariums were noted as positive features, as were the shower rooms and massage chairs, television rooms and soundproof phone booths.
6 The American Airlines Heathrow airport lounge is said to aim for an 'airy' English country home ambience.

This survey gives a clear impression of what business travellers look for from the lounges which are designed primarily for their use.

Exhibition centres

Before we finish the section on user-friendly design we need to say a few words about the situation with exhibition centres. Many of the points made earlier in relation to convention centres in this chapter also apply to exhibition centres, particularly as more and more purpose-built centres combine conference and exhibition facilities. However, the emphasis in exhibition centre design is on producing multipurpose spaces, easy access for exhibitors and suppliers to deliver heavy goods, and 'processing' areas for exhibition visitors. Plenty of lifts are also required near to the goods entrances.

Designers need to ensure that there are no dark corners or other unsuitable locations on the exhibition floor that will be difficult for exhibition organizers to sell to exhibitors.

Many exhibitions aimed at the public can attract tens, if not hundreds of thousands of visitors so road access, car parking and rail station proximity is vital.

Summary

User-friendly design is clearly a matter of identifying user groups and their particular needs and then designing to meet these needs, within the available budget. There is no doubt that user-friendly design helps ensure customer satisfaction and makes repeat business more likely.

The need for industry input in the design process

One of the best ways to ensure that the business tourism physical infrastructure is user friendly is to involve the industry and its consumers in the design process. This means consulting professional bodies, buyers, intermediaries and consumers. These stakeholders need to be involved early in the design process before irrevocable decisions have been taken and their views need to be taken seriously.

However, it is important to ensure that, right at the beginning, the terms of reference for this consultation are made clear to all participants. They need to know where they can and cannot influence the design, and what influence their views will have.

The same principle is true in relation to disabled users, whose representative bodies should be consulted from the beginning of the design of any physical infrastructure in the business travel and tourism sector.

Environmental sensitivity

Designing new physical infrastructure requires sensitivity to environmental issues, whether it is an airport, a hotel, a convention centre or an exhibition venue.

Table 8.1 uses the designing of two new hypothetical business hotels with conference facilities, one in a city and one in a coastal location, to demonstrate environmental principles which should underpin the design of hotels in these situations.

While planning laws will require some of these issues to be addressed before planning permission is granted, in some countries, this is not always the case, particularly in developing countries. Here, it is the responsibility of the individual developer to design the hotel, with environmental sensitivity in mind.

The principles outlined above can, of course, also be applied to the development of convention centres and exhibition centres.

Multipurpose use

Conference and exhibition venues can often only survive if they can attract many different types and sizes of events. They, therefore, need to be designed with flexibility in mind. Usually, this means the following issues for designers:

● creating spaces which can be sub-divided to allow them comfortably to accommodate different sizes of events
● designing spaces with either non-fixed seating, or with fixed seating that can be removed so that the space can be used for exhibitions and drinks receptions as well as meetings.

Often, the need to create multipurpose spaces can cause potential problems. For example, let us imagine that a conference venue within a hotel has two meeting rooms or spaces. Space A is used for the meeting and Space B, which is adjacent and is usually used as a meeting room, is being cleared to act as the venue for the buffet lunch for the Space A group. The problem is that the delegates in Space A will be distributed as the buffet is set up in Space B.

Conference and exhibition venues often have to be used for purposes other than business tourism events. They need to be able to swap from one use to another in a few hours, which poses real challenges for designers. For example the Sheffield Arena, in the UK, is the venue for:

● exhibitions
● major shows and spectaculars
● meetings
● ice hockey and basketball games.

Table 8.1 Environmentally sensitive design principles for two new business hotels with conference facilities

Issue	City hotel	Coastal hotel
Site selection and location	● Preferably a 'brown field' site rather than a new 'green field' site, i.e. using existing buildings or derelict site ● Near to public transport to reduce need for private transport	● Do not choose site with particularly fragile ecosystem or important habitats
Scale	● Appropriate to the location	● No larger than the norm in the area ● Low rise
Form and appearance	● Aim for aesthetic quality so it adds something to the townscape	● Try to design so that it blends into the local vernacular style
Materials	● Use recycled or recovered materials wherever possible, e.g. bricks from demolished buildings	● Local, wherever possible ● Use recycled and recovered materials where possible, e.g. bricks from demolished buildings
Site layout and landscaping	● Soften the building with site landscaping and green spaces wherever possible	● Soften outlines of the buildings with landscaping using local species ● Do not over-develop the site
Facilities and services	● Limit parking to encourage public transport use	● Design swimming pool so that water can be recycled and/or use sea water rather than precious fresh water ● 'Hide' car parking by landscaping or putting car park underground
Other environmentally sensitive design issues	● Make sure conference/meeting rooms are designed so that they can make maximum use of natural light rather than having to rely on artificial light ● Design the hotel to maximize energy conservation	● Make sure conference/meeting rooms are designed so that they can make maximum use of natural light rather than having to rely on artificial light ● Develop wildlife habitats in the grounds ● Design the hotel to maximize energy conservation

Design constraints

Whatever they try to achieve, designers always face constraints that mean that their final design is a compromise between their ideal designs and these constraints, some of which are shown in Figure 8.5.

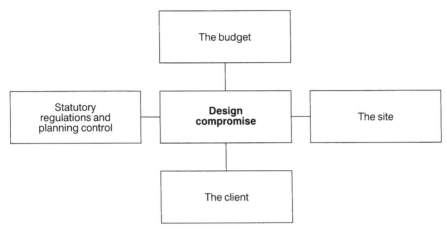

Figure 8.5   Design constraints

The budget

This will limit the quality and size of the site, the scale of the buildings and structures, the materials, the quality of finishes and detailing through to the quality of furniture and fittings.

The site

This will impose limitations on the design based on its size and shape, the quality of drainage, previous uses and their legacy, and its accessibility.

The client

Client will have their own preferences, prejudices and experience. These will influence their ideas and will shape the 'brief' which will guide the work of the designer.

Statutory regulations and planning control

Planning regulations, including zoning and building control laws, will affect all aspects of the design. This will be particularly important if the site is a recognized historic building and/or it is in an area affected by conservation legislation.

The danger of internationalization/standardization

With the growth of globalization, it appears that there is increasing internationalization and standardization of physical infrastructure. The air traveller could, in general, be forgiven for becoming disoriented in most airports, unable to tell from their design where they are.

The same is true of many modern convention and exhibition centres, together with international chain hotels. At least, in the latter case, some hotel designers now attempt to produce designs which incorporate features of the local architecture. However, this trend has not yet extended to many convention and exhibition centres.

This is obviously at odds with the concept of sustainability, which always stresses the importance of the uniqueness of place and the importance of representing that which is local. However, there is a danger that we will simply start producing kitsch pastiches of national and regional stereotypes.

What is needed, perhaps, is an approach to design that endeavours imaginatively to combine elements of local traditional architecture and local materials with modern design ideas and construction technologies.

Operational issues

The way in which physical infrastructure is designed and developed is crucial to day-to-day operations. Some of the most common operational issues related to the design and development of physical infrastructure are illustrated in Figure 8.6.

Once the infrastructure is operational, action may need to be taken to alleviate problems arising from these issues.

Costs and funding issues

So far we have focused on the design and operation of the physical infrastructure of business travel and tourism. We will now look at development costs and where the money comes from.

The first thing to say is that business tourism infrastructure is expensive. An airport costs hundreds of millions of pounds, of course. However, even a convention centre can cost millions of pounds. In 1994 it was estimated that the average cost of building a conference centre in the UK, even one on a modest scale, would be around £20 million. Some centres cost up to £200 million to develop. Traditionally, in the UK and elsewhere, convention centres were often publicly owned – 50 per cent in the UK still are. However, there has been a global trend towards more private sector ownership in this field.

The role of the public sector in this field is a controversial area, for a number of reasons:

1 The high development costs can result in the need for public sector borrowing and high debt service charges over a lengthy period.
2 Investment in business tourism infrastructure represents an opportunity cost in relation to other types of potential investment.
3 Often convention centres are operated as 'loss leaders' by public bodies to attract lucrative conventions and exhibitions to the destination bringing considerable benefits

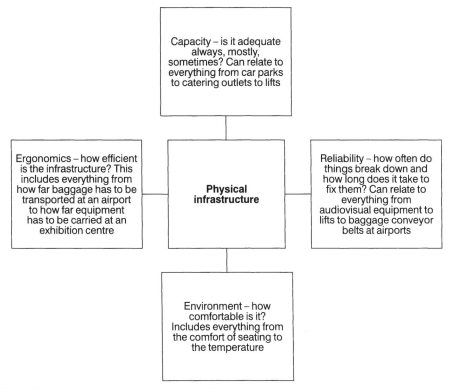

Figure 8.6 Key operational issues in relation to physical infrastructure

with them. Thus, the development of such complexes by the public sector can involve the need for significant annual subsidies to cover the losses.

4 The majority of the economic benefits of business tourism are enjoyed by private sector business; there is an issue about the extent to which the public sector should invest public money to help generate income for private sector interests.

5 Capital expenditure is required at regular intervals to refurbish or extend centres to help keep them competitive.

Those convention venues and exhibition centres developed with private money tend to be on a smaller scale than those developed by the public sector. They also are often located in existing popular business tourism destinations where the risk of developing new venues is less.

The transport infrastructure required by business travellers is generally publicly funded, such as airports, roads and railways stations, although the use of private sources of funding has generally grown in recent years. Nevertheless, necessary improvements in transport infrastructure can still be delayed for years if governments are not willing to provide funding. This can lead to congestion and delay problems for business travellers.

The hospitality sector is almost totally privately owned and most expenditure on hotels, for example, is private money, although public sector grants can be received in designated regions where incentives are given to encourage economic development and regeneration.

Conclusion

In this chapter we have seen that business travel and tourism relies on a complex variety of physical infrastructure, some of which it shares with other types of users. It has been clearly demonstrated that good design is vital to the success of all physical infrastructure in this sector, particularly in terms of user friendliness. We have also noted that there is still room for improvement in the design of business tourism infrastructure in terms of its environmental sensitivity. In the last section we have seen that there are major questions over the role of the public sector in the funding of business tourism infrastructure.

Discussion points and essay questions

1 Discuss the factors which determine the success or failure of a new convention centre.
2 Critically evaluate the ways in which the negative environmental impacts of the development of new convention centres could be minimized.
3 Discuss the arguments for and against public sector funding of convention centres and exhibition centres.

Exercise

Visit a convention centre *or* exhibition centre *or* an airport. Then produce a critical evaluation of its design in terms of its user friendliness for different groups of users.

9 The human resource infrastructure of business travel and tourism

As a labour-intensive service industry, the quality of staff, the human resource, in business travel and tourism, is of crucial importance to the success of the sector.

In this chapter we will look at several issues relating to the human resource dimension of business travel and tourism, notably:

- the nature of employment within the sector
- the types of jobs
- the people who work in the industry
- working conditions and salaries
- the key skills required by staff
- training and education.

The nature of employment within business travel and tourism

As a complex activity and sector it is not surprising that the nature of employment within the sector is also complicated. Figure 9.1 illustrates the first aspect of employment within this sector, namely, whether or not business travel and tourism is the core of a person's employment.

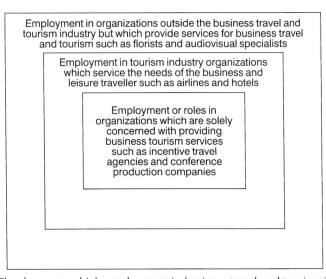

Employment in organizations outside the business travel and tourism industry but which provide services for business travel and tourism such as florists and audiovisual specialists

Employment in tourism industry organizations which service the needs of the business and leisure traveller such as airlines and hotels

Employment or roles in organizations which are solely concerned with providing business tourism services such as incentive travel agencies and conference production companies

Figure 9.1 The degree to which employment in business travel and tourism is related

Figure 9.2 recognizes that business travel and tourism-related employment can be divided three ways in terms of the functions of buyers, intermediaries and suppliers.

In Figure 9.3, we distinguish between work in business travel and that in business tourism focusing on those sectors which purely serve the needs of the business traveller/tourist.

Figure 9.4 illustrates the range of different types of organization which provide employment in this sector.

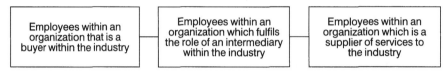

Figure 9.2   The division of employment into buyers, intermediaries and suppliers

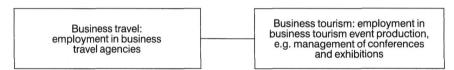

Figure 9.3   Business travel and business tourism

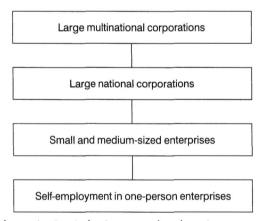

Figure 9.4   Types of organization in business travel and tourism

Because of the modernity of business travel and tourism, it is likely that most people employed in the industry are working for organizations which may well be less than twenty years old.

In the rest of this chapter we will focus upon those jobs which are within the 'core' of business tourism, that is, those involved in the management and production of conferences, exhibitions, incentive travel, and so on.

Types of jobs

The complexity of employment in the sector means that there are many different types of jobs, at all levels. Exhibit 9.1 lists some of the jobs that were being advertised in the UK business tourism sector in 2000 in *Conference and Incentive Travel.*

Exhibit 9.1 Types of jobs in the UK business tourism sector 2000

Regan & Dean + Lester

Head of Exhibitions – Proven management skills needed for top corporate production company: £50k negotiable

Commercial Manager – Marketing and sales led manager required to develop the events team at this unusual venue: £35k + car

Operations Manager – Strong leadership and logistics skills for international events team. Languages useful: £28k+

Senior Production Manager – Run the technical production department of this events company: £30k

Events Manager – Promote and manage private parties and events. Some international travel: £25k + car

Corporate Sales Manager – Great opportunity for a dynamic 'go-getter' within top events agency: £27k+

Marketing Executive – Plan and implement campaigns for this conference production company: £25k + commission

Live Events Producers – Middle to senior level for top international corporate production companies: £28–45k

Project Manager – Creative business communications consultancy needs an experienced events manager: £25–30k

Organizing Manager – Major exhibitions company needs a customer focused organizer: £26.5k

Conference Producer – Established business to business conference producers want to expand their team: £25k + commission

Event Specialist – In-house position organizing IT trade shows and exhibitions throughout Europe: £27k

Conference Assistant – Excellent administration skills are needed for this healthcare conference company: £17k

Congress Planner – Belgium office of international events company needs an experienced conference organizer: £24–30k

Account Manager – Specialists in youth culture events need someone to win and manage new business: £20–25k

Assistant Producer – Join the production team of this top corporate company. Needs fluent German: £16k

Freelancers – Producers, Production Assistants, Production Managers, Logistics, and Account Managers

Edric Audio Visual

Edric Audio Visual Limited (EAV) with offices in Bristol, Manchester and Gerrards Cross (near London) are an established company who are enjoying a period of sustained growth. Services include audiovisual sales, hire, service, video/multimedia programmes and computer graphic production. The Conference Works division of EAV specializes in total conference/event management and production.

Job vacancies:

Conference Producer (Bristol)
Will suit sales orientated creative producer seeking career advancement

Hire Operations/Logistics Manager (Bristol)
To head up a centralized operations centre

Hire Desk Co-ordinator (Bristol)
First point of contact for all hire enquiries

Sales Executives (Manchester and Bristol)
Sales of AV equipment and hire
Basic salary + commission + car

Sales Desk Co-ordinator (Bristol)
To handle all incoming sales enquiries

Marketing Assistant (Bristol)
Full range of marketing activity, CIM qualification desirable

British Association of Conference Destinations (BACD)

To assist in the Association's future growth, we are looking to appoint to the newly created position of: *Operations Manager*

Specific responsibilities include:

- Overseeing the running of the BACD office and associated systems, maximizing the use of information technology
- Managing and developing the BACD team
- Representing BACD to external bodies
- Planning, promoting and managing BACD events (exhibitions, conferences, courses)
- Maximizing revenue-generating opportunities
- Contributing to the strategic development of BACD.

The successful candidate will have a background in information technology and/or sales and marketing and/or personnel, with a proven track record in conference/ event management. He/she will be a confident communicator and a motivational team player, with a minimum of five years' post-qualification working experience.

A salary circa £21 000 is offered.

BACD is an equal opportunities employer.

Elysium Event Managers – corporate communications

Elysium Event Managers have been established since 1992 with a predominantly City and West End client portfolio. Specializing in conference and conference production, client events, staff parties, fun days and incentives.

Business Development Manager/Director

We seek a senior candidate, working alongside our managing director, to initiate and implement new sales and marketing strategies, leading to high net sales to major corporations.

- Experienced professional with the ability to activate a sales and marketing plan from concept to completion.
- Proven current sales record over the last three years.
- Presenting at director level and adding weight to senior sales opportunities.
- Computer literate with special attention to database management systems and spreadsheet packages.

Salary £ excellent basic. Earning OTE to £45 000.

New Business Sales

Ambitious, self motivated sales professional who ideally has an understanding of the event industry, who enjoys the sales process and has the desire to achieve more than the average.

- Ideally from an event or corporate hospitality background.
- Current proven sales track record.
- Enthusiastic team player who enjoys prospecting and achieving the sale.
- Support from a core team aiming for the top.
- Long-term prospects.

Salary £ excellent basic + bonus structure. Earning OTE to £23 000.

Motivation & Marketing Resources Limited

Require Sales Executive

Are offering an exciting 'once in a lifetime' opportunity to join an expanding company which has gained an enviable reputation in the design and management of incentive and conference programmes. You will have the opportunity of actively contributing to our growing market share and to developing your career further.

Your proven ability to sell to some of the country's largest blue chip companies will be essential as will be your creative flair and articulate presentation skills.

You will be responsible for increasing our client portfolio and further strengthening the company's exposure in the following markets:

- Incentive Design
- Incentive Management
- Conference Production
- Motivation Events
- Team Development
- Event Management.

Motivation and Marketing Resources Limited with the backing of its parent company *Elegant Days* (Event Manager of the year 1996 and 1997 – CHA) will provide you with impeccable credibility and support.

Greater Glasgow and Clyde Valley Tourist Board

Sales Executive
International Association Sector
Salary £16 770–20 946 (pay award pending) (scale SCP 27–34)

Applications are invited for the above post. The successful candidate will be responsible for generating new international conference business for Greater Glasgow and Clyde Valley and its members through proactive sales activity including: telesales, direct marketing and other promotional activities. In addition to highly developed analytical, communications, presentation and operational skills, the successful applicant may be required to liaise effectively with local professional and cultural communities.

At least one year's experience in the conference and meetings market is desirable.

The C/I/T/P Group PLC

Managing Director – Operations

C. £50k plus benefits

The continued growth of this dynamic group has resulted in this new senior role responsible for all the outbound operations of The Global Events Partnership and The Conference and Incentive Travel Partnership (C&IT).

Reporting to the Managing Director of these two brands, the successful candidate will have qualities that clearly demonstrate:

● Strong leadership
● Capability of managing multiple projects simultaneously
● Excellent communication and presentation skills
● High level of personal motivation
● Proven creative mind-set
● Impeccable organizational abilities
● Good interpersonal skills with serious historical man-management experience
● Unequalled understanding of the C&IT marketplace.

You may already be in a similar role or are waiting for that next career move, either way if you believe that you could more than meet the foregoing criteria then please e-mail or send an up-to-date CV and letter of application outlining your salary expectations.

We would be interested to hear from experienced operations personnel and bright graduates who are looking for a rewarding new challenge

IATA – The sky's the limit

The trade association for the scheduled airline industry, representing 260 member airlines, has vacancies in its *Hounslow office within its IATA Conference & Exhibitions Department.*

Do you have a good background in Conference & Exhibitions and are looking to move to your next challenge?

If so due to business expansion, we have excellent opportunities, both contract and permanent, awaiting you! We are currently looking to recruit Conference and Marketing Professionals in the following positions:

Conference Producer (6–12 month contract) – We are looking for an experienced Conference Producer, ideally with knowledge of the aviation industry. You will be responsible for the research and development of new events and for preparing business plans and budgets. Key tasks include liaison with internal and external contacts to initiate ideas for new events. You will be expected to work with technical advisers to develop new conference programmes and ensure that our events cover the hot topics in the aviation industry.

Conference Assistant (6–12 month contract) – We need someone to assist one of our Conference Managers with the organization and planning of our conferences and exhibitions. Duties include all aspects of event planning from venue selection to exhibition and sponsorship sales, attending international events to assist with the set-up and registration process, speaker liaison and the production of conference proceedings.

Marketing Assistant – This position is a permanent post with primary responsibility for database list selections and maintenance, handling customer enquiries and managing our e-com website. Other duties include providing administrative support to the sales and marketing team, distribution of sales material, delegate and competitor analysis.

Booking Assistant (6 month contract) – This post holder will be responsible for processing sales invoices and delegate registrations and customer booking enquiries. In addition, key tasks include the production of statistics, credit control, account reconciliation and production of delegate lists and badges.

Marketing Executive – Experienced marketing professional required for this permanent post to help with the marketing and promotion of our events. Responsibilities include preparation of marketing and production schedules, liaising with mailing house and in-house design and production staff and the preparation, layout, design and proofing of promotional materials and budgetary control. If you want an opportunity to join a fast expanding, international organization and have relevant experience, can work to tight deadlines with strong communication skills, are personal computer (PC) literate and are looking for new, exciting opportunities, then we here at IATA want to hear from you.

Hong Kong Tourist Association (HKTA)

Marketing Executive – Corporate Events and Incentive Travel

An exciting opportunity to join the specialist team within the HKTA's London office, responsible for the promotion of Conference, Exhibition and Incentive business to Hong Kong. Working within a small but highly motivated team, this key position is responsible for the prime UK market for corporate meetings and incentive travel and to assist in developing new business out of Eire and the Nordic countries.

Specific responsibilities include: liaison and negotiation, at all levels with key conference and incentive buyers, co-ordinating and participating in exhibitions, promotional events and familiarization visits, undertaking sales calls and presentations.

The successful candidate will have excellent presentation, communication and organizational skills. A creative, confident and results-oriented professional, with computer skills and the ability to manage multiple tasks/projects. Proven sales and marketing skills and a sound knowledge of the C & I industry are prerequisites. (Some product knowledge of Hong Kong would be an advantage).

A competitive salary package will be offered including private health insurance and contribution to private pension scheme.

The Marketing Organization

Account Manager – Travel

The Travel Organization is the country's largest and most successful operator of conference and incentive travel and is a division of The Marketing Organization, one of the UK's leading marketing communications agencies, employing over 100 people in Newport Pagnell.

We are looking for an Account Manager to work on our prestigious travel accounts. The primary responsibility of this role will be actively to manage and successfully deliver client business to high professional standard. This will include negotiating with suppliers, planning and executing group travel programmes and working closely and confidently with the client to ensure success on every occasion.

Whilst your activities will be centred on travel, responsibilities could well encompass the co-ordination of promotional campaigns. Suitable candidates will have excellent operational skills in conference and incentive travel, communication and social skills and proficiency in Microsoft Office.

If you have the ambition to succeed within this demanding environment, please send your CV quoting your present salary.

HARP Wallen Executive Recruitment

One incentive that should get you moving.

Account Directive – Incentive Travel – Salary c £35k. Location – Central London

Our client is a highly successful small but expanding C&I travel company, looking to expand their incentive travel business with the addition of a senior member of the team to develop and run their incentive department. This is an excellent opportunity for a self-starter keen to put their entrepreneurial flair into practice. You should be energetic, motivated, and a team player with a good sense of humour.

Sales Manager – Salary – negotiable – Location – North West England
C&I travel agency is seeking the addition of a dynamic sales professional to generate new and manage existing corporate business. You should be confident in presenting

event solutions to clients and will work closely with the operations team in the formulation and creation of these proposals. A knowledge of marketing would be useful and the ability to create and implement sales and marketing plans is a must.

C&I Sales Manager – Hotel Group – Salary – c £30k – Location – London
This is an exciting opportunity with a leading international hotel group for an enthusiastic and energetic sales manager, with full responsibility for developing group business from the UK conference and incentive sector. You should possess a proven sales track record and a working knowledge of the group's market, in addition to the desire and ability to further your sales career in a dynamic and fast paced environment.

If you are interested in the above positions or other vacancies currently being handled in the conference and incentive field, please send an up-to-date CV in the strictest confidence outlining salary details.

G.MEX Manchester ICC – Manchester International Conference Centre

Scheduled to open in May 2001 the new state of the art Manchester International Conference Centre offers three people the unique opportunity to be part of this exciting new development. Have you the knowledge and experience we require?

A National Corporate salesperson
Minimum 3 years experience in the conference industry or similar background is essential. A self starter with a proven track record, you should have the ability to work on your own initiative, and be an enthusiastic Team Player with a motivational attitude. You must be willing to work away from home and have the ability to develop new business.

A Regional Corporate/Banqueting Salesperson
1–2 years' minimum experience with a broad knowledge of the North West conference and banqueting business. A self starter, enthusiastic Team Player with the ability to work on your own initiative, you must be able to source and develop new business in this region.

A National Association Salesperson
Minimum 3 years' experience working with Association Organizers either within the industry or academia. An enthusiastic member of the Team, a self starter, with the ability to work on your own initiative and willing to travel throughout the UK.

Conference Planners

Conference Planners is a full-service live event agency. The company, founded in 1976, has a corporate headquarters in Burlingame, California, USA with additional offices in Boston and London. Client base is primarily an Information Technology Company.

For additional information please visit our web site at: www.cplan.co.uk

We are currently seeking highly motivated and experienced individuals within the Event Management Field to add to the management team of our UK offices.

Account Managers – Min. 5 years with Account Management at senior level

Account Executives – Min. 2 years experience in Event Management

Registration Manager – Excellent technology background and a proven track record

Registration Co-ordinators – To support the Exhibit Manager in sales and logistics

Production Assistant – To support the Producer and Account Team

Marketing Assistant – To work with local countries on communication programmes & Speaker Management

On-Site Travel Directors – Required for immediate work on European seminar tours and worldwide events

Technical Analyst – Responsible for analysing client needs and matching with corporate systems

Seminar Manager – Responsible for European tours, production and management of on-site staff

On-Site Travel Director – With at least 2 years' experience working on-site and will be prepared to travel around Europe as part of on-going seminar tours – approximately 2 weeks a month

All individuals must be IT literate with a good working knowledge of Word, Excel, and Powerpoint

Salaries/Benefits: Conference Planners provides an excellent benefits package and compensation package will be equal to or above industry standards. All inquiries will be kept strictly confidential.

Line Up Communications

Line Up Communications is one of the UK's most dynamic business to business communication agencies, with expanding offices in both London and Leeds. We are looking for experienced, enthusiastic people to join our team and service our expanding portfolio of international blue chip clients.

Multimedia Producer – London
An experienced multimedia producer is required to work on existing client accounts and develop new business opportunities. Working with our Leeds based design and programming team, you should be able to develop projects from initial brief to final delivery. You will need a good working knowledge of all aspects of multimedia production from creative proposals and budgeting, through to briefing of designers, programmers and video requirements.

Technical Production Manager – London
We require an experienced technical production manager to work with our in-house production teams in London and Leeds and directly with clients. You should have at least 4 years' experience of conference and event project management both in the UK and abroad, together with a good working knowledge of leading-edge technology.

Head of Logistics – London
A great opportunity for a highly experienced and self motivated individual to develop our existing logistics offer alongside our established events department. Based in our London office you would be working on a wide variety of UK and international events with both our London and Leeds based production teams.

Conference/Event Producer – Leeds
We are looking for a creative producer who will have overall responsibility for all aspects of conference/events production. You should be self-motivated with good client handling and project management skills. 5 years' relevant experience of pre-production, on-site and post-production is essential along with good communications skills and the ability to work to tight deadlines.

   All the above positions offer attractive remuneration packages, excellent career opportunities and an exciting, lively and fun working environment. All applicants will require a full UK driving licence. Please apply in writing enclosing a current CV clearly quoting the appropriate job reference.

CVL

CVL, the specialist Medical Conference and Event management agency is continuing to grow. We have developed a wider client proposition, grown our client base and now need to grow the organization again to fulfil further expansion.

We are seeking high calibre applicants for the following newly created positions:

Operations Director

The Role

Responsible for the operations division of the UK business, including Client Service Teams, Production and Medical Consultancy. Responsibilities include:

- Retention and growth of the existing client base
- Delivery of measurable high quality service
- Development of high quality client teams
- Maximize gross profit levels
- Cost base management

Applicants will have

A minimum of 8 years' management experience within an events or communications agency.

Strong leadership skills, experience of blue chip client account management and have a passion for delivering a high quality service.

It is envisaged that the successful candidate will also deputize for the Managing Director.

Business Development Director

The Role

Deliver planned business growth. This will include client development strategies, new business gains and product development. Responsibilities include:

- Major project proposals to existing clients
- New clients development
- Sales development of Martiz product to CVL clients
- CVL marketing and promotion
- CVL new product development

Applicants will have

A minimum of 5 years' sales management experience within an events or communication agency.

Strong negotiating skills, experience of blue chip client selling, excellent presentation skills, and at least one other fluent European language.

Account Manager

The Role

To ensure the retention and growth of the client portfolio. Responsibilities include:

- Allocation of work to own team
- Repeat business from clients
- Successful completion of client projects
- Management of own team

Applicants will have

A minimum of 5 years' project management experience within an events or communications agency.

Pharmaceutical/medical event management experience. Good people skills and strong attention to detail, experience of blue chip clients.

An excellent package including relocation allowances will be provided to attract the right calibre individuals.

Clearly, there are many other job types but this gives an idea of the range of jobs in the business travel and tourism industry.

There are several types of job which seem to dominate, namely:

● sales and marketing
● event organizers
● client liaison.

It is important, of course, to remember that for every job like the ones shown in Exhibit 9.1, there are probably dozens more people employed in actually delivering the service to the client, such as waiters, receptionists, audiovisual technicians, chefs, security guards, and so on.

It is now time for us to look at the types of people who work in this industry.

The people who work in the industry

There is little empirical research on the types of people who work specifically in business tourism. However, a survey by *Conference and Incentive Travel*, published in January 2000, throws some light on the nature of the workforce in the conference and incentive travel agency field in the UK. This survey found that the workforce is relatively young with a third being thirty years old or less and only 13 per cent being over fifty.

Around a third have worked for less than two years with their current employer, while only 20 per cent have worked for the same agency for seven years or more.

Rogers (1998) suggested that:

1 Many people come to the business tourism industry as a second or third career, once they recognize that they enjoy jobs that include a lot of contact with people. These people often come from a wide variety of backgrounds.
2 The industry provides opportunities for both graduates and those with postgraduate qualifications.

It is also commonly believed that in this industry women form the majority of the workforce and many of the most successful entrepreneurs in the field are female.

The four brief biographies in Exhibit 9.2 provide a good illustration of some 'typical' career paths in the conference and incentive travel sector.

Exhibit 9.2 Four biographies of professionals in conference and incentive travel

Chris McQue (Head of Conference and Incentive Travel, Capital Incentives)

Career to date

● March 1985: Account executive, Conference & Incentive Directions
● July 1986: Account director, Purchasepoint
● July 1989: Business development manager, Conference & Incentive Group Services
● November 1995: Business development manager, Page & Moy Marketing
● February 1998: Head of conference and incentive travel, Capital Incentives

Sarah Webster (Until June 2000, Executive Director, Incentive Travel and Meetings Association, ITMA)

Career to date

- Qualified in business studies with languages
- Three years as PA at Citibank Paris
- Copywriter for Philips, Holland medical/technical publications
- Worked for PR consultancy in London
- Deputy editor *Holidays and Holiday Homes*
- Manager, UK representation account for Monaco
- Executive director, ITMA

Mady Keup (Head of London Convention Bureau)

Career to date

- 1986: joined British Tourist Authority (BTA)as tourist information assistant working her way through the ranks to become business travel manager, Europe
- 1997: chief executive, Portuguese Chamber of Commerce in Lisbon
- 1998: returned to BTA as manager, central Europe based in Berlin
- 1999: joined LCB

Peter Franks (Chairman, TFI Group)

Career to date

- 1977: member of sales force, British Caledonian
- 1981: sets up TFI Group
- 1984: becomes a major shareholder in TFI
- 1991: leaves TFI to pursue consultancy work outside the industry
- 1994: returns to become TFI Group chairman
- 2000: TFI Group wins four gold medals at the annual Incentive Travel and Meetings Association awards

Source: *Conference and Incentive Travel* (1999–2000).

Working conditions and salaries

Working conditions obviously vary between sites and organizations but a *Conference and Incentive Travel* survey, published in January 2000 gave an indication of the situation in the UK.

It found that:

- while 19 per cent of people earned less than £16 000 per annum, 21 per cent earned more than £30 000
- 30 per cent of staff felt they were not adequately rewarded for their work
- only 15 per cent of those questioned worked 8 hours or less a day, while 55 per cent claimed to work more than nine hours per day. Indeed 14 per cent appeared to work seventy or more hours per week
- 63 per cent of respondents said they had occasionally or frequently cancelled holidays due to pressure of work
- 26 per cent of staff received five weeks paid holiday per annum or more
- 38 per cent of staff said they spent at least nine weeks or more travelling, related to their job, every year.

It seems that, in general, those working for conference production companies and incentive travel houses are better paid than those working for business travel agencies.

Although this data relates to the UK, the picture at present is probably also true of the industry worldwide in many ways. The picture, overall, is of an industry which is very demanding of its employees, but which offers relatively well rewarded employment compared with some other sectors of tourism.

The key skills required by staff

The technical skills required by staff to perform their duties varies with the nature of the specific job. However, there seems to be common agreement throughout the sector concerning some generic skills which, it is believed, are required by most, if not all, of those who work in business tourism.

Rogers (1998) analysed a range of jobs in the UK to see what skills were required. Common themes throughout the advertisements included:

- interpersonal skills
- communication skills, in both oral and written communication
- attention to detail
- ability to work under pressure
- analytical skills.

Given the changing nature of business tourism, there are clearly two other sets of skills that will become increasingly important:

1 *The ability to speak foreign languages.*
  As globalization develops, more business tourism events and individual business trips will take place across national and cultural boundaries. A survey of the UK conference and incentive travel agencies in 1999–2000 found that 39 per cent of staff questioned had no language skills. Of those who did, 47 per cent spoke French and 8 per cent could speak more than three languages. However, as the geography of business tourism changes, the demand may well be for people who can speak the language of the growing business tourism markets such as Russia, China, and India.

2 *Technology skills.*
  The industry is heavily dependent on different types of technologies and therefore requires staff skilled in the use of these technologies, which include:

  (a) video- and satellite-conferencing
  (b) audiovisual equipment and special effects equipment used in conference produc-
      tion and product launches
  (c) Internet marketing
  (d) computer reservations systems and global distribution systems.

As we will see in the next section, staff generally have to develop these skills though experience as the industry has not yet developed, in general, a comprehensive, sophisticated system of training and education provision.

Training and education

As a relatively new industry, it is not surprising that business travel and tourism has not yet developed an integrated provision of training and education. The fragmentation of the industry is also an obstacle to such developments.

The way in which people have gained skills and knowledge was traditionally by experience, as Penny Hanson, Managing Director of her own company, the Hanson Organization stated: 'I have never received any formal training in organizing exhibitions. My organizing skills have been developed by working up through the ranks, by working across the board on all aspects of exhibition organization, by hard work and experience' (quoted in Rogers, 1998).

Rogers noted that:

> The conference industry and the education sector have been slow to develop appropriate education and training opportunities for the industry's current workforce. The situation is now changing as educational institutions and professional associations begin to develop (courses). There is a lack of professional qualifications specific to the conference industry, although initiatives are underway to address this. (Rogers, 1998)

In spite of the growing recognition of the importance of training in all services industries, a survey of the UK conference and incentive travel agencies, published in *Conference and Incentive Travel* in January 2000 found that:

- only 21 per cent of agencies offered structured training programmes for their staff
- 64 per cent of agencies, it would appear, offered no training at all!

And there are further grounds for doubting employers' commitment to training. A readers' poll for *Conference and Incentive Travel*, published in September 1999 found that around a third of companies would not even encourage staff to work towards the National Vocational Qualification for the events industry (a UK vocational qualification). A further 20 per cent did not know what they would do while only around a half said they would support the qualification.

However, there are some valuable initiatives under way, several of which will now be discussed.

International Association of Professional Congress Organizers (IAPCO)

Since 1970 IAPCO has organized an annual training seminar for professional event organizers. Participants receive a certificate. The seminar lasts a week and covers a range of topics as can be seen from Exhibit 9.3 which relates to the 1999 seminar. While an excellent initiative only a small number of participants per annum can attend this seminar so its impact on the industry is limited.

Exhibit 9.3 The IAPCO Seminar Programme, 1999

	Sunday 24th	Monday 25th	Tuesday 26th	Wednesday 27th	Thursday 28th	Friday 29th	Saturday 30th
			Network Groups meet	Network Groups meet	Network Groups meet	Network Groups meet	Closing session and presentation of diplomas
Morning 1		Introduction to the Seminar	Governmental meetings/Intercultural awareness · Scientific programmes for medical meetings · Corporate meetings	Registration · Marketing a destination/Official carriers · Marketing a PCO company	Finance	Communication with the client · Technology marketplace	
		Coffee break					
		Introduction to the industry	Coffee break	Coffee break	Coffee break	Coffee break	
Morning 2		The role of PCO	Corporate meetings · Governmental meetings/Intercultural awareness · Scientific programmes for medical meetings	Marketing a PCO company · Registration · Making the best bid	Finance [continued]	Technology marketplace · Communication with the client	
		Lunch	Lunch	Lunch	Social programmes	Lunch	
Afternoon 1		Promotion of a congress + panel discussion on other areas of promotion	On-site management/PCO office structure · Contracts	Excursion and dinner outside Wolfsberg	Lunch	Preparation by Network Groups	
		Tea break	Tea break		Workshops	Tea break	
Afternoon 2		Sponsorship and exhibitions	Contracts · On-site management/PCO office structure		Tea break · Tutorials	Presentations by Network Groups	
		Quality Time	Quality Time		Quality Time	Quality Time	
Evening	Welcome	Dinner	Dinner		Dinner	Farewell Dinner	
	Dinner	Workshops	Cultural Entertainment		Tutorials [con]		

Source: IAPCO literature

Exhibit 9.3 (*continued*)

Themes

An overview of the conference industry

- Meeting industry associations
- Market size and value

The role of the PCO at an international congress

- Laying the foundation of the congress
- How to assist the client in formulating the objectives of the meeting
- Basic questions that apply to every congress
- Why and how to gain the client's confidence
- Understanding human needs

Promotion of a congress

- Identifying the market
- Developing a market strategy for each conference
- Addressing the market efficiently and effectively to increase delegate attendance and keep promotion costs down
- Checklist of marketing options
- New marketing options through e-mail and the World Wide Web

Sponsorship

- Providing financial support for conferences
- How to assess what you need
- Different styles of sponsorship
- Checklists of items to sponsored
- Providing the correct benefits
- How to go about getting it
- Meeting the sponsor's needs

Exhibitions related to international congresses

- Reasons for holding an exhibition with a conference
- Site selection
- Facility rules and regulations
- Registration/on-site management
- Marketing and exhibition

Three distinct market segments

- The special objectives of corporate meetings
- Governmental meetings and their special differences
- Medical meetings – how to organize the scientific programme

On-site management and PCO office structure

- Different types of PCO offices designed to suit the demands of clients with varied needs
- Receiving delegates, speakers, press, etc. and dealing with their needs on site and how a PCO company sets up the organization for it

Exhibit 9.3 (*continued*)

Contracts
A survey of contracts which must be written for a congress:

- The PCO's contract with the client
- Contracts with suppliers and hotels
- Exhibitors' contracts
- Delegate contracts
- Adequate protection for a congress

Registration systems

- Establishing an effective pre-registration system
- Registration processing, acknowledgements
- Registration forms and reply cards

Marketing strategies for a PCO company

- How to attract more congresses
- Research, advertising, direct mail
- Regional /international co-operation
- Understanding human needs
- Networking

Marketing a destination – the NTO as an ally

How to attract and promote more congresses:

- Using NTO resources
- Research, image-building, unique selling points, PR/media, sales activities
- National, regional and international co-operation
- The role of the local convention bureau

The role of the official airline

- What does it mean: partnership between the airline industry and the international meetings market?
- How can we increase the profitability for all concerned: the client, the PCO, the airline?

Making the best bid

- Bidding team
- The procedure, formal criteria and informal arguments
- Promotion and presentation

Finance

- Budgeting and budget control
- Creating a self-financing budget
- Creating a cash flow

Social events at a scientific congress
Social activities suitable for international conferences and the logistics of their organization:

- Some basic rules on social events and their planning
- Recommended treatment for VIPs and dignitaries
- Difference between scientific and corporate meetings

Exhibit 9.3 (*continued*)

Effective communication with clients and suppliers

● How to achieve your objectives

Technology marketplace

● Registration, hotel booking and abstract handling with especially
  developed software packages
● Using a fax server, e-mail and Internet (World Wide Web)
● On site: registration and teleconferencing – ISDN (telephone lines)

Event Management Program, The George Washington University, USA

This program, which was launched in 1994, is available as a day release course, through weekend classes, or by distance-learning, utilizing on-line material. The certificate level programme consists of both compulsory units and options or electives in everything from event marketing to catering design.

Professional Education Conference – Europe – Meeting Professionals International (MPI)

Each year MPI organizes a three day professional development conference at a European venue, with a packed programme of seminars led by industry professionals. The 2001 event was held at Disneyland, Paris.

Certificate in Meetings Management – Meeting Professionals International

This certificate is the first such qualification certified by a university, namely the Institut de Management Hôtelier International, which is a partnership of the leading French business school ESSEC and Cornell University. 'Students' on the programme take a number of courses to build up points, and after they attain a certain number of points they may sit the examination for the certificate. This is a very innovative course and, while not inexpensive, gives the 'student' a prestigious qualification.

MPI has also pioneered the provision of training and personal development materials via the Internet.

European Masters in Congress Management

The first ever Masters course in Congress Management was launched in 1999. It is a partnership between:

● JICS, the Joint Interpretation and Conference Service of the European Commission
● ATLAS, the Association of European Universities and Colleges which teach tourism and leisure

- Four leading European universities, namely DEUSTO Bilbao, Bologna, Berufakademie Ravensburg and Sheffield Hallam.
- Leading bodies from the event management industry.

The programme includes around twelve to fifteen months' full time study and students are able to move between institutions to progress their studies. The curriculum involves a common core taught by each university and electives which reflect the various specialisms of the four universities.

The IAPCO certificate seminars, the Certificate in Meetings Management programme and the European Masters in Congress Management course are all aimed at senior managers and potential 'high-flyers' within the business tourism industry.

A wide variety of training and education programmes are now available aimed at a wider audience within the industry. These include:

- the International Meetings Academy, a series of short courses, for staff at different levels, run by the International Congress and Convention Association (ICCA)
- the summer schools run over several days each year by the European Federation of Conference Towns (EFCT).
- the SITE annual training seminar.
- the Meetings Industry Association (MIA) which runs short courses on various topics of interest to meeting organizers.

Universities and colleges are also starting to develop degree programmes and modules in Business Tourism. Sheffield Hallam University has, since 1992, offered modules in Business Tourism and Conference and Event Management. Birmingham College of Food, Tourism, and Creative Studies has also taught modules in this field for a number of years. In 1996, Leeds Metropolitan University launched a pioneering degree in Event Management, a four-year course with a work placement included.

Finally, there has been a growth in vocational qualifications in the industry with a growing emphasis on occupational standards, skills and competences. Work began in the UK in 1993 on developing National and Scottish Vocational Qualifications specifically for the events industry. This initiative has been led by the Events Sector Industry Training Organization (ESITO), a partnership of ten professional bodies.

Perhaps what is most needed now is a review and rationalization of these various initiatives to avoid confusing the industry. This will involve the need for greater co-operation between the rather fragmented industry trade organizations.

The issue of training and education is, we believe, a major challenge facing the business tourism sector, a point that is reiterated in Chapter 14.

Conclusions

We have recognized that the quality of staff is vital to the success of the business tourism industry.

In this chapter it has been seen that there are a variety of different types of job in this industry which are interdependent if clients are to receive a good service. It has been noted that people come into employment in the industry in a variety of ways but that there are certain skills that are common to most jobs within business tourism. However, it is clear that these skills are traditionally obtained through experience in a rather ad hoc manner. Only recently has the industry begun to take training and education seriously. Today a number of useful initiatives are under way, partly thanks to the efforts of various professional bodies. There is still some way to go before the industry fully embraces the concepts of training and staff development. Nevertheless, for many people, business tourism provides interesting and relatively well-paid employment.

Discussion points and essay questions

1 Discuss the main characteristics of employment in business travel and tourism which you believe are illustrated by the advertisements in Exhibit 9.1.
2 Critically evaluate the programme of the IAPCO 1999 seminar which is outlined in Exhibit 9.3.
3 What factors do you think encourage people to seek careers within business travel and tourism?

Exercise

Interview a number of people who work in business travel and tourism in a variety of roles. Based on what they say, and your own ideas, try to devise a set of training courses for staff in different sectors of business tourism. What subjects will be covered in your courses and how will they be delivered (location, times of the year and so on) to meet the needs of the industry?

10 Marketing the business travel and tourism product

Marketing in business travel and tourism is a complex matter reflecting the diverse nature of the industry.

In Figure 10.1, the authors attempt to identify the nature of marketing in business travel and tourism, in terms of what it is that is marketed.

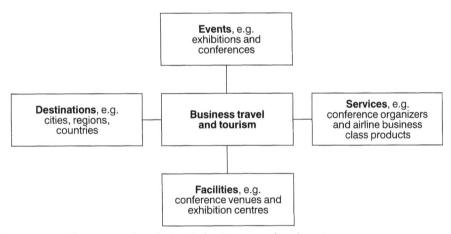

Figure 10.1 The nature of marketing in business travel and tourism

The diversity of marketing is also a function of the fact that:

- different types and sizes of organizations are involved from one-person businesses to large transnational corporations
- marketing can be international or domestic, or both.

In this chapter we will explore the following aspects of marketing in business travel and tourism:

- the marketing mix – product, price, place, promotion
- the market, notably motivators, determinants, and segmentation
- destination marketing

- key issues in marketing in the different sectors of business travel and tourism such as conferences and incentive travel
- topical issues including quality and consumer satisfaction, relationship marketing and brand loyalty, strategic alliances, women business travellers, marketing research, ethical issues and technology.

This chapter is not meant to be a comprehensive review of marketing in the industry.

Instead it is designed to highlight some key aspects of marketing in business travel and tourism.

The marketing mix and business tourism

The marketing mix consists of those variables which are controllable or heavily influenced by an organization. They are divided into the 4 Ps, namely, product, price, place and promotion.

The product

The diversity of business travel and tourism makes it difficult to generalize about the nature of the product. For example, business travellers making individual business trips will see the 'product' as the transport and accommodation services they use primarily, as well as the general facilities provided by the destination. However, the convention delegate may see the convention centre itself as the most important element of the product.

The business tourism product does, however share certain characteristics with the leisure tourism product. These are illustrated in Figure 10.2.

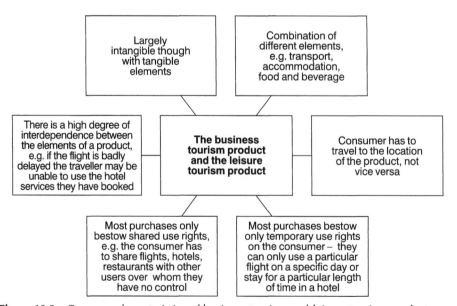

Figure 10.2   Common characteristics of business tourism and leisure tourism products

The main elements of the business travel and tourism product are outlined, in general terms in Figure 10.3. Some elements are sold separately, such as hotel rooms or airline tickets for the individual business traveller, while in other cases intermediaries package several elements together for consumers, such as incentive travel packages.

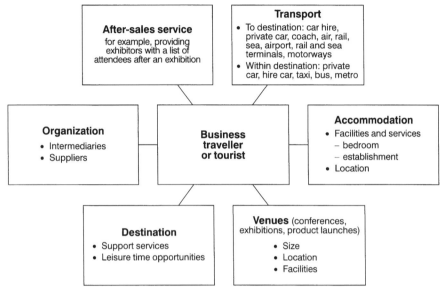

Figure 10.3 Elements of the business tourism product
Source: adapted from Horner and Swarbrooke (1996).

Like leisure tourism it could also be argued that business travel and tourism is not a product, but rather an experience. The nature of this experience will reflect, for example:

● the elements of the product
● the ambience of the destination and the venue
● the personality and experience of the business traveller.

The experience also includes three stages:

● anticipation – before the event
● consumption – during the event
● remembrance – after the event.

Furthermore, the experience can also be divided into two sets of elements, as follows:

1 Those elements which are controlled or influenced by the supplier such as hotel meeting rooms.
2 Those elements which are not under the control or influence of suppliers, but which affect the experience, such as the weather and air road congestion.

Those organizations which serve the business traveller are always trying to differentiate their services from those of other operators in the same market to help them achieve competitive advantage.

For example, for the business traveller, the hotel bedroom is not simply a place to sleep, it is instead an extension of the office. A survey published in April 1999 by *Business Traveller* compared the rooms of a number of leading international hotels to see how they differed from each other. The results of this survey are shown in Table 10.1.

Table 10.1   Facilities in hotel bedrooms for the business traveller

Hotel chain	Name of product	Features of the room	Where available	Price
Hyatt	Business Plan	Each room has a large desk with fax, phone with computer hook-up, and better lighting. Local 0800 and credit card calls are free. There is twenty-four hour access to printers, photocopiers and office supplies. The plan includes coffee-making facilities, iron and board, continental breakfast, newspaper	85 properties in the USA and Canada	$15 a day above regular room rate
Inter-Continental	Business Rooms	Large work desks with combined printer/fax machine/photocopier, a power-surge protected modem and personal computer outlets, office supplies, ergonomic chairs, halogen desk lamp, coffee-making facilities	Gradually being installed across the board, check with individual hotel	Varies according to availability, but can be the same as a standard room
Marriott	Rooms that Work	The room that works is equipped with an integrated workstation consisting of a large table and a mobile writing desk. Two power outlets and a personal computer modem jack are mounted in the tabletop and there is a movable task light and an adjustable ergonomic chair	All Marriott's full-service hotels	No additional charge
Radisson Edwardian	Hallmark Rooms	All these rooms give Internet access through the television, with infrared remote-control keyboards. They also have a fax machine, two phones and a business pack (on request). No charge for credit card calls. Full English breakfast, tea- and coffee-making facilities, paper and in-room movie are included, and there is an express checkout service	All Radisson Edwardian properties	Varies according to availability, around 10 per cent more than a standard room
Shangri-La	Horizon Club	Rooms have private fax machine, voice messaging and a large desk. The Horizon Club lounge provides business services and private meeting rooms. Breakfast, suit pressing, shoe shine, newspaper and daily fresh fruit are included in the rate	Most Shangri-La and Traders hotels (product is called Traders Club in Traders properties)	Varies according to availability, around 10 per cent more than a standard room

Table 10.1 (*Continued*)

Hotel chain	Name of product	Features of the room	Where available	Price
Sheraton	Smart Rooms	All these rooms have fax/photocopier/printer, two-line speaker phone with integral modem jack, large desk, easily accessible power outlets, high-intensity adjustable table lamp and ergonomic chair. Other services include fresh coffee and pastries for early morning checkouts, newspapers and personal incoming message delivery service	All Sheraton hotels in Europe	Varies according to availability, but can be the same as a standard room
Westin	Guest Office	Work area is equipped with an ergonomic chair, fax machine/printer/ photocopier, printer cables, speaker phone with data port and voice messaging; free local calls and long-distance access. Also included is a daily breakfast allowance, daily newspaper, late checkout facility and free access to the property's health club (where available)	Most Westin properties in North America and Asia	$20 more than the standard room rate

Source: *Business Traveller* (April 1999).

Another area where great effort has been made to attract the business traveller is business-class services on airlines. A case study relating to this subject is to be found in Part Five of the book.

All products, whether business tourism or not, have a range of factors which constitute the product. These can best be explained by using a convention centre as an example. Figure 10.4 illustrates this argument. Marketing of products such as this convention centre involves packaging all of these elements to create a satisfactory experience for the customer.

Price

Price is clearly a crucial issue in any market but it is a complex matter in business travel and tourism, for the following reasons:

1 There are direct and indirect costs for the traveller. Direct costs include, for example, fees for attending conferences or the price of an air ticket. There are also indirect costs such as the need to buy a visa when travelling to some destinations.
2 Prices for a similar product vary dramatically around the world. Some examples taken from *Business Traveller* magazine will illustrate this point as follows:
   (a) A non-residential one-day conference for 500 people including room hire, lunch, two tea/coffee breaks and taxes, would cost £9745 in Helsinki but £19 100 in Copenhagen (*Business Traveller*, May 2000).

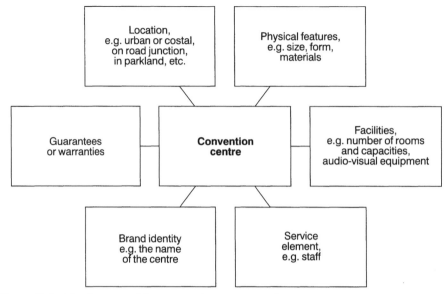

Figure 10.4 The features of the convention centre product

(b) A cocktail party for ten VIP guests in January 2000 including two-night suite hire, dinner and breakfast for one person included would have cost £2775 in Cyprus but £3350 in Rome (*Business Traveller*, January 2000).

(c) A three-night full-board stay for thirty people in fifteen rooms in a leisure hotel with golf facilities in spring 2000, would have cost £9630 in Mauritius but £17 000 in Florida (*Business Traveller*, March 2000).

3 Even within one country prices can vary significantly. For example, the twenty-four hour delegate rate at the end of 2000 was £105 at the Britannia Adelphi Hotel, Liverpool, £195 at the Balmoral Hotel, Edinburgh, and £220 at the Grand Hotel, Eastbourne (*Conference and Incentive Travel, January 2001*).

4 For many purchasers/users, price is perhaps less important than perceived value for money. This term is concerned with the relationship between benefits received and price paid. For example, in January 2000 a survey published in *Business Traveller* found that 80 per cent of readers felt that conference delegates were offered better value for money from hotels in mainland Europe than in the UK. Of course, value for money is a wholly subjective concept.

5 Most purchasers do not pay the published price, particularly for hotel accommodation and airline tickets. Negotiation is commonplace, which creates real challenges in terms of revenue planning and yield management.

6 Discounting is also rife based on criteria such as seasonality, volume of business or whether the customer is a regular user of a particular product or service.

7 Some elements of the business tourism product are sold below their market value for various reasons. For example, many municipally owned conference venues are hired out to organizers at low, even no, cost to attract conferences because of the spin-off benefits they will bring to the area.

8 Destinations usually make no direct charge for entry to the resort, city or region or for use of its facilities such as beaches, parks and even the climate. Yet these elements of the

destination may be a major factor in the decision to locate a conference or incentive travel package in a particular location.

9 Some costs are compulsory, such as travel costs, while others are voluntary, like having a drink at the end of the working day.

Place

Place or distribution is concerned with how business travellers or tourists actually purchase the products they need. There are several dimensions to this:

1 Customers can buy whole packages such as an incentive travel package or individual elements such as air tickets, venues and accommodation.
2 Customers can purchase products directly or make use of the services of specialist intermediaries, of the kind we discussed in Chapter 4.

As with leisure travel and tourism, the Internet is beginning to play a big role in distribution in business travel and tourism. By providing both information and an opportunity to purchase simultaneously it is blurring the distinction between two of the 4 Ps, namely, place and promotion. This leads us neatly on to the final P, promotion.

Promotion

To many people, promotion is synonymous with marketing; it is the visual face of marketing. However, promotion is simply one element of the marketing mix, fulfilling the function of making potential customers want to purchase a particular product. Figure 10.5 shows the different methods of promotion. Organizations combine these different

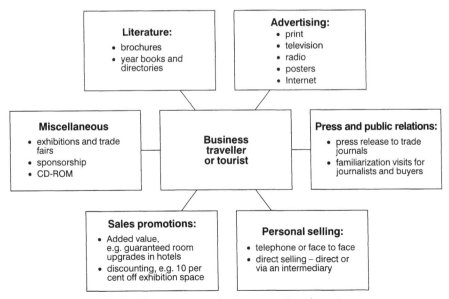

Figure 10.5 The methods of promotion in business travel and tourism

methods to create their own promotional strategy or mix. Several of these methods are discussed in more detail below. You will find case studies of some of the methods in Part Five of this book.

Advertising

Advertising, particularly in trade journals is a major weapon in the promotional armoury of many business travel and tourism organizations. As business travel and tourism is a high-spending activity, advertising tends to be glossy and colourful.

To be successful, however, advertising has to:

- be undertaken frequently to remind customers of brand names
- be integrated with other promotional techniques.

The Internet

Just as in leisure travel, the Internet is beginning to play a growing role in business travel and tourism, both in terms of finding information and making reservations.

A readers' poll published in *Conference and Incentive Travel* in February 2000 found that:

- while 35 per cent of readers preferred to book travel and accommodation via the Internet, 60 per cent still preferred other means
- only 15 per cent of readers felt that conference venue web sites offered the optimum of information for conference organizers.

It is clear, therefore, that more work needs to be done on developing this medium in the business travel and tourism field.

Trade journals

Business travel and tourism is still a relatively small industry but it is a world in which buyers are always looking for information on new products or services. The trade journals therefore play a very important role in promoting products and allowing communication between buyers, suppliers and intermediaries.

There are a large number of journals, most of which focus either on a sector (e.g. exhibitions) a region (e.g. the USA) or a particular angle (e.g. consumer advice for the business traveller). Furthermore, new journals are being launched all the time, around the world.

For example, a new journal, *CEI Asia Pacific*, was launched in September 2000 covering conferences, exhibitions and incentives. Focusing on this region where business tourism is a major phenomena this journal promised its readers, that it would 'publish industry news features, comments, and opinion from corporate buyers together with a regular series of interviews and corporate case studies. CEI Asia Pacific will be produced to the highest editorial standard' (*Conference and Incentive Travel*, June 2000).

Personal selling

In an industry based so much on interpersonal skills and trust, it is not surprising that personal selling plays a major role in promotion in business travel and tourism. The main areas for personal selling are as follows:

● venues selling their services to buyers
● airlines and hotels selling to buyers and intermediaries.
● incentive travel agencies and professional conference organisers selling their services to potential clients.

Telephone and face-to-face negotiation plays a vital role in marketing in this industry.

Familiarization or educational visits

Decisions about the destination and venue of conferences, exhibitions, product launches and incentive travel packages involve purchases where the level of expenditure can run into millions of pounds. As one would expect, therefore, very few buyers make their decisions based on brochures, videos or advertisements. They must see the place and venue for themselves, check it out, ask questions and meet the people they will be working with before they decide to contract a particular venue or other service. The familiarization or educational visit, which is the name given to this process, is therefore very important in business travel and tourism.

The market

It is now time briefly to turn our attention from the marketing mix to the market itself. Here we will simply consider the issues which are of greatest interest to marketers, namely, motivators, determinants and segmentation. Further discussion of the market is to be found in Chapter 3.

Motivators and determinants

We discussed the motivators in Chapter 3 and focused on the different motivators between the customer (usually the employer) and the consumer (usually the business traveller). We also noted that motivators varied between different types of business tourism such as conferences, exhibitions and incentive travel.

It is important that marketing people should understand motivators so that they can design products and promote them effectively.

However, we also have to recognize that while motivators are important, determinants are the factors that influence what customers will actually be able to do in reality. These determinants can be either internal or external, both relating to the customer and/or the consumer.

Determinants affect whether any trip will be made at all and, if so, what kind of trip will be taken. To illustrate what we mean by determinants in concrete terms, let us imagine an employee who wishes to attend a professional conference in another country.

First, he or she will have to persuade their employer that attendance will be worth the cost in terms of time and money. If the employer agrees the employee may not be able to attend if, for example:

- by the time the decision is made all flights and/or hotels and/or conference places are fully booked
- the financial situation of the travellers' organization deteriorates and a decision is taken to cut back on travel expenditure.

Even if this trip goes ahead, its characteristics will be determined by a wide variety of factors, including perhaps:

- what level of expenses the company has given our traveller for the trip
- the weather in the destination at the time of the conference
- whether or not our traveller already knows some of the other delegates
- the quality of accommodation in which the delegate is staying
- the cost of living in the destination.

For individual business trips the main determinants of what kind of business trip will be taken is often where the company has business interests.

Past experience and perceptions can also be a major determinant of behaviour. Business tourists travelling to new destinations may well like the security of using airlines and hotels with which they are already familiar and satisfied.

Those readers wanting to read more about motivators and determinants, in general, might find *Consumer Behaviour in Tourism* by Swarbrooke and Horner, useful.

Market segmentation

Until recently, marketers tended to view markets as single homogeneous entities. However, one must realize that every population or market is subdivided into segments – subgroups with shared buying characteristics. This issue is considered in more detail in Chapter 3.

It is important to recognize that segmentation is a very important technique for marketers today. The business travel and tourism market could be divided into a number of segments. Some potential segments are shown in Table 10.2. Each of these segments should, according to marketing theory, require a different marketing mix.

Clearly some of these criteria can change, such as purpose of travel, while others will normally stay the same for each individual, for instance, sex.

Destination marketing

As we saw in Chapter 5, destination marketing is a difficult activity because:

1 Destinations exist at different geographical levels from individual towns to countries or even continents.
2 Tourist perceptions of destinations rarely match the official boundaries of the agencies set up to market destinations.

Table 10.2 Methods of segmenting the business travel and tourism market

Criteria	Comments
Geographical	● Place of residence and/or language(s) spoken ● Whether business trip is domestic or international ● Type of destination
Demographic	● Age ● Sex ● Race ● Religion ● Family life-cycle stage
Purpose of travel	● Individual business trip – sales, networking, problem-solving ● Attending a conference ● Exhibiting at an exhibition ● Visiting an exhibition ● Taking part in an incentive travel trip
Frequency of travel	● Frequently ● Occasionally ● Rarely
Employing organization	● Public sector ● Private sector – large or small enterprise ● Self-employed
Job function	● Strategic manager ● Departmental manager – sales, finance, human resource management ● Technical specialist
Personality	● Gregarious, extrovert ● Shy, introvert

3 No direct charge is usually made to visit a destination unless there is a visa charge or tourist tax. Destination marketers therefore cannot directly use price as a demand management tool.
4 Most destination marketing is a public sector activity but most of the product is in the ownership of the private sector. Destination marketing, therefore, often focuses on promotion because it cannot control product or price.

The rise of partnership marketing

There has been a growing recognition that the public sector cannot do everything itself and there needs to be partnership between key players in destinations.

These partnerships can be of several types, notably:

● all organisations, both public and private, within a given geographical area
● between sectors, for example, airlines and hotels or venues and hotels
● within sectors, for example, convention centres.

The first type of partnership is now popular at local level through the rise of visitor and convention bureaux.

Visitor and convention bureaux

These organizations tend to be jointly funded by the public sector via a grant, and the private sector via membership fees and contributions to marketing campaigns. They

Table 10.3   Estimated budgets of North American convention and visitor bureaux, 1998 (US$ million)

Las Vegas	159.8	Salt Lake City	10.3
Honolulu	35.5	Cleveland	10.0
Orlando	31.6	Philadelphia	10.0
Reno	28.3	New York	9.9
Kissimmee	25.6	Indianapolis	9.4
Los Angeles	25.5	San Jose	8.9
Atlanta	19.9	Seattle	8.9
Miami	19.8	Denver	8.8
San Francisco	18.2	Boston	8.7
St Petersburg	16.5	Baltimore	8.6
San Antonio	16.3	Whistler	8.6
St Louis	15.5	Anchorage	8.5
Dallas	15.3	Myrtle Beach	8.5
Detroit	14.9	Anaheim	8.4
Montreal	14.9	Washington	8.3
Little Rock	14.0	Milwaukee	8.2
San Diego	13.5	Pittsburgh	8.1
Virginia Beach	12.8	Toronto	8.1
New Orleans	12.4	Fort Lauderdale	7.8
Atlantic City	12.2	Palm Beach	7.7
Vancouver	12.2	Cincinnati	7.5
Chicago[1]	11.5	Albuquerque	7.1
Houston	11.0	Galinburg, Tennessee	7.1
Key West	10.6	Louisville	7.0
Phoenix	10.5	Fort Myers	6.7

Notes: 1 Includes both Chicago Convention and Visitors Bureau and Chicago Office of Tourism.
Budgets are for 1997 or 1998 (latest figures available).

Source: IACVB, individual convention and visitor bureaux, *Travel and Tourism Intelligence City Reports* (2000).

usually have a number of roles, including brochure production, advertising, attending trade fairs, direct mail campaigns, organizing familiarization visits, preparing tenders for major events, public relations, and so on.

The budgets of these bureaux vary dramatically as can be seen in Table 10.3, which gives details of the estimated budgets of the top fifty bureaux in the USA in 1998.

National tourism organizations

National tourism boards, recognizing the importance of business tourism are now becoming increasingly involved in promoting their respective countries as business tourism destinations. However, there are great variations in their commitments as can be seen from Table 10.4 which is based on a survey published by *Conference and Incentive Travel* in June 2000

Table 10.4   The marketing activity of national tourism organizations in relation to conferences and incentive travel

Destination	Promotional budget for conference and incentive travel	Existence of dedicated conference and incentive travel department
Antigua and Barbados	£5 000	Yes
Canada	£46 000	Yes
Cyprus	£50 000	Yes
Denmark	£245 000	Yes
France	£150 000	Yes
Hungary	£83 000	No
Malta	£1 500 000	Yes
Mauritius	£30 000	No
New Zealand	£2 000 000	No
Thailand	£80 000	Yes
Turkey	£10 000	No

Source: *Conference and Incentive Travel* (June 2000).

Co-operation between destinations

Some destinations are realizing that, if they can find partner destinations with complementary attractions, then co-operation can be better than competition. Recently, for example, a co-operative promotional campaign was mounted aimed at the incentive travel market by the Singapore Tourism Board and the Indonesian Department of Culture and Tourism, under the title, 'Start with a dry martini, then wet your pants' (white water rafting!)

The importance of destination image

Destination image is important in marketing business travel and tourism, in several ways:

1 Conference and exhibition organizers and incentive travel agencies choose destinations for their events, partly based on their perceptions of these destinations.
2 Conference delegates often choose to attend conferences partly based on the perceived attractions or otherwise of the place.
3 Partners choose to accompany business travellers visiting a destination only if they perceive it to be an attractive place.

The attraction of a destination is a function of a combination of factors, including climate, scenery or townscape, safety and security, the attitude of local people towards tourists, the

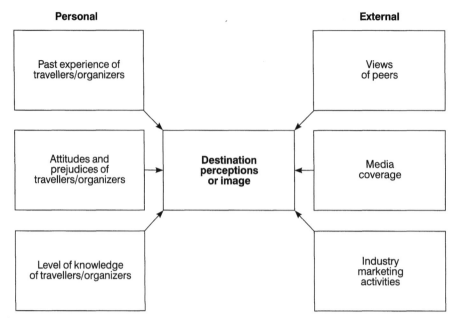

Figure 10.6 Factors affecting perceptions of destinations held by travellers and organizers

quality of the infrastructure, price levels, and so on. But destination image is a subjective and abstract concept, where perceptions are more important that reality. Figure 10.6 illustrates some of the factors affecting perceptions of a destination.

In recent years a number of destinations have succeeded in developing positive destination images, realistic or not. For example it is widely believed that:

● New York is safer than it once was
● Dublin is a lively, sociable, friendly city
● Singapore is an efficient, good value, high-quality service destination.

The above images bring real benefits for these destinations in terms of business travel and tourism.

Key issues in the different types and sectors of business travel and tourism

Each type of business tourism and sector of the business travel industry has its own distinct characteristics and pattern of marketing activity. These differences are illustrated in Table 10.5.

Table 10.6 looks at the key issues in marketing within the different sectors of the business travel and tourism industry. This is clearly a simplification of a very complex picture.

It is now time for us to move on to look at several key topical issues in business travel and tourism.

Table 10.5   Characteristics of marketing of different types of business travel and tourism

Type of business travel and tourism	Key marketing issues
Conferences and meetings	• Destinations and venues have to sell to professional agencies and/or actual clients[1] • Professional organizers and/or clients have to sell to delegates • Professional organizers have to sell their services to clients
Exhibitions	• Destinations and venues have to sell to organizers • Organizers have to sell simultaneously to exhibitors and exhibition visitors
Incentive travel	• Destinations and venues have to sell to professional organizers and/or clients • Professional organizers have to sell their services to clients • Professional organizer has to convince staff of the value of incentive with help of client
Product launches	• Destinations and venues have to sell to organizers and/or clients • Professional agencies sell their services to clients • Professional organizers and/or clients have to sell to prospective attendees
Training courses	• Destinations and venues have to sell to professional organizers and/or clients • Professional agencies sell services to client organizations • Organizers and/or clients sell package to the staff/participants

Note: 1 The client is the customer, who may organize an event themselves or employ a professional specialist agency or organizer.

Topical issues

Marketing in business travel and tourism, as in other industries, is going through a period of great change. Some of the most important issues and changes are briefly discussed in this section.

Quality and customer satisfaction

Everyone today believes in the importance of quality and customer satisfaction, even if they cannot actually define what it means. In business travel and tourism we need first to establish who the customer is, for, as we saw earlier in the book, there are customers and consumers in our industry.

Customers are generally the organizations which employ business travellers or organize business tourism events, while consumers are those who actually attend the events and use the services of the industry. And, of course, they both want different things. Quality and satisfaction to the customer will mean low price, while for the consumer it will mean comfort and status, as well as reliability which is of interest to both of them.

As frequent travellers, business tourists tend to be demanding, knowledgeable and able to compare the products of competing organizations.

Table 10.6   Key marketing issues in the different sectors of the business travel and tourism industry

Sector of business travel and tourism industry	Key marketing issues
Retail travel	• Selling services of agency to organizations which generate business travel trips • Developing relationships with professional organizers of business tourism events • Negotiating deals for clients with key suppliers
Airlines	• Selling services directly to the travel departments of organizations • Selling services to professional specialist organizers of business tourism events • Selling services via intermediaries including travel agencies, consolidators and the Internet • Developing brand loyalty schemes • Developing links with suppliers in other sectors such as hotels • Developing their business class products
Hotels	• Selling services directly to the travel departments of organizations • Selling services to professional specialist organizers of business and tourism events • Selling services via intermediaries such as travel agencies, incentive travel agencies and on the Internet • Developing brand loyalty schemes • Developing products specifically to meet the needs of business travellers
Venues	• Selling services to clients via professional specialist agencies or directly • Attracting bookings that will fill the venue for up to ten years in advance
Destinations	• Promoting to clients directly or via professional specialist organizers, to attract both short-term and long-term business

We need to make the following points about the concept of quality and satisfaction in business travel and tourism:

1 The main criterion for judging quality and satisfaction is 'fitness for purpose', products and services which do what they are supposed to do. In other words quality means flights that operate on time and venues that enable conferences to take place efficiently. Reliability, again is the crucial issue here.

2 The concept of 'critical incidents' is important because there are many occasions in business travel and tourism when the overall experience hinges on a single incident, such as a delayed flight, a problem with the audiovisual equipment at a venue or overbooking at a hotel. A customer may well be very satisfied if the organization turns the critical incident from a negative to a positive through its actions.

3 Quality has to be related to the price the customer or consumer is willing or able to afford. For example, a leisure traveller who has bought a £250 last-minute economy discount ticket from Paris to Singapore cannot expect to enjoy the same benefits as a

First Class passenger who has paid £3000 for the same journey. On the other hand, whatever price has been paid customers and consumers have a right to expect certain basic benefits such as safety.

Organizations which serve business travellers are always trying to ensure that the quality they offer matches, or preferably exceeds, the expectations of their clients. Customer questionnaires are a crucial element of such activities. Exhibit 10.1 gives an example of one such questionnaire for the Hilton Hotel at Amsterdam Schipol Airport in the Netherlands.

Exhibit 10.1 Customer satisfaction questionnaire, Amsterdam Schipol Hilton Hotel, the Netherlands, 2000

Hilton
Amsterdam Airport Schiphol

GUEST QUESTIONNAIRE

Dear Guest,

We are delighted to have you with us and hope you are pleased with our facilities and services. It is our aim to create and maintain a courteous and friendly atmosphere for you to enjoy, recognizable as typically Hilton.

We are always looking for guest feedback and would appreciate if you could take some time to fill in this questionnaire. Whether you leave the completed questionnaire at the front desk or mail it back to us, I can assure you that it will receive my personal attention and follow-up.

Thank you for your kind assistance.

Ronald A. van Weezel
General Manager

Service on arrival and check-in. Was it prompt and courteous?

excellent ☐
good ☐
satisfactory ☐
insufficient ☐
below standard ☐
your comments:

_____

_____

Your room. Was it clean, comfortable and properly supplied?

excellent ☐
good ☐
satisfactory ☐
insufficient ☐
below standard ☐
your comments:

_____

_____

Restaurants and Bar, please specify:

EastWest		**Teppanyaki Table**	
excellent	☐	excellent	☐
good	☐	good	☐
satisfactory	☐	satisfactory	☐
insufficient	☐	insufficient	☐
below standard	☐	below standard	☐

your comments:

_____

_____

The Greenhouse		**Stop over bar**	
excellent	☐	excellent	☐
good	☐	good	☐
satisfactory	☐	satisfactory	☐
insufficient	☐	insufficient	☐
below standard	☐	below standard	☐

your comments:

_____

_____

Telephone service. Were your messages handled efficiently?

excellent ☐
good ☐
satisfactory ☐
insufficient ☐
below standard ☐
your comments:

_____

_____

In-house services, porter, laundry etc. Were your personal
possessions well looked after?

excellent ☐
good ☐
satisfactory ☐
insufficient ☐
below standard ☐
your comments:

_____

_____

Individual employees. How well did we respond to your needs?

excellent ☐
good ☐
satisfactory ☐
insufficient ☐
below standard ☐
your comments:

_____

_____

Temperature, lighting, plumbing. Were you comfortable?

excellent ☐
good ☐
satisfactory ☐
insufficient ☐
below standard ☐
your comments:

_____

_____

Meeting 2000 Business Centre. Did we do everything to
assist you?

excellent   ☐

good   ☐

satisfactory   ☐

insufficient   ☐

below standard   ☐

your comments:

_____

_____

Service at check-out. Did it go smoothly?

excellent   ☐

good   ☐

satisfactory   ☐

insufficient   ☐

below standard   ☐

your comments:

_____

_____

Hotel shuttlebus. Was it on time? Did it run frequently enough?

excellent   ☐

good   ☐

satisfactory   ☐

insufficient   ☐

below standard   ☐

your comments:

_____

_____

If you return to this location, would you choose to stay with
us again?

Yes ☐

No ☐

If no, please comment:

_____

_____

_____

_____

Why did you select this hotel?

Satisfactory previous visit ☐

Visits to other Hilton International Hotels ☐

Recommendations ☐

Airport Location ☐

Travel Agencies ☐

Airline bonus system ☐

Hilton Honors ☐

How did you make your reservations request?

Directly to this hotel ☐

Through Hilton Reservations Service ☐

Through a Travel Agent ☐

Through an airline ☐

Through your company or organization ☐

Through Internet ☐

The purpose of this visit was:

Business ☐   Pleasure ☐   Both ☐

Do you have any further suggestions or comments which would help us to make your next visit more enjoyable? Did you miss any services or facilities?

_____

_____

_____

_____

_____

_____

_____

_____

_____

_____

_____

_____

_____

_____

Your name (please print) _____

Home address _____

City _____ State_____ Postal Code_____

Date of Arrival _____ Room No._____

HHonors

We participate in the HHonors loyalty programme
and many frequent flyers programmes.
For further information please contact
the reception desk.

PO Box 7685, 1118 ZK Schiphol Centrum
email: info_schiphol@hilton.com
Tel. (020) 7104000, Telefax (020) 7104080

Apollolaan 138, 1077 BG Amsterdam
email: info_amsterdam@hilton.com
Tel. (020) 7106000, Telefax (020) 7106080

Weena 10, 3012 CM Rotterdam
email: info_rotterdam@hilton.com
Tel. (010) 7108000, Telefax (010) 7108080

Internet Hilton International Co.
http://www.hilton.com

Hilton
Amsterdam Airport Schiphol

Herbergierstraat 1
1118 CA Schiphol-Centrum
tel.: 020 - 710 40 00, fax: 020 - 710 40 80

The industry recognizes the importance of quality and organizes various awards. Exhibit 10.2 lists the winners of the various categories of the Incentive Travel and Meetings Association Awards, 2001, for example.

Exhibit 10.2 Incentive Travel and Meetings Association Awards, 2001

Grand Prix Platinum Award

IKEA (UK)
Agency: Global Event Solutions

The Gold Award Winners

Automotive
Starwood Hotels & Resorts Worldwide Award
Ford Motor Company
Agencies: Imagination/Maritz Travel

Consumer products
Le Méridien Award
Hotpoint
Agency: Line-Up Communications

Financial
Millennium Hotels & Resorts Award
Clerical Medical International
Agency: Skybridge

Food and drinks
World Travel Market Award
Matthew Clark Brands
Agency: Poulter Partners

Health, pharmaceutical and cosmetics
Maison de la France Award
SmithKline Beecham
Agency: HP:ICM

Information technology
Société Des Bains De Mer Award
IBM
Agency: Skybridge

Travel, leisure and entertainment
Concorde Hotels Award
Gala Bingo
Agency: Poulter Partners

Best conference
Switzerland Convention & Incentive Bureau Award
IKEA (UK)
Agency: Global Event Solutions

Best incentive
Mexico Tourism Board Award
SmithKline Beecham
Agency: Grass Roots Travel Awards

Best UK event
JLA Award
Hotpoint
Agency: Line-up Communications

Best overseas event
International Confex Award
IBM
Agency: Skybridge

Best product launch
Kempinski Hotels & Resorts Award
Ford Motor Company
Agency: Imagination/Maritz Travel

Best promotional communication
Cannes Convention and Visitors Bureau Award
Mercedes-Benz UK
Agency: TMO

Best integrated solution
Grimaldi Forum Monaco Award
Toshiba
Agency: TFI Group

Best low-cost solution
Conference Centre at Church House Award
IKEA (UK)
Agency: Global Event Solutions

Best use of a venue's facilities
Silversea Cruises Award
IKEA (UK)
Agency: Global Event Solutions

Best use of logistics
British Airways Award
Tivoli Systems
Agency: TMO

Source: *Conference and Incentive Travel* (March 2001).

Magazines, such as *Business Traveller*, which are aimed at the consumers also have awards, based on the opinions of their readers. The results of the 1999 poll are shown in Exhibit 10.3, based on the views of nearly 1000 respondents.

Exhibit 10.3 *Business Traveller* Readers' Poll Awards, 1999

Best Airline	British Airways
Best Short-Haul Airline	Swissair
Best Long-Haul Airline	Singapore Airlines
Best North American Airline	American Airlines
Best Eastern European Airline	Lot Polish Airlines
Best Business Class	Virgin Atlantic
Best Economy Class	Virgin Atlantic

NEW Best Low-Cost Airline	easyJet
Best Frequent Flyer Programme	British Airways
Best Airport in the World	Singapore Changi
Best Airport in Europe	Amsterdam Schipol
Best Airport in North America	Chicago O'Hare
Best Airport for Duty-Free Shopping	Singapore Changi
Best Business Hotel Chain World-wide	Sheraton
Best Business Hotel Chain in the UK	Hilton
Best Business Hotel Chain in Western Europe	Inter-Continental
Best Business Hotel Chain in Eastern Europe	Inter-Continental
Best Business Hotel Chain in North America	Hyatt
Best Business Hotel Chain in the Middle East	Inter-Continental
Best Business Hotel Chain in Asia/Pacific	Shangri-La
Best Mid-Market Business Hotel Chain World-wide	Holiday Inn
Best Business Hotel in the World	The Oriental, Bangkok
Best Business Hotel in the UK	The London Hilton on Park Lane
Best Business Hotel in Western Europe	Hotel Arts, Barcelona
Best Business Hotel in Eastern Europe	Marriott, Warsaw
Best Business Hotel in the Middle East	Hotel Inter-Continental, Dubai
Best Business Hotel in North America	The Plaza, New York
Best Airport Hotel	Radisson Edwardian, Heathrow
Best New Business Hotel in the World	The Jumeirah Beach Hotel, Dubai
Best Car Rental Company World-wide	Hertz
Best Car Rental Company in Europe	Avis
Favourite Business City	London
NEW Best Travel Website	British Airways

Source: *Business Traveller* (November 1999).

While such surveys are perhaps quite influential in shaping perceptions, they are based on very small samples.

There are relatively few studies of the levels of satisfaction of business travellers with particular destinations. Leong Mau Wai and Leong Mau Ngan (1999), however, have produced an interesting study relating to Macau.

It is clear that the growth of competition has led to this growing interest in quality and customer satisfaction as organizations and places seek to achieve advantage over the growing number of competitors. We will therefore now turn our attention to this issue of competition.

Competition

There is growing competition in most sectors of business travel and tourism. Figure 10.7 illustrates some of the ways in which competition is increasing.

Let us now look at some of the ways in which the business travel and tourism industry has sought to respond to this more competitive situation.

Relationship marketing and brand loyalty

It has often been said that it is easier to keep an existing customer than find a new one. Therefore, business tourism suppliers, in common with other industries, have started to

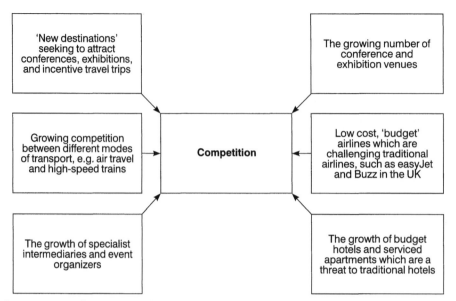

. **Figure 10.7**   Different types of competition

focus on relationship marketing and brand loyalty. Airlines have led this trend and a case study of airline frequent flyer programmes is to be found in Part Five. However, hotels have also developed similar brand loyalty schemes.

Table 10.7 shows a comparison of the programmes of five leading international hotel chains.

However, some of these schemes can seem self-defeating because:

- consumers often realize that they must accumulate many points to receive even modest benefits, and so they lose interest
- consumers often join more than one scheme and use the one which offers the most benefits
- employers – the customers – often object to schemes which benefit their employees rather than themselves.

Nevertheless brand loyalty schemes are a widely accepted aspect of modern marketing.

However, they are, as yet, little used by destinations or many venues. This may be because they only work if the consumer can use them for visits to many different places. Nevertheless, for 'footloose' events, brand loyalty rewards could be a useful marketing tool.

Strategic alliances

In an industry where capital costs are often great and barriers to entry generally high, takeovers and mergers can sometimes be impractical. In these cases, we have seen a growth in strategic alliances, often linked to brand loyalty programmes.

Strategic alliances come in different forms, including:

- alliances within sectors such as between airlines
- alliances within geographical areas such as consortia of visitor attractions on hotels
- alliances between sectors such as airlines and hotels.

Strategic alliances allow benefits for both organizations and consumers. The former gain economies of scale and the ability to offer a wider range of products to their customers while consumers enjoy access to the broader range of products and a more 'seamless' transition from one service to another.

The airline sector has spearheaded this trend. The 'Qualiflyer' group for example includes:

- twenty-five airlines, including Sabena, Swissair, TAP Air Portugal, Austrian Airlines, All Nippon Airlines, Cathay Pacific, Qantas and US Airways – travellers gain points towards a 'consumer brand loyalty programme' by using the services of any of these airlines
- nineteen hotel groups
- five car hire companies
- two credit card companies
- duty-free shops at airports
- a telephone company.

In all, there are five major airline alliances, namely, Air France/Delta, One World, Qualiflyer, Wings and the Star Alliance, although these are changing all the time. These airline alliances are often criticized on the following grounds:

1 They lead to code-sharing where, to reduce costs, airline A may stop flying a route that is also flown by airline B. The flight will be operated under the separate codes of both airlines but will only be flown by airline A's aircraft and crews. If airline A is lower in quality standards than airline B this could lead to dissatisfied customers who may feel cheated.
2 These mega-alliances make life difficult for small independent airlines, and could be seen as being anti-competitive. Ultimately this could lead to a reduction in choice for consumers as smaller airlines are squeezed out of the market.

Again, as yet, neither venues nor destinations have really begun to make use of strategic alliances, effectively. Furthermore, they are less used in the field of 'intermediaries' where 'barriers to entry' are fewer and acquisitions are a feasible option.

The rise of women business travellers

So far we have focused on corporate strategy and marketing. But what about market trends themselves? For example, in recent years, we have seen a dramatic rise in women business travellers, particularly in Europe and the USA. A paper by Westwood et al., published in 2000 noted that:

- even in the early 1990s, nearly 40 per cent of all business executives in the USA were women
- in the UK, there were 3.5 million women in management or professional jobs in the mid-1990s
- in the mid-1990s a quarter of British Airways long-haul passengers were women
- in the USA around 40 per cent of business travellers are women.

This picture seen in the USA and Europe is also spreading to other regions of the world.

Table 10.7 The loyalty schemes of five hotel chains, 2000

Hotel chain/group	Number of hotels	Programme name/fees	How to earn points	Partners	Membership benefits
Bass (including Crowne-Plaza Holiday Inn, Inter-Continental, Staybridge Suites): www.bass.com; www.crownplaza.com; www.holiday-inn.com; www.interconti.com; www.staybridge.com	2600	Priority Club World-wide (three levels). Free	Ten points per US dollar spent on non-discounted room rates	24 airlines, including American Airlines, Continental Airlines, Delta Airlines, KLM, Lufthansa, Qantas, Swissair, United Airlines. Car rental: Hertz	Free stays, upgrades, express check-in, express checkout, late check-out, free Staybridge family stays, free newspaper, 20 per cent discount on some hotel services, members can earn airline credits instead of points
Hilton and Conrad International: www.hilton.com	400	Hilton Hhonors (four levels). Free	10 points per US dollar spent at business rates at non-resort hotels; 500 points per stay at resort hotels or on non-business rates; 250 points for using Hhonors travel partners in conjunction with a qualifying stay	32 airlines, including Air France, All Nippon Airways, American Airlines, British Airways, British Midland, Cathay Pacific, KLM, Lufthansa, Qantas, Singapore Airlines, Swissair, United Airlines. Car rental: National, Alamo, Avis, Sixit, Thrifty	Free stays, room discounts, late checkout, spouse stays free, free newspaper, free use of health club facilities, free gaming chips, points can be exchanged for air miles, VIP members can exchange points for vacation packages
Hyatt: www.hyatt.com; www.goldpassport.com	191	Gold Passport (one level). Free	5 points per US dollar spent; 300 bonus points for using airline or rental partners	Airlines: America West, British Airways, Delta, Midwest Express, Northwest, Singapore, TWA, United, US Airways. Car rental: Alamo, Avis	Free stays room discounts, express check-in, express checkout, late checkout, free newspaper, free use of health club facilities, choice of points or air miles on each stay

Hotel group	Points	Earning	Airline and car rental partners	Benefits
Marriott (including Courtyard, Fairfield Inn, Marriott, Residence Inn, Spring Hill Suite, TownePlace Suite): www.marriott.com; www.marriottrewards.com	1650	Marriott Rewards (one level). Free	10 points per US dollar spent at Marriott, Courtyard, Fairfield Inn, Renaissance and Spring Hill Suite; 5 points per US dollar spent at Residence Inn and TownePlace Suite; 1000 points per stay at new Otani in Asia, up to 1000 points per Hertz rental, or 3 air miles per US dollar spent at Marriott and Renaissance, or 1 air mile per US dollar spent at Courtyard, Fairfield Inn, Residence Inn Spring Hill or TownePlace Suite	19 airlines, including American Airlines, British Airways, Cathay Pacific, Continental Airlines, Delta Airlines, KLM, Lufthansa, Qantas, Singapore Airlines, Swissair, United Airlines. Car rental: Hertz	Free stays (including selected Ritz-Carlton Hotels), free car rental, free Eurostar travel, free cruise or golf packages, free theatre tickets, free Whitbread Leisure vouchers, free selected theme park entry
Starwood (including Caesar's World, Four Points, Sheraton, St. Regis, W, Westin): www.starwood.com; www.preferredguest.com	650	Starwood Preferred Guest (three levels). Free	2 points per US dollar spent on room rates and services; 50 points per day on Avis car rental; one point per US dollar spent on AT&T long-distance calls; 5000 points when buying Iridium World satellite service/phone	Airlines: Air France, Air New Zealand, Alaska, Alitalia, American, America West, Ansett, Asiana, Canadian, Cathay Pacific, Continental, Delta, EVA, Japan, KLM, Northwest, Qantas, Saudi Arabian, Thai, United, US Airways. Car rental: Avis	Free stays, room upgrades, free room service, AT&T, Land's End and Saks Fifth Avenue gift vouchers. Points (minimum 2000) can be exchanged for air miles

Source: Business Traveller (January 2000).

The business tourism industry has not always recognized this trend. Many female business travellers still seem to experience discrimination from hotel and airline staff. For example, in 1996 a female *Financial Times* journalist reported that a male flight attendant, 'clearly thought that I was the wife/mistress/daughter of the chap sitting next to me, with no thought at all that a woman might be travelling in her own right in business class. For the rest of the flight I did not get offered second drinks, coffees, anything' (Daneshku, 1996, quoted in Westwood et al., 2000).

Attitudes are changing, but prejudices still remain. However, it would be a mistake for the industry to feel it can meet these trends by tokenistic action like that seen in hotels with full-length mirrors in hotel bedrooms and peepholes in doors!

Perhaps women travellers will respond best to those organizations which:

- show them respect and recognize their right to equal treatment with their male counterparts
- recognize that the needs of male and female passengers are generally similar, namely, reliability, good service, punctuality and safety.

The implications of cross-cultural business travel

Globalization and the economic development of formerly less developed countries is increasing the volume of international, and inter-cultural, business travel. This has great implications for the industry, particularly as many of these travellers are from countries which have previously generated few international tourism trips. These countries include China, India and Russia, to name but three.

The implications of this trend for business travel and tourism suppliers are outlined in Figure 10.8. The secret is to avoid stereotyping and conduct good customer research to allow 'concrete' action to be taken that actually meets the real needs of tourists from different cultures.

Marketing research

Like all industries, marketing is about identifying and meeting the needs of target markets, effectively. This implies a strong role for marketing research, yet this activity is currently underdeveloped.

At last work is going on to endeavour to achieve greater standardization of statistics relating to business travel and tourism between different countries. However, it is a long process and there is still a considerable way to go.

There are still great problems in obtaining up-to-date, reliable figures on the number of business tourists visiting a particular destination or the market for incentive travel in a specific country. This situation partly reflects the difficulties involved in defining these travellers and markets, but also the apparent lack of willingness of governments to invest in researching these matters.

As barriers to travel, such as visas, are decreasing it is even more difficult to collect such data. Only countries with strict immigration control policies, such as China, Russia and Turkey for example, can have reliable business tourism statistics.

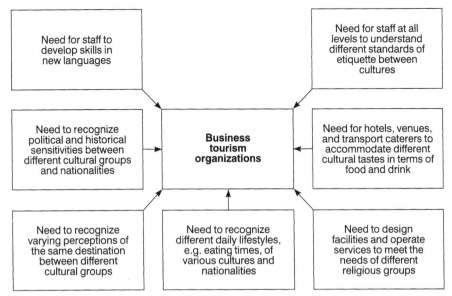

Figure 10.8 The implications of cross-cultural business travel for business tourism organizations

However, statistics are not our only problems. Marketing requires good qualitative research to help marketing people decide how and when to intervene to influence the customer's decision-making processes. There are currently great weaknesses in this respect in business travel and tourism, including:

1 A lack of empirical research on how individuals and organizations make decisions to locate conferences or incentive travel packages in a particular location, including the factors they take into account the relative weighting of these factors
2 A dearth of data on how people decide whether or not to attend a particular conference or exhibition.
3 While some good work has been done in recent years we still know relatively little about how the perceptions of destinations which are held by business travellers develop.
4 There is little empirical research on the relationships between buyers and specialist intermediaries and between the intermediaries and suppliers.
5 At a time when the business tourism market is becoming increasingly multicultural, we still have relatively little empirical research about cultural differences in behaviour and expectations, and the implications of these differences for marketing.
6 We still have little longitudinal research showing how the purchase behaviour of business travellers changes over time.

Considerable research is conducted, of course, by business tourism organizations such as convention centres, retail travel companies, airlines and hotel chains. However, this is commercial research carried out solely for the benefit of the organization in question. It rarely, if ever, is made public.

This lack of up-to-date data on the business travel market and customer/consumer behaviour is a real problem for the industry. It is also a challenge for academics.

The role of technology

As we saw earlier in this chapter, the Internet is starting to have a significant impact on business travel and tourism marketing. It is blurring the distinction between promotion and place or distribution by allowing customers to gain information and buy products and services simultaneously.

The following selection of sites gives an idea about how the Internet is being used by the industry:

● www.phoenix.cub.com – details of hotel services for groups in Phoenix, USA
● www.tq.comm.au/ – Queensland – Conventions-Incentives – details of convention facilities and incentive opportunities in Queensland, Australia
● www.huntpalmer.co.uk – specialist guide to air charter for conference and incentive organizers
● www.LateRooms.com – availability of over 150 000 rooms at discounted rates
● www.wcities.com – details of attractions and venues in a number of cities around the world
● www.-qeiicc.co.uk – details of facilities at a specific major London conference centre
● www.british-airways.com – details of the services provided for business travellers by this airline.

Technology also has other implications for business travel and tourism marketing.

Virtual Reality (VR) is already having an impact on training courses – on the one hand it can help bring such events to life and make the training more effective. For example, surgeons can now try out new surgical techniques, using VR, without risking the lives of real patients. However, in the longer term, VR could be a threat to business travel. If a surgeon can use VR to learn new techniques at her or his own hospital, they will no longer need to travel to learn the techniques at another hospital.

On the other hand, VR could also become a positive benefit to business tourism marketing through its role as a promotional tool. If we can allow the customer, artificially, to experience, for example, being a conference delegate relaxing on a beach in Bali, it must be a more effective way of promoting Bali as a convention destination than via a brochure or video.

The rise of smart-card technologies also has implications for business tourism marketing, particularly in terms of customer service. For example, it can speed up airline check-in and allow the business traveller to arrive later than usual and still catch the flight.

Improvements in reservation systems, notably the rise of Global Destination Systems, are making it easier for the retail travel sector to construct complex, tailor-made itineraries, easily and quickly, for clients.

Increasingly, sophisticated computer-based database mailing systems are also making it ever easier for us to target our marketing much more precisely.

Finally, the development of communication and entertainment technologies is forcing organizations which serve business travellers to modify their products and services, including:

● at-seat mobile phones, computer games, and even casinos in aeroplanes
● special effects equipment in convention centres
● computer access points and mini-offices in hotel bedrooms.

Over the next few years, technological innovations are set radically to change the way we travel on business. In particular, the mobile phone will play an increasing role by providing the traveller with Internet access as well as telephone services, creating a virtual mobile office.

Ethical issues

Business travel and tourism marketing does raise several ethical concerns, notably:

1 The nature of some of the services offered, from excursions to red-light districts and lap-dancing clubs to incentives to fragile wilderness environments. The products, particularly incentive travel trips, often also encourage 'conspicuous consumption' often in destinations where the local population enjoys a poorer standard of living than the traveller

2 The pricing of business tourism services is often high and aimed at the lucrative international markets. This practice discriminates against domestic business travellers in poorer countries and the less affluent international business traveller.

3 Brochures and advertisements, in some destinations, often rarely feature local people but simply foreign business travellers, particularly if the local people have a different skin colour to the target market. Local people may only feature in such promotions as waiters or receptionists for example.

4 The distribution network includes ownership relationships between suppliers and intermediaries which influence the options which the intermediary offers to their clients. However, the customer may be unaware of these links and how they are affecting the service they receive.

5 The brand loyalty schemes reward the traveller rather than their employers and encourage travel that may not be wholly necessary simply so that the traveller can accumulate greater rewards.

Other ethical issues are discussed in Chapter 5, which is concerned with the impacts of business travel and tourism.

Overall, it has to be said that, in contrast to leisure tourism, relatively little attention has been paid by the industry or commentators, to the ethical challenges involved in the marketing of business travel and tourism. This will probably change in the future as the idea of ethical or socially responsible, business gains greater recognition.

Currently, we could be forgiven for thinking that business travel and tourism is a rather self-indulgent world in which consumers are free to do pretty well as they like, providing they – or their employer – are prepared to pay the bill.

Conclusions

In this chapter we have explored the complexities of marketing in business travel and tourism, beginning with an examination of the marketing mix in this industry. We then looked at issues relating to the market before focusing on the specific question of destination marketing. In a brief section we discussed the key issues in marketing different types of business tourism and in the different sectors of business travel and tourism. Finally, we looked at a number of topical issues in the field. We have seen that business travel and tourism marketing is going through a period of change and faces numerous challenges. Some of these challenges will be discussed further in Chapter 14, which looks at the future of business travel and tourism.

Discussion points and essay questions

1 Critically evaluate the concept of the marketing mix in relation to *both* a convention centre *and* an airline, of your choice.
2 Discuss the factors which make destination marketing such a complex activity.
3 Discuss what you consider are the three greatest challenges facing those involved in the marketing of business travel and tourism products and services.

Exercise

Select ten Internet sites of organizations offering services and facilities for business tourists and travellers.

Evaluate each site in terms of its ease of use, quality of information, and ease of booking if it has such a facility. Then present your results in a report, with recommendations for how each site could be made more user-friendly and effective as a marketing tool.

Conclusions to Part Two

In Part Two we have looked at the development of business tourism facilities, the management of human resources within the industry, and the marketing of business travel and tourism products.

We have noted the importance of good design and user friendliness when designing new physical infrastructure for business travel and tourism. In Chapter 9, we focused on the people who work in the industry, the nature of their jobs and their education and training. In the final chapter of Part Two we looked at how we market products in business travel and tourism including destinations.

It is now time for us to focus on the practical side of business travel and tourism, namely, the organization of events.

Part Three
The Practice

Part Three focuses specifically on the skills and techniques required in order to manage business tourism events. It endeavours to concentrate on the practical side of the management of business tourism in some detail.

Chapter 11 examines a wide variety of issues that have to be taken into account by anyone planning any type of business tourism event. These include matters such as venue selection, budgeting, transport arrangements, project planning, timescales and crisis management. It also looks at the topical question of managing cross-cultural differences.

The next chapter offers a range of concrete examples of successful business tourism events, highlighting the reasons why they were a success. Wherever appropriate, problems experienced are identified together with how they were solved.

In the final chapter in Part Three the reader is invited to put theory into practice. Through seven interactive exercises the reader has an opportunity to increase their understanding of how to organize events from a conference to an incentive travel trip. The reader also has a chance to design a new convention centre or market a business tourism destination; and just like in real life, there are unforeseen complications to be handled.

11 The organization of business tourism events

In some ways, now, we come to the heart of this book, for in this chapter we focus on the practical side of business tourism. This section endeavours to offer the reader some guidelines concerning the successful organization of business tourism events. This chapter uses the experiences of the authors as well as that of specialists in this field such as Seekings and Rogers.

The chapter offers advice which is common to all types of business tourism events. It also looks at the key issues which are specific to different kinds of business tourism events. It is hoped that the chapter will help you tackle the challenges which are to be set in Chapter 13.

Finally, in introduction, this chapter does not claim to be comprehensive; it is simply a set of general guidelines. Readers should consult the specialist references contained in the Bibliography if they wish to explore this matter in greater detail.

Generic event management tasks and skills

In this section we will consider those tasks and skills which are required for the organization of all successful business tourism events.

Objectives

Sometimes it is all too easy to slide into organizing an event with no clear idea of why it is necessary or what we want to achieve. It follows that we need to have clear objectives.

These objectives could include:

- encouraging networking between people with common interests
- launching a new product to a particular audience
- increasing the level of knowledge of a specific issue among a group of people
- making a certain amount of money by organizing an exhibition.

Objectives should guide every aspect of the organization of the event and each aspect of the planned event should be tested, explicitly or implicitly, in terms of whether or not it meets the objectives?

The setting of objectives should take place, even if the event is one which happens regularly, for it is still important to review the event and ensure that the needs of participants are reflected in the objectives.

An event can have a number of objectives but they should be as precise as possible. As Seekings says of conferences: 'Objectives should be short statements ... lengthy discussions are usually woolly and obscure. Without (objectives) discussion is usually unstructured or aimless' (Seekings, 1996).

The same point can be applied to all other types of business tourism events. We must also recognize that a business tourism event may not be the best solution to meeting an objective. The use of video or satellite conferencing could be a more cost-effective way of meeting our objectives for sharing ideas between a small group of people, for example.

Planning timescales

Any business tourism event takes time to arrange. A common failing is not leaving enough time to organize an event properly. This can result in:

- the ideal venue not being available
- key speakers being unavailable
- many members of the target market being unable to attend
- the organizers having to pay a premium price because they have no alternative suppliers they can turn to because they have left it so late.

Everything takes longer than expected and, therefore, the following should be considered as minimum typical time frames for organizing a successful event:

- specialist small-scale seminar – several months
- medium-size product launch – six months
- large training course – one year
- major international association conference – two to three years.

The planning team

Planning an event requires a range of expertise which suggests the need for a planning team. Often, for association conferences for example, there will be a group of organizers, a committee, who can each handle a particular aspect of the event.

Alternatively, a team needs to be put together that will encompass all the necessary skills to achieve the tasks, including for example:

- financial control
- marketing
- operational management
- specialist services such as audiovisual.

Planning teams should meet regularly to ensure that everyone is making satisfactory progress and to share experiences and information.

Anyone trying to organize an event on their own will face great problems as they will have no one off whom they can bounce ideas, or from whom they can seek advice or to whom they can delegate tasks.

The planning process

Good event organization is a systematic process, which is summarized in general terms in Figure 11.1.

Events occur at a particular moment, so, all planning must be geared to ensuring everything is in place at the appropriate time.

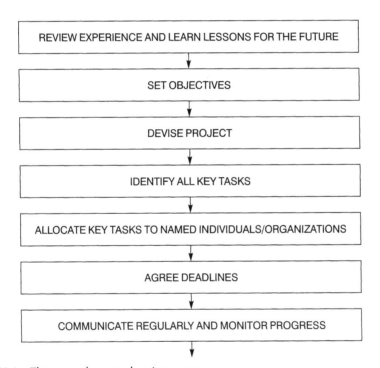

Figure 11.1 The general event planning process

One technique which is useful in this respect is Critical Path Analysis (CPA). This technique:

- identifies when tasks need to be completed
- identifies the interdependence of aspects of event management.

Figure 11.2 illustrates this fact with a simplified CPA for the organization of a small training course.

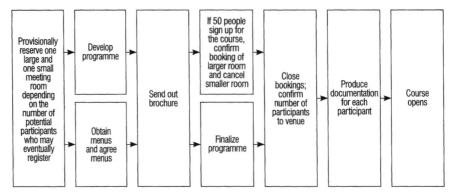

Figure 11.2   A simplified Critical Path Analysis for a hypothetical training course

The target market

In many ways, this is the most important aspect of any event. Successful events are those which meet the needs of their audiences, whoever these may be. It is therefore crucial that, from the beginning, organizers have a clear idea of who the target audience is.

First, we have to recognize that there can be more than one audience. An exhibition organizer usually has two audiences, namely, exhibitors and visitors, each with different desires. Likewise, a professional organizer working on an association conference has to satisfy both the organizing committee of the association as well as the delegates.

However, if we focus just on the end user or consumer, then the organizer has to know who will be participating in the event. The organizer may need to know:

- where the attendees/participants come from, to help them plan transport and allow for journey times
- the leisure interests of participants, for incentive travel packages for instance
- if there are people present who speak a different language and may require interpretation facilities
- how many of the target audience may have special dietary requirements, for example.

There are two other criteria which are much used by organizers but which are open to criticism, namely, age and sex. For instance one often sees organizers planning social programmes around activities they believe will appeal to women, such as shopping, as they assume most partners will be women. This is clearly becoming a very outdated stereotype and many organizers are changing their approach. It is important, therefore, that when event organizers segment markets they do it on the basis of reality not stereotyping.

Calculating numbers

Even if we have a clear idea of our target audience we still have to calculate how many people will attend. We will see the vital importance of this issue, when we look later at

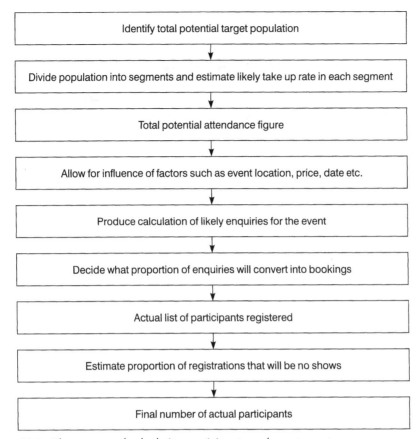

Figure 11.3 The process of calculating participant numbers at events

budgets. Early in the planning process, we have to estimate likely numbers of participants. This is a process with several stages and is illustrated in Figure 11.3.

As we have seen this is a long process, involving a series of 'guestimates'. The actual number of participants can be affected by a wide variety of factors, some of which are mentioned in Figure 11.3. Competing events could be another factor, which brings us nicely to our next planning issue.

Selecting dates

Sometimes organizers have no choice over dates, or the dates may be suggested by tradition, in other words, 'we always hold our conference in the first week in September'.

However, in many cases, organizers have a large amount of discretion in when events take place. Table 11.1 suggests some of the factors that should be taken into account when fixing the dates for an event.

All commentators seem to be agreed that, as far as possible, organizers should be flexible about dates, as this will give them more freedom to negotiate good deals with venues.

Table 11.1   Factors influencing the selection of dates for events

Demand-side factors	Supply-side factors
• Public holidays and religious holidays in target markets • Weather, e.g. good weather will increase attendances • Some days of the week are, rightly or wrongly, perceived to be better than others for meetings and trade fairs • A timescale that allows sufficient time for the planning of the event • The availability of key people as guest speakers	• Availability of venues • Price levels at different times of the year and on different days of the week • Availability of transport services • Weather, e.g. danger of disruption due to bad weather

In-house versus use of intermediaries

When an organization decides it needs to organize any kind of event it has a major decision to make. Will it organize it in-house or use a professional organizer. Table 11.2 lists the advantages and disadvantages of both approaches.

There is clearly a trend towards the use of professional organizers but many organizations still prefer in-house organizations largely for financial reasons. However, this can put great pressure on non-specialist employees to deliver a successful event. It can also be a false economy because professional organizers may be able to negotiate better deals with suppliers than the organizations' inexperienced employees.

Choosing suppliers and intermediaries

Let is imagine our hypothetical organization has chosen to organize its own event, the choice of potential suppliers is mind-blowing. How does an organization choose from

Table 11.2   In-house organization versus the use of a professional organizer

	Advantages	Disadvantages
In-house	• Understand own aims best • Less expensive in money terms • Can keep better control	• Can be unable to view the event objectively • Can be very time-consuming • May lack experience and expertise
Professional organizers	• Experience and expertise • Can view event objectively and professionally	• Can be expensive financially • May not care as much about the event as organizer/client • May not fully understand the client's needs

hundreds of destinations and thousands of venues? This is an issue we will turn to later in this chapter. It is also a question of which florist, photographer, or audiovisual specialist to use.

Suppliers and intermediaries will often, of course, be selected on the basis of price, although value for money may be a better criterion. We must ensure that, if possible, we are not persuaded just by smart presentations and slick sales people. We should ask about the track record of our potential partner and ask for references from satisfied clients that we can check up on later.

It is also important to make decisions only, when in full possession of the facts, and not allow ourselves to be railroaded into signing a contract by a 'for today only' discounted price.

Choosing the destination

If ever there was a case of the classic 'chicken and egg' situation it is the 'which comes first, the destination or venue' question! Most respected commentators appear to suggest that the specific building or buildings where the event will take place – rather than destination (the geographical location of the event) – should take precedence. This clearly does not apply to incentive travel which is all about destinations and their leisure attractions.

However, clearly the destination is important, in a number of ways, including the following:

1 A destination which is not perceived as attractive may reduce the number of participants who might take part in an event compared to if it had been held in a more 'attractive' location.
2 Sometimes, the destination is dictated by the subject of the event or the organization behind the event. For example, a conference about the coal industry should, perhaps, take place in a coal-mining region, while the annual general meeting of a regionally based company should perhaps take place in that region.
3 An event may require a large volume of accommodation or particular specialist facilities that may only be available in particular destinations.
4 Events where social or partner programmes are an important element may gravitate towards a place with many leisure attractions.
5 Exhibitions aimed at the general public will usually take place in large towns or cities which have a large resident population.
6 International events which involve many participants flying in to attend the event, will often need to be in places which have their own airport or have an airport within one hour's travel time.

Let us now move on to look at the venue itself.

Venue selection criteria

Successful events are those which have the right venue, so great attention must be paid to venue selection. Investigation or reconnaissance visits to potential venues are required as well as simply brochures and sales people's promises. The organizer also needs a clear idea of what the ideal venue would be for their event, together with a checklist of criteria to test any venue against.

Let us look at the criteria to take into account when choosing a venue.

First, we have to choose the type of venue we would prefer.

1 Would it be more appropriate to hold our event at a residential venue which has accommodation or a non-residential venue which does not, and
2 Are we looking for a venue in a particular location such as road junction, countryside or city centre, and
3 Are we looking for a conventional or a more unusual venue?

Unusual venues could typically include the following:

● universities and colleges
● historic houses and castles
● museums
● theme parks
● racecourses
● sports stadia
● theatres
● golf courses.

It could also be a floating venue, in other words, a cruise ship. For example, in March 2000 Royal Caribbean and Celebrity Cruises advertised their conference facilities. Exhibit 11.1 shows them advertising their facilities by answering hypothetical questions from organizers.

However, in relation to venue selection criteria, let us imagine that we have chosen to use a conventional venue, such as a hotel with conference facilities.

The criteria we might use for selecting our venue are outlined in Table 11.2.

The question then arises of where and how to find information about potential venues. The following sources should be of assistance:

● directories of conference venues such as the *Blue Book* and *Green Book* and *Venue*, all of which are annual publications
● computer software, e.g. *Viewpoint Conference Guide* which is produced twice a year and the twice yearly *Venue Directory for Windows*
● trade exhibitions, e.g. International Confex and EIBTM
● the trade press such as *Conference and Incentive Travel* and *Meeting Planner International*
● conference placement agencies
● local visitor and convention bureaux.

Of course, some organizations prefer to use a specialist organizer to ensure they select the correct venue for their event.

There is no doubt that venue selection is the key to successful events. But not everything can be covered systematically on a checklist basis, such as staff friendliness and the ambience of the venue, which while hard to quantify are vital ingredients in a successful event.

Exhibit 11.1 Royal Caribbean and Celebrity Cruises advertisement

What's included in a Royal Caribbean/Celebrity cruise at no extra cost?

- **Conference rooms and standard a/v equipment**
  Hotel? No   Cruise? Yes

- **24-hour room service**
  Hotel? Sometimes   Cruise? Yes

- **Full board**
  Hotel? Sometimes   Cruise? Yes

- **Health club access**
  Hotel? Sometimes   Cruise? Yes

- **Spouse programme**
  Hotel? No   Cruise? Yes

- **Twice-daily cabin service**
  Hotel? No   Cruise? Yes

- **Free first-run movies**
  Hotel? No   Cruise? Yes

- **Night turndown service**
  Hotel? No   Cruise? Yes

- **Out-of-hours food**
  Hotel? No   Cruise? Yes

- **Nightly entertainment**
  Hotel? No   Cruise? Yes

- **Airline costs/round trip transfers**
  Hotel? No   Cruise? Yes

Source: *Conference and Incentive Travel* (March 2000).

Accommodation needs

Most business tourism events include the need to book accommodation, so let us look at some issues relating to accommodation:

1 The grade or classification of hotels. In many countries, where there is an accommodation classification system, there may seem to be little relationship between quality and the official grade. This is because the grade is often based on facilities or price, rather than actual quality. Organizations should, therefore, not rely on official grading systems.

2 Hotels are traditionally organized on the basis of departments such as sales and marketing, food and beverage, and banqueting. This can cause problems of co-ordination as the sales department makes the promise to the customer but it is food and beverage and/or banqueting which actually delivers the service.

Table 11.3   Criteria for venue selection for a hotel with conference facilities

Subject	Criteria
Location	• Situation – urban, rural, coastal • Surroundings – landscaped, concrete, derelict • Accessibility – near major road, railway station, airport • How easy is it to find?
Conference rooms	• Number and capacity – adequate for the event? • Quality – soundproofing, décor, blackout facilities, cleanliness, seating, access, power points • Partitioning – should cut out all noise
Accommodation	• Number of rooms – are there enough, are there the right number of singles/twins, doubles, family rooms? • Quality – entertainment, room service, décor, facilities, bathroom size, nice views, furnishings, etc.
Catering	• Quality of food • Speed of service in day time • Variety of food • Provision for specialist diets, e.g. vegetarian, halal, kosher, vegan, etc. • Quantity of drinks included in the price • Where will participants be fed? Is it adequate?
Hotel facilities	• Separate office in hotel for conference organizer during event? • Leisure, e.g. swimming pool, tennis courts, etc. • Quality of public areas • Car parking • Audiovisual equipment • Business centre with computer, fax, message, secretarial facilities • Availability of exhibition space of required
Human resources	• Management: is it amenable, efficient, effective, supportive? • Availability of specialist audiovisual technician • Level of training of staff • Does venue offer dedicated single contact person for the event?
Social activities	• What could delegates do in their free time? • How easy would it be for them to access these activities?
Price	• Published rate, e.g. 24-hour rate? • Willingness to negotiate? • Terms and conditions of payment
Ability to help organize specialist services	• Photographers, entertainers, florists, etc.
Miscellaneous	• Facilities for disabled participants? • Simultaneous translation facilities? • Access to meeting rooms for deliveries by vehicle? • Press facilities? • Storage space? • Courtesy shuttle bus?

3 Standard prices in hotels are called the rack rate but very few business clients will pay this price. Negotiation on the basis of bulk or regular purchase usually brings the price down significantly. This is especially true in off-peak seasons or at quiet times of the week. Negotiation is therefore essential when contracting hotel accommodation.
4 Organizers need to be clear in their dealings with hotels about:
   (a) when they must confirm final numbers
   (b) what will happen about 'no-shows' and what cancellation charges will apply.
5 Overbooking of hotels is a problem and organizers need to be aware of this risk and know what they will do in this situation.
6 Hotels are not the only option for organizers. The organizer may also increasingly make use of university halls of residence, self-catering apartments, and river cruise boats, for example.

Food and beverage

Food and beverage is an essential prerequisite for successful business tourism events. The following is a list of points which organizers should bear in mind in this respect:

1 Many people today are health conscious or vegetarian/vegan, or have dietary requirements dictated by their religion. You should ensure that venues can meet their needs with interesting options, providing of course that participants have informed you of their specific needs.
2 Heavy lunches are not conducive to productive working afternoons or to good time-keeping. Often, lunch is a light affair, served buffet-style to speed up the service.
3 There is a trend towards theming some meals during events, which combines entertainment with good food and drink. Such themes should be carefully planned and imaginative.
4 Many venues have standard menus; however these can be modified, through negotiation, to meet the tastes and/or the budget of the organizer.

The beverage side is, unfortunately, open to dishonest practices such as the substitution by staff of cheap products for well-known brands. Organizers have to be vigilant and ready to report such practices to the venue management.

Transport arrangements

If this event involves transport organization in the package, and often even if transport is not included, the organizer has to bear the following few points in mind:

1 Rail operators and airlines will often offer special fares for those attending major conferences or exhibitions, particularly if the organizer promotes their services, in promotional material, and designates them 'preferred service partners'.
2 When advising participants on travel arrangements, or making them on their behalf, please remember that delays are common. So organizers should ensure that they allow a margin of error so that if delays occur the event schedule will not be disrupted.

3 Organizers have to recognize that there are usually five types of transport needs for events, namely:
   (a) from the participant's home to the destination airport or railway station
   (b) from the home airport or railway station to the destination airport or railway station
   (c) from the destination airport or railway station to the accommodation
   (d) between the accommodation and the venue
   (e) between the accommodation and/or venue and leisure attractions and activities.

Programming issues

When deciding on the programme for an event the following points need to be borne in mind:

1 Timetables should be realistic and allow adequate time for breaks, lunches and registration, for example. Otherwise the event will start to run late which will upset many participants.
2 Try not to make participants spend too long on one activity or session or they will lose concentration and become restless.
3 Organizers should endeavour to put interesting activities or speakers on just after lunch or later in the day to maintain the interest of participants.
4 Providing scheduled free time for participants is usually a good idea, or participants will simply go missing when they feel they have had enough, which can disrupt the flow of the event.
5 Social events and excursions can help provide relaxation time for participants but can also help participants 'network' or communicate with each other. As many participants will agree, this informal networking is often the most part of the event, and organizers should plan opportunities for it to take place.

The most important aspect of any business tourism event is timing. Nothing annoys participants more than an event that does not keep to schedule.

Budgeting

Now we come to perhaps the most important issue, budgeting. Every event must have a budget. However, budgets can vary in their aims depending on the type of organization and the type of event. A budget can be based on the need to:

● generate a particular level of profit or surplus
● break even, in other words, balance income and expenditure
● operate within a given subsidy, in other words, expenditure must not exceed income by more than a particular amount.

For our purposes let us imagine we are organizing an event where the aim is to break even. First, we need to identify our costs, in terms of:

- fixed costs, those costs which will be incurred regardless of the number of participants
- variable costs, those costs which will vary directly in relation to the number of participants.

Examples of fixed costs, of course, include:

- venue hire charges
- marketing expenditure
- equipment rental.

Variable costs, on the other hand, include:

- accommodation
- food and beverage
- printing and postage.

Income can come from a number of sources. For a conference, for example, it could come from:

- delegate fees
- sponsorship
- renting stands at an exhibition linked to the conference.

It is important that we are able to calculate the breakeven point, in other words, the point at which the income from a particular number of participants will be sufficient to cover the fixed cost and relevant variable costs. This point is illustrated in Figure 11.4.

In Table 11.4 we have a hypothetical draft budget for a conference of 300 full-time delegates, that is designed to break even.

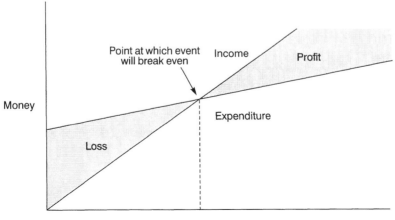

Figure 11.4 Calculating the break even figure for an event
Source: after Seekings (1996).

Table 11.4 Draft budget for conference of 300 delegates

Expenditure	*£*	*Income*	*£*
• Hire of venue	10 000	• Delegate fees at £250 per delegate	£75 000
• Food and beverage for 300 delegates	15 000	• Sponsorship	
• Accommodation for 300 delegates	30 000	– Star Air	3 000
• Speaker fees and expenses	5 000	– Sunnyvale District Council	3 000
• Social programme	5 000	– Dumpville Transport	2 000
• Marketing	3 000	• Advertisements in conference brochure	5 000
• Administration costs	8 000	• Advertising banners at conference	1 000
• Conference brochure production	1 000		**£89 000**
• Delegate transport while at conference	3 000	Nominal loss with 300 delegates = £100	
• Insurance	1 000		
• Contingencies (10%)	8 000		
	£89,000		

However, overall income and expenditure is not the only concern for organizers. They also have to be concerned with cash flow, in other words, when money comes in and goes out. This needs to be balanced to avoid short-term problems where expenditure exceeds income for a particular period.

The best cash flow will be achieved if organizers:

- stimulate income early in the project through deposits from delegates, for example
- delay payment to suppliers, including the venue, for as long as possible.

Nevertheless, there is likely to be a period when reserves will be needed to keep the project solvent until income begins to flow.

In the event of possible cancellation of the event, it is important for organizers to ensure they have enough money to meet the costs which will arise even if the event does not take place, such as venue cancellation charges.

Organizers will often find themselves having to reduce expenditure by cutting costs such as food and beverage. This must not be done at the expense of the overall quality of the event.

The art of negotiation

The organization of most business tourism events involves a considerable amount of negotiation; most things are negotiable in this dynamic market-driven activity, so let us say a few words about the art of negotiation.

Organizers will probably be most successful as negotiators, if they:

- ensure that the person with whom they are negotiating feels that they too are gaining from the agreed solution; in other words, if there is a 'win-win' situation
- try not to get into a position where they have no room for manoeuvre, on dates for example.

Cotterell (1994) also put forward some advice for event organizers:

- prepare – for example, know the prices charged by the venue to other clients and know the prices charged by similar venues in the area
- be nice but gain respect
- do not lie
- be flexible
- never reveal deadlines
- 'name drop'
- hint at other business to be placed in the future
- be patient
- disclaim responsibility for the final decision
- do not underestimate the sellers.

Of course, the organizer has to know what may be open to negotiation. In 1997 Carey published a list of such areas. These are outlined in Table 11.5.

Negotiation skills require practice and learning lessons from good and bad experiences. In business tourism, it is important to recognize that most things are negotiable!

Table 11.5   Potential areas of negotiation with a venue or accommodation

Areas where the venue could be asked to reduce or waive a charge	Areas where the venue could be asked to include items within its overall charge
<ul><li>Partner rates and single supplements in hotels</li><li>Early check-in and late checkout at hotels</li><li>Meeting room charges if considerable expenditure is being made on food and beverage for example</li><li>Audiovisual equipment</li><li>Technical support staff</li><li>Use of an office for organizers</li><li>Parking</li><li>Signs</li><li>Extra porters</li><li>Storage facilities</li></ul>	<ul><li>Complimentary rooms for key personnel in hotels</li><li>Room upgrades for key people, in hotels</li><li>More favourable terms for payment and credit facilities</li><li>Service charges and gratuities</li><li>Continuous tea and coffee service</li><li>Upgrades to menus and wine</li><li>Welcome cocktail on arrival</li></ul>

Source: adapted from Carey (1997).

Contracts and the legal dimension

It is important for organizers to recognize that business tourism events involve large sums of money, and risks if things go wrong. Therefore, there is clearly a need for contracts to protect all parties. These contracts are usually between the venue and the organizer/client and should clearly outline:

- the responsibilities of each party
- the mechanism by which disputes will be resolved
- the process by which the agreement can be terminated
- the penalties that may be suffered by both parties if they fail to meet their obligations under the contract.

Obviously, those organizers not experienced in such methods should consult a professional organizer and/or their legal adviser before entering into such a contract.

Marketing

We now come to one of the most important issues – marketing. All business tourism events involve marketing in some way. For example:

1 Conferences have to be marketed to encourage people to register as delegates.
2 Exhibitions have to be marketed to both visitors and exhibitors.
3 Incentive travel trips have to be internally marketed to the staff who may wish to become participants in them.
4 Product launches have to be sold to the target audiences, whether they be the media, retailers or consumers in general.

Let us now look at the tools we use in business tourism to market events. First, however, as we noted earlier in this chapter, we have to be clear about our target market and market segmentation. We need to understand their desires and objectives so that we can design products and messages that will appeal to them.

Inasmuch as everything discussed in this chapter relates to the event 'product' we will focus on the other aspects of marketing, notably price, promotion and place or distribution.

Pricing is usually based on costs, of course. But we have to recognize that price also has to relate to relevant competition and to where we wish to position our event in the marketplace. There is also a psychological dimension in that £299 looks better than £300.

Often we need a complex pricing structure to reflect different types of product. For example, there will be a fee for the whole three days of a conference of that duration but there may also be day rates for those wishing just to attend for one day. Likewise an exhibition stand of 10 square metres in a prime location will be more expensive than one of the same size in a poorer location.

Promotion is a key aspect of event marketing. It can take all the usual forms, such as advertising, direct personal selling, press and public relations and sales promotions, for example. But for most events, the brochure is still the most important promotional tool.

Exhibit 11.2 provides an example of the text of a brochure used to promote an academic conference in September 2000.

Business tourism events make increasing use of direct mail and Internet marketing to contact their target markets. Accurate up-to-date databases are a vital asset, for business tourism event organizers today.

In terms of *place* or *distribution* the Internet is also breaking down the distinction between promotion and distribution, for it fulfils both roles. Potential customers can both access information and make bookings in the same transaction.

Relevant marketing issues specific to different types of event will be discussed later in this chapter.

Event booking

The forms on which participants formerly register to take part in an event need to be simple, clear and attractive. They should try, in one go, to gain all the information the organizers need. This includes:

● name and position, if representing an organization
● address, telephone, fax and e-mail
● information on accompanying persons, where appropriate
● details of arrival and departure dates
● accommodation requirements, if appropriate
● chosen method of payment
● an opportunity for participants to notify organizers of any issue they feel the organizer needs to know, such as special diets, late arrival at a hotel or disabilities
● details of any relevant social events the participants may or may not wish to attend.

Clearly the same form can also be made available via the Internet.

An example of a conference booking form, relating to the previously entitled Tourism 2000: Time for Celebration? conference, is contained in Exhibit 11.3.

Administration

Between the beginning of the marketing of the event and the day of the event, there is a need for meticulous administration. Tasks include:

● acknowledging bookings
● following up enquiries
● preparing and sending invoices
● providing documentation relating to the event
● preparing rooming lists for accommodation, wherever appropriate.

A crucial task is the monitoring of the budget situation to identify possible problems, in terms of overall income or cash flow. Constant liaison with venues and accommodation is also required to make sure everyone is clear about responsibilities, and is informed about any changes.

Exhibit 11.2 Tourism 2000: Time for Celebration? – conference brochures

Tourism 2000: Time for Celebration?

Centre for Travel & Tourism
University of Northumbria at Newcastle

Centre for Tourism
Sheffield Hallam University

Sheffield, UK

2-7 September 2000

The Major International Tourism Conference of the Millennial Year

UNIVERSITY of NORTHUMBRIA at NEWCASTLE

Sheffield Hallam University

Visit our conference website:
http://www.travel-tourism.com/conference

Cover Artwork by David Hockney, "A Bigger Splash" 1967. Acrylic on Canvas, 96x96" Copyright © 2000 David Hockney

Produced by the Department of External Relations DER107/MBA/KT/PC

Conference Sponsors and Supporters

The Conference organisers would like to thank the following organisations for their support:

Business Education Publishers
Channel View Publications
Chatsworth Estates
English Heritage
First Choice Holidays and Flights Ltd.
International Festivals and Events Association Europe
National Liaison Group for Higher Education in Tourism
Peak District National Park Authority
Sheffield City Council
Sheffield Industrial Museums Trust
Sheffield International Venues
The Earth Centre
The Leighton Group
Travel Law Centre, University of Northumbria
World Archaeological Congress

Conference Organisers

The Centre for Travel & Tourism is delighted to be working with the Centre for Tourism of Sheffield Hallam University to bring you *Tourism 2000: Time for Celebration?*

The Centre for Travel & Tourism of the University of Northumbria at Newcastle has organised and managed regional, national and international conferences and is proud of its reputation for quality, hospitality, and innovation. Above all it is proud of the contributions its previous international conferences have made to the development of tourism as an important academic discipline and to the development of a responsible, forward thinking industry.

Your Conference Directors are:

Dr Mike Robinson, Centre for Travel & Tourism, University of Northumbria at Newcastle;

Mr Philip Long, Centre for Tourism, Sheffield Hallam University.

Supported by the Conference Organising Committee comprising:

Mr Nigel Evans, Centre for Travel & Tourism, University of Northumbria at Newcastle;

Ms Dianne Lowe, Centre for Tourism, Sheffield Hallam University;

Dr Richard Sharpley, Centre for Travel & Tourism, University of Northumbria at Newcastle;

Mr John Swarbrooke, Centre for Tourism Sheffield Hallam University.

Introduction

The year 2000 stands as a bridge between a thousand years of history and a future that is, by definition, uncertain. As a large part of the world engages in one of the largest celebrations in human history, this year, more than any other, is a time of reflection, evaluation and anticipation.

With this conference we seek to reflect on the growth and development of tourism from its roots in pilgrimage and exploration to its present and future role as a vast and complex social and cultural activity, a diverse international industry, and as focus for academic discourse. The capacity of tourism to bridge cultural divides and forge understanding, together with its ability to generate social and economic benefits has given us much to celebrate. The invention and creativity of tourism, and its function in providing us with a myriad of pleasurable experiences, are very much accepted in the 'first' world as integral to culture and something we will carry with us as we move into the 'new age'

However, there is also much to question. As tourism continues to grow and permeates the most distant of environments and remote cultures, it continues to raise ever-more challenging issues relating to equality, identity, futurity and meaning. It forces us to look at how we manage tourism and how we achieve balance. To learn we must ask questions.

The image chosen for this conference is David Hockney's 'A Bigger Splash'.

The warmth of the Californian summer, the cloudless sunny day, the lure of the swimming pool, imaginings of sitting by its side in quiet relaxation would seem to capture the spirit of much contemporary tourism in the westernised world. This is the tourism of reward, hedonism, and escape.

But the absence of any person in the picture askes the questions for us: 'where is everyone?' All we see is an indicative splash and the vacated solitary folding chair. Here is the latent draw of the picture that awakens our curiosity beyond its initial aesthetic impact. We arrive at the picture with a view and we leave it with a question mark.

With the *Tourism 2000: Time for Celebration?* Conference we begin with a great many question marks, but hopefully all those involved will leave with a clearer view.

Conference Venue

The Conference will be held at Sheffield Hallam University in the heart of the City of Sheffield. Sheffield is easily accessible by air, rail and road.

The City of Sheffield is England's fourth largest City and occupies a position at the meeting of two rivers, the Sheaf and the Don. Though some traces of medieval Sheffield exist, notably in the Cathedral and at nearby Beauchief Abbey dating from 1175, the City is very much the result of Victorian industrialism and commerce. The City is world famous for its steel making and in particular the manufacture of cutlery. From the middle of the 19th century, Sheffield grew rapidly to become the world's foremost steel manufacturing centre. Despite recent decades of economic re-structuring, Sheffield now produces more steel than ever utilising advanced, clean technologies.

Whilst proud of its industrial fame Sheffield is a dynamic city that has diversified and developed its economic base. Tourism, leisure and sport have been at the forefront of a changing Sheffield. New attractions such as the National Centre for Popular Music and the nearby Earth Centre complement long established museums, art galleries, parks and gardens. Sheffield has been designated a National City of Sport and enjoys a wealth of international sports venues. The wild and beautiful landscapes of the Peak National Park are close by and provide opportunities for walking, climbing and a range of outdoor activities. The City itself is pleasantly green containing more woodland than any other English city.

Culture is at the forefront of the regeneration of Sheffield. The City offers a range of theatres and music venues ranging from the impressive Edwardian grandeur of the Lyceum, to the Studio complex in the City's Cultural Industries Quarter. Perhaps one of the most surprising links between Sheffield's industrial base and its thriving cultural and media developments was highlighted by the highly acclaimed film 'The Full Monty'. The film, about unemployed steelworkers who form a troupe of male strippers, was shot on location in Sheffield, and in October 1997 became the biggest-earning British-made film ever, overtaking 'Four Weddings and a Funeral'.

Sheffield, Funeral Gate

Conference Accommodation

A wide range of city centre hotel accommodation is available to delegates at rates specially discounted for the conference.

In addition, quality study bedrooms (single and single en-suite) are available as part of the award winning student accommodation on the edge of the Cultural Industries Quarter of Sheffield.

Demand for both hotel bedrooms and study bedrooms will be high for the conference and we suggest early booking.

Sheffield, Peace Gardens

To make it easier for delegates and to ensure you qualify for the discounted rates all accommodation should be booked through the Tourism 2000 Conference Office:

Tel: +44(0) 114 225 5335/5336
Fax: +44(0) 114 225 5337
Email: tourism2000@shu.ac.uk

Language

The official language of the conference is English for all spoken and written material.

A Welcome to Sheffield

A welcome reception will be held for delegates in the splendid Town Hall. Built in 1890 and officially opened in 1897 by Queen Victoria, Sheffield Town Hall with its 210-foot clock tower still dominates the city centre skyline. The clock tower is capped by a statue of Vulcan, Roman God of fire and metal, symbolic of the City's traditional industries of iron and steel making. The imposing entrance hall with its grand staircase, decorative stonework, two vast figures representing electricity and steam, and an elaborate chandelier decorated with signs of the Zodiac are typical features of this Victorian architectural extravaganza.

Sheffield Town Hall

The Conference Dinner

The conference dinner will be held in the unique Cutlers' Hall.

The Company of Cutlers in Hallamshire was incorporated by Act of Parliament in 1624 and, in 1638, the Company bought a piece of land on Church Street for £66.12s and built their first Hall. The present Hall, the third, a Grade 2 listed building, was built on the same piece of land in 1832. It has been extended twice, in 1867 and 1888, and is regarded as one of the finest Halls in the North of England. The Cutlers' Company owns a world famous silver collection that is displayed in the Hall.

A Chatsworth Reception

Cutlers' Hall

Chatsworth, home of the Duke and Duchess of Devonshire, is one of the great treasure houses of England, set in the heart of the Peak District. This is the venue for a special reception for conference delegates. The palatial Chatsworth House was built on the banks of the River Derwent for the Duke of Devonshire between 1687 and 1707. The 26 richly decorated rooms that are open to visitors house an outstanding art collection including works by Rembrandt, Veronese, Gainsborough and Freud. For this year 2000 and to celebrate their 50th year at Chatsworth, the Duke and Duchess have chosen favourite treasures from their private collection to show visitors - from illuminated manuscripts to family portraits by Lucian Freud.

The 105 acre garden laid out by Capability Brown, contains fountains, ponds and a cascade, together with a maze. The house and garden are set in a larger country park.

Study Visits

Delegates will have a choice of the following themed half-day study visits:

Tourism and Industrial Heritage

- Abbeydale Industrial Hamlet, a former 18th century steel and scythe works and;
- Kelham Island Museum which presents the industry and life of Sheffield complete with the most powerful working steam engine in Europe.

Regeneration through Leisure and Sport

- Behind the scenes at Don Valley Stadium - a centre for national and international sports events;
- Sheffield Ski Village - Europe's largest artificial ski resort which boasts an 'alpine atmosphere'.

Issues for Tourism in Rural Areas

- The rural community and tourist centre of Castleton;
- The Upper Derwent Valley.

Interpreting Heritage for the Tourist

- Brodsworth Hall and Gardens.

Tourism and Millennium Projects

- The Earth Centre.
- Magna - a major visitor attraction in the making focusing on the steel industry and being created from the vast structure of the former Templeborough steel works.

Chatsworth House

Accompanying Person's Programme

A programme of visits and activities will be organised for accompanying persons and will include:

- An excursion to the ancient City of York;
- A visit to Meadowhall - one of Europe's largest indoor shopping and leisure complexes;

Accompanying persons will also be invited for:

- The Conference opening ceremony;
- Conference dinner;
- Visit to Chatsworth House;
- Conference study visits.

Registration for accompanying persons includes:

- Accompanying persons programme of excursions
- Pre-conference welcome reception at Sheffield Town Hall
- Conference opening ceremony
- Choice of study visits
- Reception and tour of Chatsworth House
- Grand conference dinner at Cutlers' Hall
- Yorkshire farewell event
- Access to all conference exhibitions
- Use of Sheffield Hallam University sports facilities and access to the leisure and international swimming pools at Ponds Forge International Centre during the conference period

Please complete the enclosed conference booking form and return it as soon as possible to: Tourism 2000 Conference, Conference 21, Stoddart Building, Sheffield Hallam University, Sheffield, S1 1WB, UK   Fax +44(0) 114 225 5337

Booking Conditions

Cancellation Policy

Registration fees will be refunded, less a £100 administrative fee if it is received in writing by the conference office prior to 31st July 2000.

After this date, no refund will be given however, confirmed substitutes will be accepted.

General Conditions of Registration

1. The fees listed for the conference are to be those set out on the preceding page. All registrations must be enclosed with appropriate payment by the Conference organisers in advance of the conference.

2. It is expressly agreed that the Convenors and Organisers of the Conference "Tourism 2000: Time for Celebration?" and their legal representatives, directors and employees, and their agents, officers and servants shall not be liable for any loss, injury or damage of any kind whatsoever suffered directly or indirectly by the person, possession of property of any conference participant or other person during or in connection with the events on the programme or any other activities of the conference "Tourism 2000: Time for Celebration?" for any reason whatsoever no matter howsoever caused.

3. It is agreed that the Convenors and Organisers of the Conference "Tourism 2000: Time for Celebration?" and their agents and officers reserve the right to cancel at any time any or all of the programmed or other activities if this should appear necessary as a result of events which are beyond their control or which they cannot reasonably be expected to influence or for which they are not responsible. Without limiting the generality of the foregoing, such events shall include force majeur, disorders, riots, obstruction or curtailment of transport and/or transmission facilities, international or other crises, or any other undesirable occurrence.

4. Decisions regarding any aspect of the conference shall be taken by the Convenors and Organisers – or their agents at their sole discretion and shall be final.

Conference Associates

International Festivals and Events Association Europe

Founded in 1992, IFEA Europe is the European affiliate of IFEA World which has more than 2,400 members. IFEA Europe has members from over 19 countries and provides a forum for the managers, organisers, producers, public relations directors, fund-raisers and sponsors of festivals and events.

Through its international co-operations, its conferences and 'Behind the Scenes' workshops IFEA Europe is committed to increasing the professionalism of festivals and events for all concerned. As well as being important activities for local communities to celebrate cultural traditions and innovations in the arts, festivals and events also have a vital role to play in tourism, attracting visitors from far and wide. New and innovative partnerships with tourism organisations are thus increasingly important.

World Archaeological Congress

The World Archaeological Congress (WAC) is a non-profit making, international forum for discussion for anyone who is genuinely concerned with the study of the past. WAC was formed in the mid 1980s and is based on the need to recognise the historical and social role and political context of archaeology, and the need to make archaeological studies relevant to the wider community. As part of its work WAC holds major international Congresses every four years, with the most recent held in Cape Town, South Africa (1999).

WAC also seeks to promote interest in the past in all countries, to encourage the development of regionally based histories and international academic interaction. As part of its particular interests, WAC is increasingly aware of the issues surrounding the relationship between heritage and tourism and is pleased to be working in association with the Tourism 2000 Conference.

The National Liaison Group for Higher Education in Tourism (NLG)

The National Liaison Group for Higher Education in Tourism (NLG) was established in 1983 as an independent membership organisation to provide a focus for the development of tourism studies at degree and postgraduate level.

The NLG seeks to promote the development and recognition of tourism as a subject for study within UK Universities and to encourage high standards and best practice in course provision. It promotes links between education and the tourism industry and liaises with other bodies nationally and internationally on issues relating to tourism in higher education.

Sheffield International Venues

Sheffield International Venues operates a prestigious range of sporting and leisure facilities of world-class standard.

Sheffield Arena is one of the most impressive concert venues in the UK and many of the entertainment world's most celebrated stars – including Tina Turner, Elton John and Michael Jackson – have appeared here. The Arena can also be transformed into an ice hockey pitch and can host major trade and public exhibitions.

For Olympic standard facilities the Don Valley Stadium with its huge seating capacity attracts international athletics meetings and also hosts large concerts.

Ponds Forge International Sports Centre with its modern architecture boasts a breathtaking 'state of the art' Olympic size swimming pool and has hosted numerous national and international swimming and diving events. With over 3,200 square metres of cater for a wide variety of sport and leisure activities. With over 3,200 square metres of business facilities Ponds Forge is able to provide for exhibitions and conferences.

Hillsborough Leisure Centre with its pool areas and 'beachside' atmosphere provides top class sport and leisure facilities for families in the Sheffield area.

Don Valley Stadium

Centre for Travel & Tourism

The Centre for Travel and Tourism is the research, consultancy, conference and publications body of the University of Northumbria covering all aspects of international travel and tourism. Established in 1986 the Centre has an excellent reputation for its work with the travel and tourism industry. As a University body it is able to draw upon a wide range of expertise, research resources and a truly international body of knowledge and examples of best practice.

The work of the Centre focuses on three key themes: tourism development, tourism and culture, and travel industry management. Staff are closely involved with the travel and tourism industry at regional, national and international level. The Centre boasts an unrivalled source of information, ideas and contacts which, together with genuine objectivity, distinguishes the Centre for Travel and Tourism as one of the UK's leading research and consultancy bodies. The Centre endeavours wherever possible to transfer the research and practical experience of its staff to the University's teaching programme.

Centre for Tourism

The Centre for Tourism was established in 1989 and is responsible for tourism education, research, publication and consultancy in Sheffield Hallam University. The Centre consists of tourism staff who specialise in the provision of high quality, intellectually demanding and professional tourism education which enjoys an international reputation. All Centre for Tourism staff are active in research and publication.

Current academic research in the Centre for Tourism includes work on sustainable tourism, tourism and consumer behaviour, as well as tourism and urban and rural regeneration. The Centre for Tourism can also draw on the professional expertise of teaching and research staff in related disciplines such as leisure management, countryside recreation, arts and hospitality management. The Centre for Tourism team offers tourism education, research and consultancy services to clients which reflect team members' wide-ranging expertise and builds upon their practical experience of completing projects regionally, nationally and internationally.

Source: Conference Organisers

Exhibit 11.3 Tourism 2000: Time for Celebration? – conference booking form

Conference Booking Form (Charges per person & inclusive of tax)

Post or fax to:
Tourism 2000 Conference, Conference 21, Stoddart Building, Sheffield Hallam University, Sheffield S1 1WB, UK
Tel +44 (0) 114 225 5336,   Fax +44 (0) 114 225 5337,   Email tourism2000@shu.ac.uk

REGISTRATION FEES - FULL CONFERENCE ATTENDANCE		No. of Persons	Amount
Delegates	£495		
Groups (5 or more delegates from the same institution)	£445		
Full time research students (See note 1)	£250		
Accompanying persons	£195		

REGISTRATION FEES - INDIVIDUAL DAY ATTENDANCE	Including conference publications	Excluding conference publications (See note 2)	No. of Persons	Amount
Sunday	£195	£120		
Monday	£195	£120		
Tuesday	£195	£120		
Wednesday + Thursday (2 days)	£195	£120		

REGISTRATION TOTAL   £_____

Discounts are available on the full attendance rate of £495 and individual day attendance rates of £195 for members of:
IFEA, WAC and **ATLAS** (discounts are not available on any other rates)

Please complete in **BLOCK CAPITALS.**
Cheques and Banker's Drafts should be made payable in Pounds Sterling to Sheffield Hallam University.

Prof / Dr / Mr / Mrs / Miss / Ms (please circle)   Surname ....   Forename ....

Position/Title ....

Name of Organisation ....

Address ....   Post/Zip Code ....

Telephone ....   Fax ....   Email ....

Method of Payment (please ✓)	**Please charge my Credit Card Account:**
Cheque/Banker's Draft ☐	Cardholder's Name ....
Credit Card (See note 3) ☐	Card Number ....
Invoice to Organisation ☐	Card Expiry Date ....
Official Order Number	Card Address (if different from invoice address) ....
....	....

Please state any special dietary/access requirements ....
....

I am a member of the following (please ✓)   IFEA Europe ☐   WAC ☐   ATLAS ☐

Please see over for Notes and Booking Conditions ▷▷▷

Source: Conference Organisers

Organization on the day

If the planning has been good and no unforeseen problems arise, everything should go smoothly on the day. The key tasks on the day of the event are to:

● welcome and register participants
● ensure that everyone knows what is happening and where it is happening
● deal with queries
● receive payment from participants wherever appropriate
● resolve short-term operational difficulties.

Staff on the day have to be flexible and prepared to work long hours.
Let us now focus on what happens if things do not go to plan.

Risk and crisis management and contingency plans

There is always a chance that things can go wrong and then we are in the business of crisis management. In the authors' experience, some of the commonest problems include:

● keynote speakers who are unable to attend because of illness or travel problems
● participants being seriously delayed or unable to attend at all due to transport difficulties or bad weather
● overbooked hotels
● fire alarms and bomb threats
● failures of audiovisual equipment.

All these risks and others are foreseeable and the organizer should have in place contingency plans to implement if they arise – what we might term the 'what if' approach.

This may involve having an alternative schedule in reserve, or a suitable additional set of audiovisual equipment available. However, it is important that everyone on the team knows about these contingency plans.

An article in *Conference and Incentive Travel*, in October 1998, looked at possible crises and contingency plans in relation to incentive travel, in particular. The author gave organizers the following advice:

1 Wherever possible clients should take out event insurance.
2 It is always prudent to have a back-up destination in mind in case the first plan falls through.
3 Ensure there is availability at alternative facilities – investigate all possibilities.
4 Draw up a crisis plan to cover all conceivable eventualities – do not assume anything.
5 Make sure partners on the ground know what to do in an emergency.
6 Check to see whether there are alternative means of reaching a destination – in case of air strikes or road blockages for example.
7 To be safe, include a doctor in the party for adventure or wilderness trips.

Event evaluation

At the end of an event it is very easy to simply breathe a sigh of relief and retire to the bar or to bed! However, we need always to evaluate events to see how successful they have been and how well clients feel they have been organized. The organizer, first, has to decide when to evaluate – before, during or after the event, or a mixture of the three. Then there is the question of what to evaluate and how. Questionnaires are the most used method, although interviews and focus groups are also useful.

With questionnaires, of course, we have to be careful to avoid bias or ambiguity with the questions. We also need to give incentives or apply a little light pressure to maximize the response rate.

A follow-up evaluation after an exhibition, for example, addressed to the exhibitor might ask questions like:

1 How satisfied were you with the quality/quantity of visitors to the exhibition?
2 Do you think exhibitions are a cost-effective form of promotion for your organization?
3 How would you rate the efficiency of the organizer of the exhibition?
4 How could the exhibition be improved for future years?
5 How likely is your organization to exhibit at next year's exhibition?

Nick Purden, writing in *Conference and Incentive Travel* in May 1998 advised organizers, when evaluating events to:

● set measurable objectives
● take time to design a questionnaire that will enable them to get the information they need
● agree a realistic budget
● allocate the necessary personnel and resources required to follow evaluation through
● use electronic audience response systems, which give instant feedback
● evaluate at the event while there is a captive audience
● consider offering an incentive to encourage delegates to respond
● enclose a reply-paid envelope if doing a postal questionnaire
● follow up initial responses to enable you to refine messages for future events.

After the event

There are, finally, a number of tasks to be completed after the event is over and the participants have all gone home. These tasks include:

● reviewing how the event went, its strengths and weaknesses including the results of the evaluation exercise discussed above
● paying all the bills
● chasing outstanding payments from participants
● sending 'thank you' letters to participants

They may also include starting to plan the next event if it is a regular event.

Conference management skills

In this chapter we have looked at all the tasks involved in conference management. The conference organizer, clearly, requires a wide variety of skills. According to Rogers (1998), these skills include:

- organizational skills
- attention to detail
- willingness to be flexible and work long hours
- creativity and flair
- ability to work under pressure.

Other desirable attributes of organizers are skills such as:

- marketing
- budgeting
- people motivation and management
- tact and diplomacy
- calm assertiveness
- negotiation.

Clearly, this is a demanding job, requiring a multi-talented person!

An iterative process and the triumph of compromise

It would be simple if event organizers could simply follow a linear checklist with each action leading effortlessly to the next until the event took place. However, this is not what actually happens.

In reality, unforeseen circumstances – changes of mind by the client, and so on – mean that things are changing all the time. This means that events are the results of an iterative process where aspects of the event are revised several times before they can be finalized. The interdependence of all the elements of an event means that changing one will have a knock-on effect to all the others. Often the end result is a compromise between desires and constraints. Let us see how this could happen, in practice, using a small hypothetical example, illustrated in Figure 11.5.

Key issues with different types of business tourism events

The first part of this chapter has explored the generic skills required by the organizer of any business tourism event. In the final section of the chapter we will look at the issues which are specific to the different types of event.

Meetings and conferences

Meetings and conferences have a number of specific attributes in terms of their organization. Table 11.6 offers a checklist for organizing such events. Exhibit 11.4 offers an American checklist, produced by Sheraton Hotels and Motor Inns.

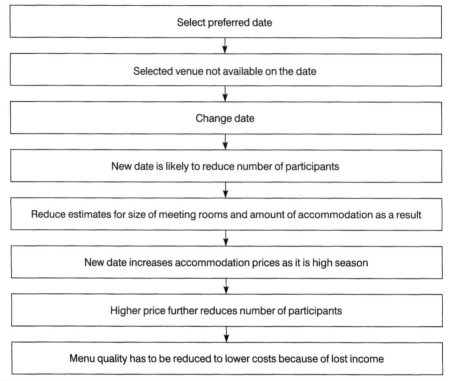

Figure 11.5   The iterative process in event planning

Exhibit 11.4 Convention planning checklist – Sheraton Group

Convention Planning Guide and Checklist

So many things go into planning a successful convention that no human being could keep all of them in mind at one time. This checklist was developed to aid planners with this problem. With its help, perhaps you may be saved the headache of overlooking some item that might spoil an otherwise perfect convention.

Helpfully yours,

Sheraton Hotels & Motor Inns

---

1. **ATTENDANCE**
    Total number of convention registrants expected

2. **DATES**
    Date majority of group arriving
    Date majority of group departing
    Date uncommitted guest rooms are to be released

3. **ACCOMMODATION**
    Approximate number of guest rooms needed, with breakdown on singles, doubles and suites
    Room rates for convention members
    Reservations confirmation: to delegate, group chairman or association secretary
    Copies of reservations to . . . .

4. COMPLIMENTARY ACCOMMODATION AND SUITES
Hospitality suites needed – rates
Bars, snacks, service time and date
Names of contacts for hospitality suites, address and phone
Check rooms, gratuities

5. GUESTS
Have local dignitaries been invited and acceptance received
Provided with tickets
Transportation for speakers and local dignitaries
If expected to speak, even briefly, have they been forewarned
Arrangements made to welcome them upon arrival

6. EQUIPMENT AND FACILITIES
Special notes to be placed in guest boxes
Equipment availability lists and prices furnished
Signs for registration desk, hospitality rooms, members only, tours, welcome etc.
Lighting – spots, floods, operators
Staging – size
Blackboards, flannel boards, magnetic boards
Chart stands and easels
Lighted lectern, Teleprompter, gavel block
PA system – microphone, types, number
Recording equipment, operator
Projection equipment, blackout switch, operator
Special flowers and plants
Piano (tuned), organ
Phonograph and records
Printed services
Dressing rooms for entertainers
Parking, garage facilities
Decorations – check fire regulations
Special equipment
Agreement on total cost of extra services
Telephones
Photographer
Stenographer
Flags, banners, Hotel furnishes, US, Canadian, State flags
Radio and TV broadcasting
Live and engineering charges
Closed circuit TV

7. MEETINGS
Floor plans furnished
Correct date and time for each session
Room assigned for each session: rental
Headquarters room
Seating number, seating plan for each session and speakers' tables
Meetings scheduled, staggered, for best traffic flow, including elevator service
Staging required – size
Equipment for each session (check against Equipment and Facilities list)
Other special requirements (*immediately prior to meeting, check*)
Check room open and staffed
Seating style as ordered
Enough seats for all conferees
Cooling, heating system operating

PA system operating: mikes as ordered
Recording equipment operating
Microphones: number, type as ordered
Lectern in place, light operating
Gavel, block
Water pitcher, water at lectern
Water pitcher, water, glasses for conferees
Guard service at entrance door
Ash trays, stands, matches
Projector, screen, stand, projectionist on hand
Teleprompter operating
Pencils, note pads, paper
Chart stands, easels, blackboards, related equipment
Piano, organ
Signs, flags, banners
Lighting as ordered
Special flowers, plants as ordered
Any other special facilities
Directional signs if meeting room difficult to locate
If meeting room changed, post notice conspicuously
Stenographer present
Photographer present (*immediately after meeting, assign someone who will*)
Remove organizational property
Check for forgotten property

8. **EXHIBIT INFORMATION**
Number of exhibits and floor plans
Hours of exhibits
Set up date
Dismantle date
Rooms to be used for exhibits
Name of booth company
Rental per day
Directional signs
Labour charges
Electricians' and carpenters' services
Electrical, power, steam, gas, water and waste lines
Electrical charges
Partitions, backdrops
Storage of shipping cases
Guard service

9. **REGISTRATION**
Time and days required
Registration cards: content, number
Tables: number size
Tables for filling out forms: number, size
Chairs
Ash trays
Typewriters, number, type
Personnel – own or convention bureau
Water pitchers, glasses
Lighting
Bulletin boards, number, size
Signs

Notepaper, pens, pencils, sundries
Telephones
Cash drawers, number, size
File boxes, number, size
Safe deposit box (*Immediately prior to opening, check*)
Personnel, their knowledge of procedure
Policy on accepting checks
Policy on refunds
Information desired on registration card
Information on badges
Ticket prices, policies
Handling of guests, dignitaries
Programme, other material in place
Single ticket sales
Emergency housing
Hospitality desk
Wastebaskets
Mimeograph registration lists (*If delegates fill out own registration cards*)
Set up tables away from desk
Cards, pencils in place
Instructions conveniently posted
Tables properly lighted (*During registration, have someone available to*)
Render policy decisions
Check out funds at closing time
Accommodate members registering after desk has closed

10. **MUSIC**
    For: reception   recorded or live
            banquet   recorded or live
            special events recorded or live

    Shows
            entertainers and orchestra rehearsal

    Music stands provided by hotel or orchestra

11. **MISCELLANEOUS**
    (*Entertainment*)
    Has an interesting entertainment programme been planned for men, women and children
    Babysitters
    Arrange sightseeing trips
    Car rentals

12. **PUBLICITY**
    Press room, typewriters and telephones
    Has an effective publicity committee been set up
    Personally called on city editors and radio and TV programme directors
    Prepared an integrated attendance-building publicity programme
    Prepared news-worthy releases
    Made arrangements for photographs for organization and for publicity
    Copies of speeches in advance

Source: Astroff and Abbey (1995).

Table 11.6   Checklist for organizing a conference or exhibition

Procedure		Breakdown	Important
Objectives	What for	For whom. Where. When. Organizers. Meetings	Send early notification to delegates
Main features	Dates	How long. Arrive/Depart. Venue rates. Provisional booking	End the meeting before midday on Friday
	Invitations	VIPs. Guests. Exhibitors. Mailing list. Dates	
	Agenda	Timetable. Speakers. Handouts. Equipment. Publicity. Printer	
	Finance	Budget. Policy. Administrator. Credit arrangement	
	Social activities	Functions. Outing. Entertainment. Wives [*sic*]	
Provisional programme	Timetable	Rooms. When. Facilities. Transport. Personnel	
	Speakers	Booking. Equiment. Talk. Length. Fee. Transport	
	Exhibits	What. Exhibitor. Accommodation. Room space	
	Confirmations	Venue speaker. Entertainment. Speeches. Standbys	
Venue bookings	Budget	Rates. Extras. Menus	Vary the menus
	Accommodation	Protocol. Rooms. Dining. Functions. Exhibits. Parking	Check the cancellation list
	Service	Hospitality. Suites venue manpower [*sic*]. Contacts	Have you considered the non-resident?
Timetable	Function	When. Where. Who. Seating. Equipment. Manpower [*sic*]	Avoid a tight schedule
	Information	Schedules. Seating plans. Organizers. Venue staff. Rates	
Social activities	Functions	Dinners. Speeches. Staffing. Equipment. Room plan	
	Outing	Transport. Babysitters	
	Entertainment	Times. Fee	Choose entertainment to suit audience
Joining instructions	Objectives		Dispatch as soon as possible
	Place	Accommodation. Residential/non-residential	Send venue brochures and local literature
	Time		
	Timetable	Transport. Agenda. Meals	
	Facilities		

Table 11.6 *Continued*

Procedure	Breakdown			Important
Equipment	Speakers	What. When. Where	Power points	Can everyone see and hear?
	Functions	PA system	Light switches	Do you need extension leads?
	Exhibits	Floor plan. Room plan	Compatibility	Have spares ready. Leave time to set up equipment Can the rooms be blacked out?
Catering	Morning coffee Lunch	When. Where When. Type. Where. Pre-lunch drinks		Cater for dietary requirements Appoint one man (sic) to control the bar
	Afternoon tea Evening meal	When. Where Style. Function or private		Observe protocol
Check-back	Objectives Timing Communication	Functions. Deadlines. Duty rotas Venue staff. Organizers. Complaint contact. Phone numbers		Get a 'crisis' contact
	Information	Delegates. Guests. Exhibitors. Mailing. Literature		
	Finance	Policy. Budget. Administration. Payments		
Registration	Information	Spare literature and agendas. Signs. Badges		Has a message board been set up?
	Personnel	Administrators		
Welcome	Protocol Social	VIPs. Honorarium. Welcome services. Bar. Payment. Speech		Personnel
Session checks	Functions	Signs. Seating. Lighting. Heating. Ash-trays. Water		Handouts prepared?
	Equipment	Working. Position. Plugged in. Volume. Lights. Scripts. Space		
Security	Personnel Documentation Equipment Materials			
Emergencies	Spares Briefing Services	Rooms. Equipment. Literature Schedules. Duty rotas Medical. Lost and found. Replacement. Insurance		
	Back-up	Personnel. Crisis contact		
Conclusion	Equipment Accounts	Exhibits. Returned. Removed Settled		

Source: Meetings World (1969) Group Ltd.

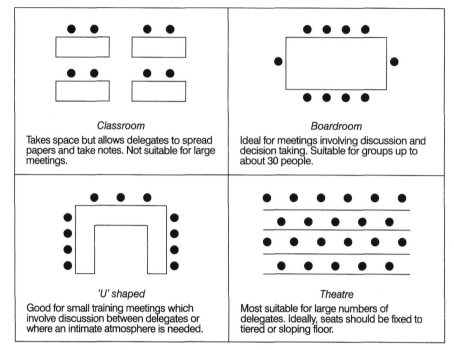

Figure 11.6   Four main types of meeting room layout
Source: Seekings (1996).

The first issue, when organizing a venue, is perhaps, number and capacity. This, of course, depends on room layout. Several styles are common, as can be seen in Figure 11.6.

Clearly, layout will relate to capacity, as can be seen from Table 11.7.

For larger events, theatre-style seating is, of course, the only one which is generally satisfactory.

Often we have to organize social programmes too, as well as the meeting or conference. These may include everything from excursions to historic houses, themed dinners and theatre visits, to treasure hunts. These may well include the need for the transporting of guests from place A to B and back again. It is important to remember that:

- travel times can be greatly increased at peak times due to heavy traffic
- delegates will often not enjoy a long journey to a social activity after a hard day's work.

Partner programmes may also be required, to provide things to do for the partners of delegates during the conference sessions. The main thing here to remember is that partners will not, as some organizers still seem to believe, always be women. An increasing number are men. The number of partners can also be very small and organizers may feel it is not always viable to offer a partners programme.

A conference or gala dinner is usually organized at larger events. It is often better if this is away from the main conference venue, to give delegates a chance to see something new.

Finally, often conferences will have an associated exhibition which is often used as a way of bringing in extra income. However, it is important that this exhibition is located where

Table 11.7   Room size and number of delegates

Number of people	Approximate area (m²) needed for		
	Classroom layout	Theatre layout	Reception/tea/coffee
10	16	*	*
15	24	*	*
20	32	15	*
25	40	19	*
30	48	23	18
40	64	30	24
50	80	38	30
75	120	57	45
100	200	75	60
125	230	93	75
150	**	112	85
175	**	130	100
200	**	150	115
250	**	190	145
300	**	230***	175
400	**	300***	235
500	**	400***	300
1000	**	745***	600
1500	**	1120***	900
2000	**	1500***	1200

Notes: Room capacities are reduced when other than simple audiovisual aids are to be used.
* Even small numbers of people will be cramped if the room is too small.
** Loose tables and chairs are not recommended for these numbers; use tiered lecture theatres with writing facilities or theatre-style layout.
*** Consider using theatre with fixed seating for these numbers.
Source: Seekings (1996).

delegates will pass all the stands regularly or the exhibitors may be unhappy and feel they have not received value for money; they may even refuse to pay the bill!

Exhibitions

Exhibitions, or trade fairs, are a specialist field in their own right. Organizers usually hire a venue and then have to subdivide it into 'stands' – separate portions of space. Figure 11.7 illustrates the layout of a typical exhibition. Stands cost different amounts depending on their size and location (for examples of modular stands, see Figure 11.8). For example, in Figure 11.7, stand 110 would be very expensive as it is large and located directly opposite the entrance. Stand 532 would be considerably less expensive because it is small and is in a block, away from the main entrance.

As well as simply selling stand space, organizers may sell modular stand packages which will include floor space plus, typically, walls and ceilings, lighting, and so on. Sometimes the modular stand is just a shell but at other times it can be a fully developed stand. If it is just a shell the organizers will provide an opportunity, at extra cost, for exhibitors to

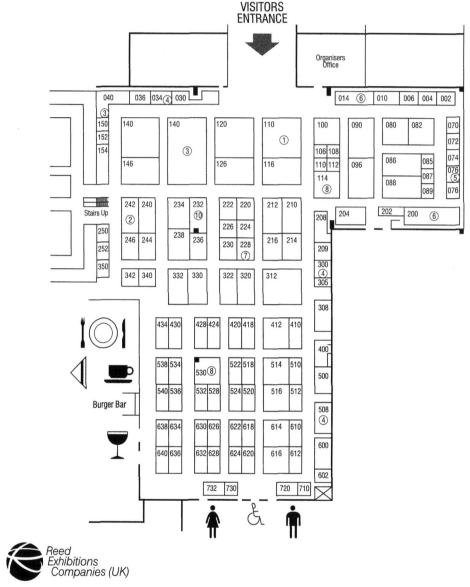

Figure 11.7 The layout of a typical exhibition
Source: Reed Exhibitions Companies (UK), cited in Cartwright.

purchase their needs (from floors to furniture, lights to telephones) from the appointed contractor. Organizers clearly can make extra income from this 'service' through fees from exhibitors as well as money from contractors who wish to be the sole official supplier of some product or service.

Selling stand space tends to be an example of tactical marketing with lots of negotiation based on supply and demand. Stands left unlet near to the exhibition date may be offered at a considerable discount because empty stands look bad for the whole exhibition.

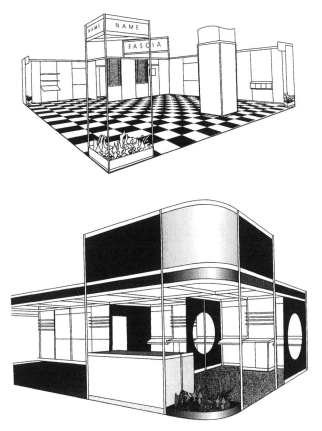

Figure 11.8 Typical modular stands
Source: Cartwright.

Apart from the sale of exhibition stands, marketing effort also has to be spent on attracting sufficient quality visitors to satisfy the exhibitors, whether it is an exhibition for the general public, trade visitors only, or both. This means, among other things, deciding how much it will cost to visit the exhibition. This depends on whether entrance fees from visitors are seen as a significant potential source of income or not.

It also depends on whether maximizing visitor numbers or attracting a smaller number of high-quality visitors is the main aim. Free entry would probably achieve the former while a substantial fee could help achieve the latter.

Many exhibition are annual events and the exhibitors' perceptions of the volume and quality of last year's visitors will determine whether or not they are likely to book for this year's event.

Incentive travel

When organizing incentive travel packages it is important to remember that incentive travel is leisure travel with a business purpose. Much of the material in this section is based on published information by SITE.

First, SITE identifies the following stages in the development of an incentive travel programme:

1 Examine the company goals and objectives so that a complementary programme can be developed.
2 Develop specific programme goals and objectives including targets where possible.
3 Develop a detailed budget for the programme, either a fixed sum or the 'profits' from extra sales generated by those being rewarded by the programme.
4 Create detailed, fair, easily understood qualification criteria for the programme so that would-be participants know what they have to do to gain the reward.
5 Choose the destination, which must be viewed by participants as motivational.
6 Design the programme and market it.
7 Deliver the programme.
8 Post-programme evaluation and review.

Many incentive travel programmes involve:

● an educational or business element in the programme, as well as the leisure activities
● partners attending the incentive along with the 'winners'.

The incentive package has to be special, and tailor-made for each client. It must be unique, and cannot be a package which the client could buy themselves, off the shelf!

The marketing process is, first, to the client company by the specialist incentive travel agency, selling the package they can offer, and then to the employees who are the eventual beneficiaries of the package.

Product launches

The key to product launches is they have to work perfectly first time, otherwise the effect is lost and the brand image could be damaged, which in turn could cost the company heavily.

Most product launches feature a number of elements including the following:

● a 'spectacular' unveiling of the product, usually involving a celebrity
● a press conference
● an opportunity to sample/try out the product
● an important guest speaker, usually a representative of the company.

The needs of product launches often include sophisticated special effects and unusual themed catering.

The key to success is attracting the right audience which can include:

● company staff
● intermediaries in the distribution system
● trade and general media
● the public.

Often, of course, these different audiences will be catered for by separate, but related, events, which may take place simultaneously or consecutively.

A major issue at product launches is security, in terms of the product, in that the product must not be seen by any unauthorized person before the appointed time.

Training courses

When designing training courses, we have to focus on their objectives, which should determine the duration, content, and format of the event. For example:

1 If the aim is largely to impart factual information, then a formal style of event may be appropriate, within a conventional training centre or hotel meeting room for instance.
2 If the objective is to encourage interaction and discussion, then a more informal environment is called for, but probably in a similar venue.
3 If team-building or character development is the aim, then physical activity in the outdoors is one of the most popular ways of achieving this objective.

However, whatever the main purpose of a training course, it is important to recognize the value of social activities and free time to encourage networking between participants.
  Training courses usually require:

● specialist tutors or instructors, who may not be experienced event organizers
● a large number of different rooms or spaces, preferably with flexible seating, to allow interaction and to provide space for group activities.

It is important to get the programme right, because training can be a tiring process for participants. There should, normally, therefore, either be regular breaks or a relatively early finish to the working day.

Organizing mixed events

Many business tourism events today are a mixture of two or three different types of events, such as:

● an exhibition with seminars or a conference with a supporting exhibition
● a training course that is also designed to be an incentive
● a product launch which is also an incentive.

When organizing such a mixed event it is important to ensure that both (or all three) elements of the event meet their respective objectives.

Conclusions

In this chapter we have seen that a large number of tasks and skills are required to plan and manage all types of business tourism events successfully. We have also seen that each separate type of event also has its own specific organizational issues.

Hopefully, the material in this chapter will prove useful to you when you tackle the challenges set out in Chapter 13.

Discussion points and essay questions

1 What do you think are the *three* most important factors in the organization of a successful conference *or* exhibition?
2 Discuss the ways in which the organization of a product launch is different to the organization of an incentive travel package.
3 Discuss the factors you would take into account, in order of importance, when organizing a major international association conference.

Exercise

You should design a brochure to market a hypothetical:

- incentive travel package, or
- international conference, or
- exhibition.

12 *Examples of good practice*

In Chapter 11 we looked at the principles and techniques behind the successful organization of business tourism events, while in the next chapter we will challenge you to try to plan a hypothetical event of your own. We thought it would be helpful, therefore, for us to give you some real-world examples to show you how professionals plan such events in practice.

The authors have endeavoured to provide a range of examples to cover all forms of events including conferences, meetings, exhibitions, incentive travel, product launches and training courses. However, as we will see, it is difficult to categorize events in this way for often they are combined, for example:

- sales meetings and incentives
- conferences with supporting exhibitions
- training courses and meetings.

Most of the case studies here are taken from the pages of *Conference and Incentive Travel* magazines, and relate to the UK primarily. The authors have simply selected aspects of each event which illustrate points made in Chapter 11.

Conferences and meetings

Here are some examples of the choices made, and actions taken, by UK conference organization professionals in relation to a series of very different conferences and meetings.

1 In November 1999, leading china company Wedgwood held its biannual conference at the Radisson SAS Hotel, Manchester Airport, UK. Several interesting points emerge from this event, notably:
   (a) the company chose a modern hotel deliberately to reflect the new, modern image they wish to portray
   (b) the venue was chosen for its convenience for the 230 delegates who were coming from the UK and Ireland

(c) starting the programme with a relaxed free day to allow delegates to 'get into the mood' for the event

(d) celebrities including comedian Ken Dodd were used to contribute and motivate or amuse the delegates

(e) to make an evening fashion show work well, the hotel staff helped Wedgwood change the room around in just one hour.

2 In April 1999, Sony held a major meeting at the Copthorne Hotel in Stuttgart, Germany. This was a combination team-building exercise and conventional meeting, with the following interesting features:

(a) a good balance between professional and leisure activities

(b) a go-kart race was organized on the first evening to 'break the ice' and start team-building

(c) a dramatic event at the end of a formal conference session, namely, a darkened room and the arrival of cocktails topped by fiery sparklers maintained participant interest

(d) a themed dinner based on famous musicals from the West End in London.

3 In February 1998 World Event Management organized an event for 350 pan-European delegates in Malta. The strengths of this event were as follows:

(a) selecting a destination with mild winter weather for the comfort of delegates

(b) negotiating with Air Malta so that they varied their schedule to meet the needs of the delegates

(c) finding two hotels that could accommodate all the delegates between them

(d) finding suitable venues for the two team-building activities

(e) transport delays were prevented because the event took place in the off-peak season

(f) negotiating good rates with the hotel because it was the off-peak season.

4 Niagara Health Care of the UK held a conference and incentive event for 180 people in January 2000 at the Four Points Sheraton Hotel in Eilat, Israel. The event involved the following interesting points:

(a) warm weather was guaranteed, even in January

(b) the destination offered a wide range of attractions which were important because the event had a leisure element, as it was also an incentive

(c) the excellent, attentive service provided by the staff.

5 In June 1999, international Sterling Software support group held a conference for around 700 delegates at the Edinburgh International Conference Centre, UK, with a budget of £400 000. The key factors behind the success of this event were as follows:

(a) the venue provided the right mixture of meeting rooms, lecture theatres, and exhibition space

(b) a whisky-tasting took place at the beginning of the event to create a relaxed mood

(c) the support exhibition allowed delegates to find out the latest information on new software products

(d) when the original conference dinner venue fell through, the organizers were able to find a suitable substitute

(e) the use of inspirational speakers at the end of the event to ensure that it ended on a high note

(f) the venue team was very professional and supportive.

6 The store group, BHS, held its annual management conference for 400 delegates at the Grand Hotel, Brighton, UK over two days in July 1999 at a cost of £78 000. The positive features of this event included:

(a) the use of a professional communications agency to help them stage manage the event

(b) a wake-up aerobics session in the morning to energize the delegates

(c) the hotel had enough bedrooms to accommodate most of the delegates.

7 BG Technology Forum, in July 1999, ran an event for fifty overseas guests at Stapleford Park, Leicestershire, UK over a period of four days. The event succeeded because:

(a) the venue offered a special environment and had all the necessary facilities

(b) ample opportunity was given for participants to network and have fun together, including a Scalextric racing game and a Jenga game.

8 Apple Mac Information Systems organized a conference for 250 customers in October 1998 at the Rochester Town Park Hotel in Cork, over three days. Key features of the event were:

(a) the location allowed the customers to visit the company's factory at Cork

(b) the hotel was large enough to accommodate most of the delegates at the event

(c) the excellent staff and quality of service at the hotel

(d) the good programme of entertainment provided by the hotel.

9 The Association of British Travel Agents (ABTA) held its annual conference in 1999 in Cairns, Australia, at a cost of around £750 000. The organizers were pleased with the following aspects of the event:

(a) Cairns was one of the few resorts that had the facilities of a major city including a large convention centre that could accommodate 1800 delegates

(b) the organizers were able to negotiate a very competitive air fare for the flight to Australia.

A number of issues arise from this set of examples, notably the importance of good staff, surprises and unusual activities, and the quality of the venue.

Exhibitions

Exhibitions and trade fairs usually succeed because they attract enough visitors to satisfy the exhibitors and enough exhibitors to satisfy the visitors. Here are some examples of exhibitions that have been successful and the reasons why:

1 *World Travel Market, London* This is arguably the most important tourism industry trade fair in the world, which over twenty years has achieved its success by:

(a) being located in one of the world's most attractive and exciting cities, in a country which is both a major generator of outbound tourism and a receiver of inbound tourism

(b) its reputation, which has been built up over twenty years

(c) ensuring that the exhibition includes all the major destinations and suppliers to the tourism industry which gives buyers a great incentive to visit

(d) using a well-established, easy accessible venue

(e) effective marketing to the target markets

(f) providing entertainment to provide light relief for visitors

(g) providing a programme of seminars of interest to tourism industry professionals, which provides a further motivation for visitors.

2 *Motor Show, NEC, Birmingham* This well-established event attracts large numbers of trade and public visitors because it:
  (a) is located at a venue which is easily accessible by air, rail and road
  (b) uses a highly professional venue with excellent facilities for both exhibitors and visitors
  (c) attracts a considerable amount of media attention which provides free publicity for the event
  (d) is used to launch new products which gives people an incentive to visit the event.
3 *EIBTM, Geneva* This annual event is one of the major MICE industry trade fairs in the world. It has become successful because:
  (a) it attracts exhibitors from all over the world and from all sectors of business travel and tourism which gives a motivation for visitors to attend
  (b) it offers a programme of seminars for professionals provided by the leading professional bodies in the industry
  (c) of the gala dinner which provides exhibitors and visitors with an opportunity for networking and social activity
  (d) it is an annual event and can therefore build up brand loyalty over time
  (e) Geneva is perceived as a safe, efficient destination.

The success of exhibitions seems to be about targeting the right markets, providing enough attractions to motivate the potential visitor, and an accessible venue.

Incentive travel

Incentive travel combines both business and pleasure, and is thus a complex phenomena. Here are some examples of successful incentives and the reasons for their success:

1 Compaq held a biannual incentive, over five days in February 2000 for thirty-five people, in Dubai. This had the theme of 'Arabian Adventure' and was built on the success of the company's 1998 'Spirit of Adventure' incentive which had won three industry awards. The strengths of this package were as follows:
  (a) the event was planned by two specialist agencies who worked together, Travel Impact and Motivation in Management
  (b) having clear objectives for the event, namely to encourage improvements in sales performance and building relationships within the company
  (c) careful selection of the participants to make sure the right thirty-five, out of a potential market of nearly 10 000, took part in the incentive
  (d) making clear to potential participants how they could earn a place on the trip
  (e) Dubai has excellent infrastructure, does not require a visa and is well connected to the UK by air
  (f) the use of a local destination management company
  (g) the accommodation of participants in a five-star hotel
  (h) a wide variety of leisure activities, including driving high-performance cars and helicopter rides.
2 SAAB Great Berlin, in June 1999, organized an incentive for forty-two dealers in Berlin. Its success was due to the following factors:
  (a) the destination and programme matched the interests of the group in good food and wine

(b) the conference dinner was held in an exclusive residence with the owners personally looking after the clients

(c) the programme was well structured.

3 Texaco, in September 1999, took fifty-two distributors of their products on a five-day combined incentive and conference to Tuscany, Italy, at a cost of around £200 000. The incentives aspect of the event succeeded because:

(a) it was a new, exciting destination for the company

(b) the city of Florence, the main destination, is compact and easy to move around

(c) the destination combined a great historic city with beautiful countryside

(d) there was a motivational after dinner speaker, former racing driver, Jackie Stewart

(e) the inclusion of competitive business simulation games in the programme

(f) a relaxing day of country pursuits in the Tuscan countryside

(g) a surprise luxury banquet on the last evening.

4 In February 2000, over five days, a company ran an incentive trip for sixty-five information technology professionals in Finland, at a cost of £2300 per person. This event was exceptional for the following reasons:

(a) it took place in Northern Lapland, a unique destination

(b) unusual activities were included in the programme, notably husky dog sled rides, snowmobiling, and ice-fishing

(c) the ground arrangements were made by an experienced Helsinki-based destination management company

(e) several 'surprises' for participants were planned including a pretend coach breakdown in the countryside

(f) participants met local Lapp people.

5 Car manufacturer, BMW, organized an incentive or 'internal' competition prize for service staff, in Paris, in 1999. The event was successful because:

(a) the participants were carefully selected

(b) the organizing company made an inspection visit to identify the best destination and venue

(c) the programme included classic Paris sightseeing such as the Eiffel Tower and a cruise on the Seine, which appealed to those for whom this trip was intended.

6 In April 2000, Memorex Talex organized an annual incentive or 'awards conference' for sixty-five staff in Cardiff Bay, Wales at a cost of £26 000, over two days. It featured:

(a) the theming of the event – secret agents and James Bond specifically

(b) the optimum duration, long enough to have the necessary impact, but not too long for interest to wane or make it too expensive

(c) unusual activities for participants such as powerboat racing.

From these six examples it is possible to see that some of the key attributes of a successful incentive travel package are unusual activities and events, a clear set of objectives, the use of a local destination management company where possible, and a memorable special dinner or 'happening' to end the trip.

Product launches

Product launches are usually one-off events where everything has to work perfectly, over a short period of intensive activity. Here are some lessons from several successful launches:

1 Cordis launched a new pharmaceutical product in Athens in March 1999, with an audience of 300 and a budget of £500 000. The key features of the launch were as follows:

  (a) the destination was easily accessible to the target audience
  (b) the staff at the hotel venue were helpful and supportive
  (c) there was a high-quality awards dinner on one night during the two-day event.

2 In 1999 the Vauxhall motor company launched its new Omega car to 1400 dealers at two venues in Bedfordshire and Northamptonshire in the UK at a total cost of £1 million. The success of this event was due to the following factors:

  (a) the venues reflected the image the company wanted for its new car, namely, relaxing and stylish
  (b) the venues were both ideal for their purpose; a testing track to show off the car and a castle
  (c) dealers had ample opportunity to test drive the car.

3 In October 1998, Peugeot launched its new 206 car to 7500 staff and general public, at a cost of £1.6 million, over seven days. The event was special because:

  (a) it took place in a city centre, Birmingham, rather than behind closed doors in a hotel, or exhibition venue
  (b) around 4500 members of staff had to be brought by coaches from the factory at nearby Coventry
  (c) dealers were able to drive the new cars away to their dealership
  (d) there was a daily sound and light show in the city centre
  (e) the main venue, the International Convention Centre was very professional.

4 In February 1998 Vauxhall launched its new Astra car to 17 000 dealers and staff from twenty-three centres in Marrakesh, Morocco. This massive event was a success because:

  (a) the company chartered a fleet of aircraft to transport participants to the event
  (b) the lead agency involved in organizing the launch had ten years' experience of working with Vauxhall
  (c) of a pleasantly warm winter climate at the destination
  (d) there was a well-planned programme featuring presentations, workshops, test drives and entertainment
  (e) the local roads were ideal for test drives because they carried relatively little traffic
  (f) of good forward planning including numerous inspection visits
  (g) of the use of an experienced local destination management company
  (h) there was clear agreement between the four agencies involved as to who was responsible for which aspect of the event.

5 In 1996, Jaguar launched its XK8 car in Canada to 1400 leading dealers and their partners. The event was exceptional because the car was launched in the open air, based on a famous hole at a local golf course, which juts out into the sea. The actual launch was a surprise; people thought they were attending a social event or that the car would be launched the next day in more conventional surroundings.

These examples show that the most successful product launches have meticulous planning, an element of surprise and ensure that the venue and programme matches the image of the product which the manufacturer wishes to promote.

Training courses

Training courses take a variety of forms but, as we will see from the following examples, success is usually due to a few common factors:

1 Over two days in January 2000 consultancy firm, Arthur Andersen, ran a training course in London for forty business advisers, with a budget of £5000. The factors behind the success of this event were as follows:
   (a) the venue, the four-star Shaw Park Plaza Hotel, had enough syndicate rooms to accommodate the break-out sessions of the course
   (b) the venue was convenient for the majority of participants who arrived by rail
   (c) because it was new, the venue was not heavily booked and therefore offered a very competitive price
   (d) the hotel was able to offer the group the use of a wide range of audiovisual equipment
   (e) the bedrooms impressed the participants with their quality.
2 In 1999, a legal firm, Dibb Lupton Alsop, organized an event to explain the the importance of mediation to some of their clients. It was a success because:
   (a) they put their message across in a novel way, by role-playing a fictitious scenario in a mock court setting
   (b) scripting and the acting were largely carried out by professionals.
3 KPMG, the consultancy firm, in April 2000 organized its annual team-building event in the Lake District, UK, as part of its training activities programme. The key features of the programme were that:
   (a) it was arranged by a specialist in outdoor management development and team-building
   (b) the budget was modest at £200 per person because there was no need for luxury accommodation due to the nature of the programme
   (c) the event had clear objectives, namely the company wanted an event where there would be team-bonding but where, also, participants would have fun
   (d) the organizers provided all the necessary equipment for participants
   (e) the activities had an ultimate aim, a mission which allowed participants to focus their energies on a common task
   (e) the organizers did not put pressure on participants to take part in activities they did not want to join in with.
4 In September 1999, eighty employees from Andersen Consulting took part in a leadership training day held near Hagley Hall, Birmingham, UK, with a budget of £30 000. The success of the event was based on the fact that:
   (a) no one knew what they were going to be doing when they arrived; it was a total surprise
   (b) the event was organized by a company specializing in team-building days 'with a military flavour' which was just as well because the event was based on a mock military exercise
   (c) the venue offered 4 square kilometres of varied terrain
   (d) the event helped reacquaint a wide range of people with each other
   (e) a gala dinner at a city centre hotel provided a further opportunity for networking and socializing.

These four examples demonstrate that imagination and the unexpected, together with experienced organizers, help create successful training courses.

Conclusions

In this chapter we have seen that there are several common factors which contribute towards the organization of successful business tourism events. These include:

- adequate planning including inspection visits to the destination and venue
- using the services of experienced, professional organizers
- planning programmes which clearly meet the objectives of the event
- the use of imagination in the programming of events and the element of surprise
- the provision of good quality accommodation, food and drink
- making sure destinations and venues are easily accessible to participants.

It is also clear that, often, organizers have to produce events which are actually several different events at the same time. In other words they could be combined conferences and exhibitions, sales meetings and incentive trips, or incentives and training courses. Such events require careful management to distinguish between the different aims of each type of event.

Discussions points and essay questions

1 Identify and discuss what you consider to be the three most important factors in organizing a successful conference.
2 Discuss the extent to which the factors leading to successful conferences are different to those required for successful training courses.
3 Critically evaluate the ways in which good programming of business tourism events can maximize their chances of being successful. What are the features of a successful business tourism event programme?

Exercise

You should contact an organization which has recently organized a conference, exhibition, incentive travel package, product launch or training course. You should then talk to the organizers about the experience and identify those factors which made the event a success, as well as those factors which caused problems.

13 Major interactive exercises

We are now at the stage in this book where the reader is invited to become an active participant, putting into practice the ideas contained in this text.

The authors have devised a series of exercises which can be undertaken by a group or an individual. They are practical activities designed to give the participant a real understanding of the issues involved in organizing a business tourism event or managing an aspect of business tourism. We have tried to make them as realistic as possible. The exercises have been designed to be flexible, and to be able to be adapted to different circumstances and locations. Furthermore, the exercises can be lengthened or shortened depending on the time available to the participant.

There are, of course, no 'right answers' to these exercises but, for each one, a range of criteria has been given to guide the participant towards the development of a successful response to the challenge.

In carrying out these exercises you may need to seek the help of a wide range of practitioners in the business travel and tourism field. Please do so in a professional and polite way as these are busy people trying to do a difficult job.

You should feel free to add details and make any reasonable assumptions which you think you need to in order to make the project more realistic.

We hope you find the exercises both worthwhile and enjoyable, and we would welcome your feedback on how they could be further developed and improved.

Coping with the unexpected

You are perhaps thinking these exercises will be quite straightforward. Well, unfortunately, it is not quite that easy. To make these exercises as realistic as possible, we have built in three or four or five unforeseen surprises with each project.

So you should start working on the project, and when you are well under way, you should turn to the section entitled, 'Surprise, surprise!' Do not look now – that would be cheating!

Good luck!

Organizing a professional association conference

A major professional association is planning to hold an international conference for its members. Its members come from all over the world and are distributed as follows:

- Europe   = 50 per cent
- North and South America   = 20 per cent
- Asia   = 15 per cent
- Africa   = 5 per cent
- Australasia   = 10 per cent

The association is a medical association, and 70 per cent of the members are men. The conference must have three days of business seminars and a two-day social programme afterwards.

You must assume that the conference will attract around 300 delegates from around the world.

Around 50 per cent of the delegates will bring a partner, and 75 per cent of these partners will be women.

The fee for delegates to the conference must not exceed £1000 ($1500; €1500) for the five days, including accommodation and meals but excluding travel to the destination.

The event is supposed to take place in May or June the year after next.

You have been employed by this association to manage this event for them. Your task is to:

1 Evaluate three potential destinations for the conference and select one of them. You must give your reasons for your choice of destination.
2 Within your chosen destination you must evaluate at least two potential venues. You must then select one venue and justify your choice.
3 You must find accommodation for the delegates in single/twin/double/family rooms, as appropriate, and plan details of the catering arrangements for the conference.
4 You must devise a schedule for the business seminars and the social programme.
5 You must devise a partners programme.
6 You should devise a brochure for the event.
7 You should suggest a pricing strategy for delegates and partners that will allow the organizers to break even.
8 You must investigate travel options to the destination for delegates from all five continents.

Your findings should be presented, in report form, to the Conference Committee of the Association.

To be judged successful, your proposal will need to meet the following criteria:

- the destination should be accessible for all delegates and should be perceived as an attractive place to meet
- the venue must be able to accommodate the needs of the conference
- the accommodation and catering arrangements should be adequate to meet the needs of the delegates
- the conference schedule and programme must be realistic and workable

- the partners programme should be cost-effective and attractive
- your budget must be comprehensive and realistic
- your pricing strategy should be realistic
- your travel arrangements to the conference for delegates from different regions of the world must be accurate and practical.

In a separate report, you should outline the lessons you have learnt from undertaking this exercise.

Organizing a major trade exhibition

You are a commercial organizer of trade exhibitions and fairs. You have decided to organize a major holiday and travel exhibition in your own country.

The exhibitors will be tour operators, transport operators, accommodation providers, visitor attractions and tourist destinations.

The visitors will be members of the general public who are interested in taking holidays. They will visit the exhibition and the exhibitors will try to sell their products and services to them.

The exhibition will last for three days, in either January or February.

You anticipate that about 200 exhibitors from around the world will attend, and think you will attract around 30 000 public visitors from all over your own country.

Your task is to:

1 Select a destination for your exhibition and justify your choice.
2 Evaluate alternative venues, select one, and explain your choice.
3 Develop a package for exhibitors that includes stand space, construction of a shell stand with walls and display boards, and basic amenities such as furniture, telephones and lighting.
4 Devise a marketing strategy to explain how you will attract 200 exhibitors and 30 000 visitors.
5 Produce a budget for the exhibition.
6 Devise a pricing strategy for exhibition stands and entrance tickets.

To be successful, you will need to:

- select a destination which would be attractive and accessible to both exhibitors and visitors
- select a venue which is suitable and cost-effective
- develop a floor plan for your exhibition which offers different sizes and shapes of stands for different exhibitors, and which makes the best use of the available space
- develop a package which will be affordable for exhibitors but will be profitable for you. You will need to find the cost of providing furniture, lighting and stand construction services, for example, at your venue
- ensure your marketing strategy is realistic and cost-effective
- ensure your budget is realistic and competitive, and makes allowances for contingencies
- ensure your pricing strategy is realistic and will help you achieve your aim of making a profit equivalent to 20 per cent of the total income from the exhibition.

Your results should be presented in the form of a feasibility study for the project.

You should produce a separate report noting what you have learnt from this exercise about the issues involved in planning a major trade exhibition or fair.

Planning an incentive travel package

You are a specialist agency which organizes incentive travel packages.

You have been asked by a car dealer to organize an exciting, innovative package for fifty of their most successful sales people.

They want an intensive three-day programme, with some team-building exercises and some social events.

The destination must be outside the dealer's own country and must be a place that will be seen as special by the sales people.

The budget is £100 000, ($150 000, or €150 000) for the whole package including all transport.

Your task is to:

1 Evaluate three potential destinations before finally recommending one to the client, with a justification of your choice.
2 Choose the accommodation which the participants will use.
3 Devise an innovative programme for the three days which includes team-building exercises and social events.
4 Plan the catering arrangements for the three days with an emphasis on unusual menus and high-quality food and wine.
5 Plan the travel to the destination and within the destination, using the best quality flights you can afford within the budget.
6 Provide a budget which allows you to provide the whole programme within the £100 000/$150 000/€150 000 budget, including a fee of £10 000/$15 000/€15 000 for your services.

To be successful you must:

● select a destination that will be seen as exciting and different by the participants
● choose accommodation which will be viewed as special by the participants
● create an innovate programme that provides variety and stimulation for the participants
● give the participants the chance to enjoy imaginative, unusual and high-quality food and drink
● plan travel arrangements which are as exclusive and high quality as possible, as well as being convenient for participants
● provide a budget that includes the organizer's fees and provides a great experience for the participants, within the client's overall budget.

You should present your results in a report to your client.

You should produce a separate report which states what you have learnt from this exercise about organizing an incentive travel package.

Organizing a product launch

You are a company which specializes in organizing product launches for clients. A major perfume house has engaged your services to organize the launch of their new perfume,

'Magique'. This perfume is going to be marketed as a scent with magical properties, a mysterious essence. The launch must reflect this message.

Your client wants the launch to be a high-profile, glamorous event for a carefully selected audience, comprising the following people:

- fifty buyers from top department stores in London, Paris, Milan, Amsterdam, New York, Hong Kong, Singapore and Tokyo
- twenty-five trade press journalists, based in Paris, London and New York
- twenty-five representatives of major international newspapers and television companies from Europe, North America and Asia.

The event must last just a few hours.

Your task is to:

1 Plan a launch event that will be spectacular and will give the product the best possible introduction into the market.
2 Select the destination and venue for the event that will be in keeping with the image of the product.
3 Make arrangements for the guests at the event to be transported to the event, given lavish hospitality and, if necessary, provided with overnight accommodation.
4 Find the perfect celebrity to open the event.
5 Organize a press conference as part of the launch event.
6 Produce a detailed budget for the event.

To be successful you must:

- select an appropriate destination and venue
- devise a programme for the launch event that will be spectacular and memorable, and which will reflect the image of the product
- make all the necessary travel, hospitality and accommodation arrangements for the 100 VIP guests, that will make them feel very special
- produce a comprehensive budget that allows for a fee of £20 000 ($30 000, €30 000) for your company.

You should produce a report for your client 'selling' your ideas. There is no fixed budget for this project but you must convince the client that the budget you propose will be cost-effective for them.

You should produce a separate report which outlines what you have learnt from this exercise.

Organizing a training course

You are a management consultancy company which has won the contract to run a one-week training course for 250 newly appointed managers in the food industry. These people, who all work for the same multinational company, are food technologists who have now been promoted to management positions. They have no previous experience of general management. The training course must be designed to give them an introduction to management theory, human resource management, operations management, marketing and financial management.

The company does not want a theoretical, academic course. Instead it wants a practical, industry-related course with active participation by the managers and interaction between participants, and between the tutors and participants.

You must organize all aspects of the programme and deliver the whole package for less than £150,000/$225,000/€225 000 including the cost of the venue, accommodation, all meals, tutors and a training manual for each participant. In addition, you will need to allow for a fee of £20 000/$30 000/€30 000 for organizing this event, within this budget.

Your task is to:

1 Select a suitable destination for the training course given that all the participants are residents of your own country.
2 Evaluate three potential venues and select one, justifying your choice.
3 Design a detailed intensive programme for the participants.
4 Arrange all accommodation and meals for the one-week event.
5 Provide a detailed budget for the training course, including the cost of tutors and the production of the training manual.

To be successful, you must:

● select an appropriate destination and venue
● design a programme that will meet the needs of your client and the participants
● produce a detailed, comprehensive budget that show that you can run the course for no more than £150 000/$225 000/€225 000.

You should present your results in a report for your client.

You should write a separate report which outlines what you have learnt from the exercise about organizing training courses.

Designing a convention centre

You have been engaged as a consultant, by a town or city, of your choice, to advise them on the design of a new convention centre.

The aim is not to produce a detailed architectural design for the centre, but rather to:

1 Produce a report detailing the key points that the architect will need to take into account when producing the final designs for the centre, and suggesting possible approaches which might be taken towards these issues.
2 Identify a suitable site for the new centre.
3 Produce sketch plans of what the centre might look like.

The key issues you should address in your report should include the following:

● making the new centre user friendly for different groups of potential users such as the disabled and foreign visitors

- ensuring that the new centre is multipurpose and can also be used for exhibitions and concerts
- the need to make sure that the new centre is as environmentally friendly as possible.

You should also add any other issues which you feel are important.

When choosing a site for the new centre, you should take into account the amount of land required, and access to the site by road and public transport. The cost of the site should also be ascertained, if possible.

Finally, your sketch plans should be of two types, namely:

1 Plans of the site and the layout of the centre, in two dimensions.
2 Three-dimensional plans of what the centre might actually look like.

To be successful you must:

- identify and discuss the key issues in detail and suggest sensible approaches which should be taken towards them
- identify a site which is suitable, practical and cost-effective
- produce sketch plans which make good use of the space available and are imaginative
- show that you are aware of the lessons to be learned from the design of convention centres elsewhere in the world.

Your results should be presented in report form to your clients.

You should then produce a separate report outlining what you have learnt from this exercise about convention centre design.

Marketing a business tourism destination

You have been engaged as a consultant by a town or city – of your choice – to develop a marketing strategy for them, that will help them attract more business tourism. They are particularly interested in attracting more medium- and large-scale conferences, training courses, and small exhibitions and trade fairs.

Your task is to produce a comprehensive marketing strategy for the destination. This will require you to:

1 Critically evaluate the existing marketing activities of the destination in the field of business tourism.
2 Provide as much detail as possible on the market for conferences, exhibitions and training courses.
3 Suggest which market segments the destination should target.
4 Evaluate the current business tourism product in the destination, identifying strengths and weaknesses.
5 Analyse the competition and suggest ways in which the destination could seek to achieve competitive advantage.
6 Make recommendations relating to the promotion of the destination.
7 Suggest any potential partnerships that might be developed to help market the destination.

8 Produce a draft budget including how much it would cost to implement your strategy.

9 Suggest a range of appropriate performance indicators to help the destination evaluate its performance.

Your report should be in two sections, as follows:

1 An outline strategy for the destination covering five to ten years, focusing on the strategic dimension of the marketing of the destination.

2 A tactical, short-term marketing plan covering between one and two years.

You should tell your client how much money it would cost to implement both of these elements of the marketing strategy, and explain why this expenditure will be worthwhile.

To be successful, your report must be:

● based on sound analysis of the current situation in the destination
● realistic about the future prospects for the destination
● able to demonstrate a good knowledge of the business tourism market
● realistic about the competition faced by the destination
● accurate about the financial costs of implementing your proposed strategy
● clearly divided into long-term strategic activities and short-term tactical actions.

You are also required to produce a separate report outlining what you have learnt from this exercise about destination marketing.

Surprise, surprise!

Just when you thought things were going smoothly with your project, you receive a nasty surprise, or perhaps more than one – just like in the real world. Here is some extra information about your project that might make it a little more difficult for you.

You can choose to handle these issues all at once or one at a time.

Organizing a professional association conference

1 You have a keynote speaker as an integral part of your programme – he requires first-class air travel to the destination and a fee of £2000/$3000/€3000.
2 Long-term weather forecasters predict three or four weeks before your event that a typhoon may hit Hong Kong, Singapore and Tokyo, places where some of your delegates live, just around the time of the conference.
3 It appears that an unexpectedly high number of men are registering for the partners programme, so that as many as 50 per cent of the partners may be men.
4 A small group of delegates has just informed you that, for religious reasons, they require halal cuisine.
5 A new accommodation tax of £5 per person per night has been introduced.

Organizing a major trade exhibition

1 At a late stage, your furniture contractor goes bankrupt and is no longer able to provide furniture for the stands for your exhibition.
2 You are left with a number of small stands which you are having great difficulty selling, because they are in the less attractive locations.
3 A major national newspaper in your country wants to buy 5 000 tickets for your exhibition to give away to its readers. But it wants to buy them at a discounted rate, 40 per cent off the normal price.
4 A number of exhibitors and visitors start asking if you can book overnight accommodation for them at the destination.

Planning an incentive travel package

1 Your client tells you late in the planning stage that, following requests from participants, they would like to know if you can arrange transport from home to the airport for some or all of the participants.
2 The client needs to reduce costs and asks you how you could reduce the bill by 10 per cent in ways which would do the least damage to the quality of the package.
3 Your chosen accommodation tells you they have overbooked and cannot accommodate all of your participants. Ten of them will need to be found alternative accommodation.

Organizing a product launch

1 The client wants you to try to find a more exciting and glamorous venue than the one you are proposing, but they do not want it to cost any more.
2 One of the VIP guests wants to stay in the destination for four nights in a top-class hotel, at your client's expense.
3 A television company says it requires facilities at the launch so it can broadcast live from the event.

Organizing a training course

1 Late in the planning process, the client says you will need to make sure there are ten personal computers available at the venue for the participants to use.
2 The client would like you to organize a big social event for the participants on the last evening of the course.
3 You suddenly discover that ten of the delegates are vegetarian and two require a gluten-free diet.

Designing a convention centre

1 A lobby group representing people with hearing difficulties does not think you are giving enough thought to their needs. They have given a story along these lines to a major newspaper.
2 Your client tells you they are particularly concerned about energy consumption and want your advice on how to design the centre to minimize energy consumption.
3 At a late stage in the project, your preferred site is taken off the market, so it is no longer available.

Marketing a business tourism destination

1 Your client destination asks you how their prices compare to those of their major competitors.
2 Your client says they have been given £200 000/$300 000/€300 000 to spend on a 'one-off' marketing campaign for the destination. They want you to tell them now how they should spend the money.
3 The hoteliers in the destination say they are dissatisfied with how your client markets the destination. They think marketing the destination should be handed over to a consortium of leading local entrepreneurs.

Conclusions to Part Three

In Part Three, we have concentrated on the practical side of the industry, in other words, the organization of business tourism events.

Chapter 11 identified the key issues that need to be taken into account when organizing different types of business tourism events. In the following chapter, the authors offered some examples of good practice, in the organization of a range of events.

Finally, in Chapter 13, the reader was challenged to deepen their understanding of the subject, through seven major practical exercises.

It is now time for us to look at the future of business travel and tourism.

Part Four
The Future

14 Twelve key challenges in the management of business travel and tourism

As we enter the new millennium, business travel and tourism is generally in a healthy state, and looks set to continue to grow in the coming years. However, the industry faces a number of challenges which could have an adverse impact on its future development if they are not tackled successfully.

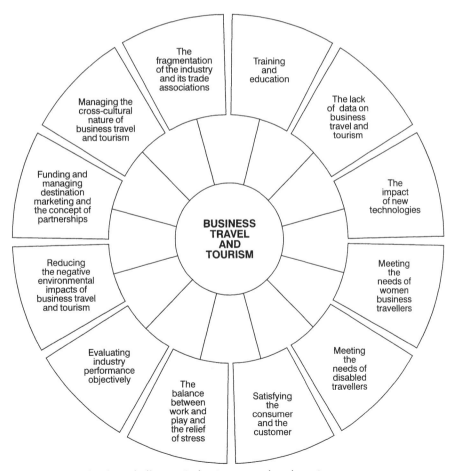

Figure 14.1 Twelve key challenges in business travel and tourism

Some of these challenges affect one sector in particular but, in general, they have an impact on all sectors of business travel and tourism, albeit in different ways.

In this chapter we will focus on twelve of these challenges. These are illustrated in Figure 14.1.

The fragmentation of the industry and its trade associations

There is general agreement that the business travel and tourism industry does not receive the attention it deserves from government. This is, perhaps, partly because it is a very fragmented industry with no single body speaking for the whole industry, even in an individual country, let alone globally.

The lack of a single body may reflect the very diverse nature of the industry, which has three main dimensions, as follows:

1 There are great differences in terms of structure, key players, and market characteristics between different sectors of business travel and tourism such as incentive travel and exhibitions.
2 The suppliers, intermediaries and buyers are usually distinctly different types of organization with different objectives and ways of operating.
3 There are distinct geographical differences around the world within business travel and tourism. For example, even the terms used vary from place to place, around the world. Conventions in the USA are usually called conferences in the UK and congresses in much of mainland Europe.

However, these reasons do not offer a full explanation for the fragmentation that we see in business travel and tourism. In some other industries, the problems identified above are also present, but they are more united and speak as industries with fewer different voices than business travel and tourism.

There is no doubt that this 'fragmentation' and the lack of a clear, single voice representing the industry is a real problem for the industry in terms of influencing politicians and public policy, in individual countries and globally.

The fragmentation of the industry is clearly illustrated by a brief look at the 1999–2000 edition of the influential guide, *Venue – The World-wide Guide to Conference and Incentive Travel Facilities*. This guide listed no fewer than *sixty-four* professional associations, and this list does not claim to be fully comprehensive! These bodies often market themselves to try to attract new members, sometimes at the expense of other associations.

For the sake of the industry, there is clearly a case, therefore, for greater co-operation and partnership, together with rationalization of the trade associations in the industry. This is now being recognized by many in the industry and some useful initiatives are under way.

In the UK, for example, the Business Tourism Partnership (BTP) was set up in 1999 to give a single, strong voice to the industry. This group has thirteen members and was set up in response to the UK government's new tourism strategy which was published in January 1999. Among other issues the BTP is seeking to persuade government in the UK to reduce value added tax (VAT) on hotel accommodation and devote some money from the new air passenger duty tax for investment in business tourism facilities. It is also interested in qualifications and training for the industry, as well as the need for better data on business travel and tourism.

However, there is still greater scope for further partnership and co-operation to give the industry a strong single voice, while recognizing the differences between sectors and countries.

Training and education

The fragmentation of the industry, as well as its relatively recent origins, may also explain why there is as yet not a well-developed system of training and education within the industry. Failure to develop such a system will also delay recognition of the industry as a mature, professional industry.

The provision needs to encompass skills training for general staff, together with management development for managers. To reflect well on the industry, and to be effective, the provision needs to:

● allow progression from level to level as staff move up the hierarchy
● lead to qualifications which are recognized throughout the industry and in different countries
● balance theory and practice, and allow participants to make valuable use of their experience
● be available to people throughout their career in the industry
● offer the generic skills such as marketing and finance while reflecting different practices and issues within different sectors
● be offered through flexible methods of teaching such as open- and distance-learning so people can study while they work
● complement existing in-company training.

The question will arise about who should offer and manage training and education programmes on business travel and tourism, namely, professional bodies, specialist commercial trainers or academic institutions. Perhaps a partnership of all three groups would be beneficial.

There are already several excellent initiatives in training and education within the field of business and travel. Three of these are briefly described below:

1 IAPCO, has since 1970 run an annual seminar for professional congress organizers. The 1999 event, held at Ermatingen in Germany, lasted for seven days and had seventeen main themes. Tutors came mainly from the industry and at the end of the event they were given a Certificate of Attendance.
2 The highly respected body, MPI, which is based in the USA but also has an office in Brussels, has developed the first 'universally certified global professional designation for meeting professionals'. It was developed in co-operation with the widely renowned Institut de Management Hôtelier International, Paris, a European affiliate of the Cornell University School of Hotel Administration. The Certificate in Meetings Management (CMM) involves:
   (a) a self-assessment to determine programme eligibility
   (b) home study

(c) a five-day residential full-immersion course

(d) a three-part examination.

This is an exciting initiative that could be further developed in the future.

3 In 1999 a new European Masters degree in Congress Management was launched by four European universities in partnership with EMILG. This project is being developed in co-operation with the Joint Interpretation and Conference Service of the European Commission.

These programmes show what can be done, but there is still considerable scope for further development and for co-ordination of the initiatives.

Not all the initiatives have been directed at management training. In the UK, in 1999, a new vocational qualification for operational skills was introduced. The National Vocational Qualification (NVQ) is part of a nationwide system of qualifications for staff in most industries. The NVQ was developed in conjunction with the industry.

There is a need for a unified system that will provide an 'umbrella' for all the initiatives or the industry will simply become confused and may then not take full advantage of what is on offer.

A final issue is how to persuade more academic institutions to take business travel and tourism more seriously. Some universities offer undergraduate courses in meetings management and diplomas in trade-fair organization, while more have modules on different aspects of business tourism.

However, the lack of academic provision in this area also means there are few academic researchers in this field. This is partly the cause of the next problem we will address, namely, the lack of reliable data.

The lack of data on business travel and tourism

Wherever business travel and tourism professionals gather together, it will not be long before the conversation turns to the lack of good research in the field – applied research that can be used by the industry. This is a problem shared with leisure travel and tourism but it is even worse in the field of business tourism. There are a number of areas where research is currently weak, including:

● the lack of detailed reliable data on key markets such as the different types of national association markets including professional associations, voluntary associations, trade unions and religious organizations

● the dearth of data on how buyers make their purchase decisions so that marketers can know how to influence them

● information on the perceptions which buyers hold of particular destinations, venues, and organizations

● the lack of longitudinal research to help us identify trends in the market

● the absence of comprehensive data on cross cultural and national differences in the demand side of the business travel and tourism market

- the underdevelopment of economic impact studies which monitor the costs and benefits of business travel and tourism
- the failure to focus enough attention on attempting to predict future developments in the industry.

An industry can only be successful in the long term if it understands its markets and how the latter keeps changing. It is vital, therefore, that the quantity and quality of research in business travel and tourism improves. This means encouraging more academics to research in this field, as well as persuading government to give a higher priority to such research.

Finally, there is a need for more co-operation between countries to harmonize definitions and match research methodologies around the world so that data from different countries can be easily compared.

The impact of new technologies

Business travel and tourism is at the forefront of technological developments, and these innovations represent both opportunities and threats for the industry. Figure 14.2 illustrates this situation.

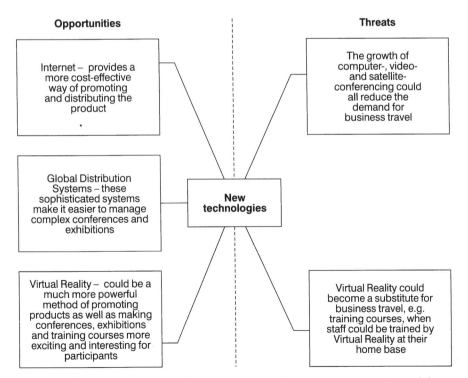

Figure 14.2   New technologies and business travel and tourism: opportunities and threats

Figure 14.2 clearly offers a highly simplified picture. Reality is far more complex in three ways:

1 Some technologies such as the Internet may benefit the supplier and buyers but be a threat to the intermediaries by reducing the need for their services.
2 Some technologies have great importance for some sectors but relatively little for others. Computer- and video-conferencing are a highly relevant development for the meetings sector but are of little importance for the incentive travel sector.

There are three other important issues that will affect the future impact of new technologies on business travel and tourism:

1 As always, the crucial issue will be how organizations respond. Those that anticipate the impact of technological changes and plan accordingly may be able to turn the developments into opportunities, while for those that do not, they may be a threat.
2 The pace of technological change and the nature of new development may render much current investment obsolete, very quickly. This could be very expensive for organizations that invest too heavily in technologies that will soon be outdated.
3 The future success of the industry may also depend on areas where current technology is not keeping pace with changes in demand. For example, the future of business travel will be constrained if we cannot find technological solutions to the problems of crowded airspace and airports.

We must make sure we neither overestimate nor underestimate the impact technology will have on the industry in the future.

Meeting the needs of women business travellers

Across the world the number of women business travellers is growing, albeit at a different rate in different countries. This has implications for the business travel and tourism industry.

However, surveys have shown that many women business travellers do not want to be treated differently to male travellers. For example, in 1998 a study published in the *Journal of Travel and Tourism Marketing* showed that women considered cleanliness, in-room temperature control and smoke detectors as important characteristics in the selection of hotel rooms. It is highly likely that this view would be shared by male travellers. Women, in this survey, were also concerned with general security, as are many male travellers. On the other hand, the women interviewed for the survey clearly did not consider the provision of women-only floors or special arrangements for single female travellers as important factors when selecting a hotel room. This is bad news for those hotels which have tried to target the female market as if it were very different from the male equivalent.

If we look at how business travel services are promoted, however, then there is a problem. Most advertisements and brochures assume that the business traveller is a man, being looked after by women. We suggest you look at a range of advertisements and brochures for airlines business-class services and duty-free shopping in magazines aimed at the business traveller to see how true this is. Most women are seen in subordinate roles or as patronized partners. In an industry like business tourism where many buyers and intermediaries are women, this is a very old-fashioned and unwise approach to marketing.

There is clearly a need for more research on women business travellers to ensure that their needs are met, as they become an increasingly important part of the market.

Meeting the needs of disabled travellers

In different areas of the world, at different paces, legislation and public opinion is leading to a growth in demand for business travel by disabled people. However, for many people with disabilities, life as a business traveller is still difficult.

We must recognize that there are a wide variety of disabilities, including being wheelchair-bound, having other mobility problems, impaired hearing and sight problems.

The design of business tourism infrastructure is vital to meeting the needs of business travellers with different kinds of disability. Buildings should be accessible for wheelchairs and, wherever there are steps, ramps or lifts should be provided. Information can be provided for sight-impaired travellers in Braille while induction loop systems can help the hearing-impaired traveller.

The operational management side also needs to take account of the needs of disabled travellers, through the provision of sign language interpreters to help hearing-impaired travellers, for example.

Clearly, all of this involves a cost but, increasingly, legislation will demand provision for disabled travellers to be provided as a matter of course, throughout the world. In the meantime, being proactive could attract extra business, particularly from charities concerned with disabilities, and will lead to fewer complaints from disabled travellers.

The business travel and tourism industry has yet to be seen to tackle this issue effectively; it will need to do so in the future. This will mean working in partnership with disabled people and their representative bodies.

Satisfying the consumer and the customer

It is one of the truisms of management theory that success means satisfying your customer. However, the problem in business travel and tourism is that we have both customers and consumers to satisfy.

In general, the customers are the employers and organizations which pay the bill for people to attend conferences, exhibitions, training courses, and incentive travel packages. They, naturally, are most likely to be satisfied if the cost to them is kept to a minimum.

On the other hand, the consumer who is the actual traveller is usually an experienced business traveller. His or her satisfaction is largely related to factors such as comfort and quality of service.

At the same time, they are both interested in reliability. Nevertheless, the different perspectives of customers and consumers mean it can be difficult to design products and services which will please both customers and consumers.

This is a major challenge for the business tourism industry and there are some problems to solve. For example, many frequent flyer programmes are more popular with consumers or travellers than with the customers who would prefer lower prices from airlines.

Ultimately, the customer who pays the bill is more important than the consumer, but it is the consumer who uses the service, passes on negative feedback to other consumers and customers, and complains vigorously to front-line staff.

The balance between work and play, and the relief of stress

A major concern today is stress, both physical and mental. Nowhere is this seen more than in business travel. The business tourist is often away from home for long periods, works very long hours and is badly affected by travel delays.

The business travel and tourism industry needs to take these problems seriously. It should look at the following issues:

1 Providing more opportunities for active leisure within the programmes of events, or in the working day on business trips.
2 Building more free time into conference programmes.
3 Planning travel itineraries to reduce jet lag and stress. For example, flights which involve short times to catch a connecting flight are very stressful and should be avoided.
4 Making available on aircraft, in hotels, and at venues, relaxation exercises and classes.
5 Ensuring that for part of the day travellers are free of mobile phones and computers, which are again, a constant source of stress.
6 Making it as easy as possible for travellers to contact their families and friends while on business trips.

The industry and employers must recognize that a stressed traveller and a workaholic traveller is not an efficient, productive traveller, and so must do what they can to alleviate the problem.

Evaluating industry performance objectively

The business travel and tourism industry is still young and trying to prove itself. At the same time, it is a highly competitive industry in which companies boast about their strengths and successes to gain competitive advantage. Both these factors mitigate against the objective evaluation of performance within the industry.

Performance evaluation is crucial in every aspect of business tourism including:

● how successful visitor and convention bureaux are in marketing their destinations
● how well or badly an event goes from the point of view of the users
● how successful, or otherwise, companies are within the industry.

Quality improvement means objectively analysing performance, in terms of weaknesses as well as strengths. However, the great competition and hype that surrounds the industry can make such analysis difficult, or even impossible, as well as being seen by some as undesirable.

Future success and the long-term health of the industry may well depend on organizations being more willing objectively to evaluate what they do and how well they do it.

Reducing the negative environmental impacts of business travel and tourism

Business travel and tourism have often been criticized for their negative impact on the environment, particularly in terms of the transport sector. They are particularly criticized for the pollution and fuel costs of air travel, and the use of the private car to take the business traveller from one destination to another.

As a result of international legislation, airlines have already done a lot to reduce their environmental impact but the use of the private car is still a major problem around the world.

We must also ensure that new convention and exhibition centres are designed in an environmentally friendly manner. At the same time, incentive travel organizations must be sensitive to the impact of tourism on fragile environments when planning their programmes.

Some welcome action has already been taken. For example, the organizers of EIBTM, one of the conference industry's major trade fairs, have 'for a number of years given their support to environmental initiatives by publishing an annual "Green Directory", and sponsoring their "Greening of Business Tourism Awards"' (Rogers, 1998).

Nevertheless there is still a lot to do, and business tourism organizations will have to give more attention to this issue if it continues to grow in importance worldwide, with both public and politicians.

Funding and managing destination marketing and the concept of partnership

In many parts of the world the promotion and management of business tourism destinations is a public sector activity, run by central and local government bodies. Many of these organizations, however, lack the resources to compete in this highly competitive market. In some countries they also lack staff with the skills and knowledge to operate effectively in this field.

For this reason many destinations have accepted the concept of partnership where the public and private sectors work together to market and manage destinations. They pool their financial resources and expertise to achieve greater impact in the market, on the model of the visitor and convention bureaux of the USA.

However, even these bodies are often underfunded as we can see from the following examples, taken from a survey reported in *Conference and Incentive Travel* in September 1998.

In 1997, in the UK, London earned an estimated £1.35 billion from conference business but spent only £300 000 on conference-related marketing. Birmingham earned £250 million in the same year but spent only £20 000 on conference-related marketing. In York, conferences in 1997 were worth £80 million approximately, but only two staff were involved in conference-related marketing. The situation is better in some countries than in the UK, but there are also countries where things are even worse.

There is clearly much still to be done to create ways of funding and managing destination marketing so it is well resourced, and paid for by those who gain most from business tourism, financially.

Managing the cross-cultural nature of business travel and tourism

Globalization and the development of economies in Asia, Africa and South America, means that business travel and tourism is more and more a truly cross-cultural activity, in terms of the demand side. Yesterday's stereotypical business traveller was American, German or Japanese. Today he or she is increasingly likely to be from Malaysia, Korea or Russia. Tomorrow they may come from China or Brazil.

This development has great implications for the business tourism industry in terms of the product and how it is marketed. The product needs to take account, for example, of different religious beliefs about diet and the practise of prayer. Marketing, particularly advertising, has to also take account of religious beliefs and values in different cultures, and how they affect the acceptability or otherwise of different types of advertising.

Staff also need to understand what constitutes protocol and polite behaviour in different cultures so that offence is not caused to guests.

Labour mobility has also created a truly multicultural workforce in business tourism. Managers have to understand different cultures to ensure that they manage their staff as fairly and effectively, as possible.

The cross-cultural nature of business travel and tourism will grow in future, and all organizations must recognize the implications of this development and take appropriate action. Otherwise the new markets will take their business elsewhere and customer satisfaction levels will decline.

Conclusions

In this chapter, the authors have endeavoured to identify some key challenges for the business tourism sector today that will continue to affect it in the future. The emphasis has been on what the industry needs to do about these factors but the authors are aware that most of the issues are being increasingly recognized. Nevertheless, it is clear that the industry, which is young and only just reaching maturity, will face a number of major challenges in the next few years. It needs to deal effectively with these issues or they will threaten the continued growth and development of the industry in the future.

Discussion points and essay questions

1 Critically evaluate the suggestion that marketing research in business travel and tourism is underdeveloped and unreliable.
2 Discuss the likely impact of the increasingly cross-cultural nature of the international business travel and tourism market on suppliers and intermediaries in the industry.
3 Discuss the difficulties involved in developing a unified, globally recognized system of training, education and qualifications for the business travel and tourism industry.

Exercise

Select one of the issues illustrated in Figure 14.1. Investigate your chosen issue and try to find out about initiatives that are being taken by the industry in this field. Evaluate the likely success or failure of these initiatives, and try to identify aspects of the issue which are still not, in your view, being adequately addressed by the industry.

Part Five
Case Studies

This section of the book contains a number of case studies, designed to give real world examples of topics covered in the text.

These case studies are generally of two types:

- studies of individual organizations or destinations
- studies of specific issues.

While it is generally accepted that case studies only tell us about a particular organization, destination or issue at a particular time, they do illustrate points which are probably applicable more widely.

List of case studies

We have divided the case studies into four sections, namely, intermediaries, suppliers, venues and destinations.

Intermediaries

- Page and Moy Marketing (UK)
- The role of trade fairs in meetings and incentive travel marketing

Suppliers

- Hilton – services for the business traveller
- Historic Conference Centres of Europe (Austria)
- Business services and loyalty programmes offered by major hotel groups
- The business class product of airlines
- Frequent-flyer programmes – Lufthansa and Air France
- Airports and business travellers – Singapore Changi airport

Venues

- The British Universities Accommodation Consortium
- Disneyland® Paris Business Solutions
- LEGOLAND® Windsor (UK)
- Amsterdam RAI International Exhibition and Congress Centre

Destinations

- Business tourism in Hong Kong – City of Life
- Switzerland Convention and Incentive Bureau (SCIB)
- Iceland
- The marketing of Portugal as a business tourism destination

15 Page and Moy Marketing*

Page and Moy Marketing is a corporate marketing services agency providing a range of business-to-business motivation, incentive and marketing communications services. It is an established company that has an annual turnover in excess of £25 million, in a total market for incentive travel that has continued to grow over the last ten years. The company employs a range of personnel drawn from a variety of backgrounds. The corporate aim of the company is to provide the best motivation, communication and reward services to improve their clients' business performance. The company aims to differentiate itself by offering high levels of client servicing and technical excellence. This case study reviews the way in which the business is broken down, and looks at some examples of programmes that the company has organized.

The Page and Moy Marketing business

The company relies on the fact that large companies from a range of industrial sectors like to arrange motivation and incentive events using a specialist motivation agency such as Page and Moy Marketing. These events can range from those that are specially designed to reward staff, customers or distributors, to those that are designed to launch a new product or service. The key industrial sectors that organize and hold events of this kind include the automotive, computers/information technology, fast-moving consumer goods (fmcg), financial services and pharmaceutical companies. A recent survey conducted by Page and Moy showed that companies from these sectors ranked the different kinds of reward systems available to them in order of preference as being – travel/cash (equal first), vouchers (third), merchandise (fourth), and UK sporting events/leisure weekends (fifth). Many of the companies involved in these programmes are looking for more exciting and novel incentive and motivation schemes. The company therefore organizes many events that involve travel and hospitality either in the UK or overseas, and constitutes an important intermediary in the business travel world.

The division of the Page and Moy Marketing business is shown below.

---

* Page and Moy Marketing has now been renamed P&MM Limited.

The Page and Moy Marketing business

Motivations and incentives

The solution to boosting corporate performance is a combination of many factors. Innovation, creativity and logistical expertise are crucial. So is a sound grasp of the key issues in your industry; the kind of knowledge which only comes with experience.

Our account management service includes programme development, creative design and media, performance measurement and reporting.

But of course, at the heart of any motivation programme lies the reward. Naturally this motivational trigger is different for everyone, and so we offer a supremely flexible and comprehensive service which includes:

- merchandise
- store vouchers
- UK events
- travel (groups or individual)
- Dream Machine – to help fulfil an individual's personal ambition.

The wide choice of reward is supported by a variety of options for redemption; post, telephone, twenty-four hour automated telebanking or remote access via the Internet.

Conferences and video production

Creativity and efficiency are the cornerstones of our Conference and Video Production service. Our aim is to find the best possible medium with which to communicate your message. With a wide portfolio of client case histories, we can clearly demonstrate our experience in handling conferences, videos, roadshows, product launches and exhibitions.

Event management

In the UK or abroad, our expertise ensures that even complex logistical tasks are handled in the most professional and cost effective way. Our comprehensive services takes your project from brief to completion, monitored throughout with the latest event management software. This not only ensures accuracy and fast, effective reporting; it also provides a fee collection and billing facility, and where required, an electronic badge swipe registration system.

Escapades

Our Escapades division provides innovative tailor-made corporate hospitality events including:

- fly for lunch and champagne weekends
- multi-activity days
- team-building and special events

Whatever your needs, we are an exciting source of ideas.

Incentive and conference travel

With thirty-five years of experience, we are ideally equipped to deliver a first-class group travel service. We use the latest computer technology, to ensure optimum efficiency in pre-departure, on site and post-event operations. We are committed to providing innovative incentive and conference travel solutions which take advantage of all the latest developments in both ground facilities and flight routes worldwide. Financial and professional security is provided through our ATOL (Air Travel Organizers' Licence) bond, IATA (International Air Transport Association) licence and our professional indemnity insurance. We are also members of the ITMA.

Business improvement programmes

Business improvement is our key focus. We provide a service that applies our core skills of programme design, systems development and process administration to an entirely bespoke marketing programme requirement.
   This covers areas such as:

● staff and customer loyalty
● quality standards improvement
● research
● customer satisfaction
● telemarketing
● skill development.

Where required we will set up specialist teams to handle your outsourced marketing services programme.

Source: Page and Moy Marketing literature.

New trends in incentive travel

Escapades which is the small group adventure brand of Page and Moy Marketing has been working hard at reflecting new demands in the market that link to the general changes in consumer behaviour in the tourism industry.
   The reduction in time needed to travel to far flung destinations and the consumer demand for existing and adventurous experiences has been reflected in the types of programmes that Escapades is developing for their clients. 'We are seeing more and more clients respond favourably to challenging programmes. Although still a relatively new market it is not replacing the main client programme but is seen as more of an alternative or enhancement to it' (John Silvester, Marketing Director, Page and Moy Marketing).
   Examples of the new breed of incentive travel destination include areas of the globe that have previously been inaccessible to groups. Some of the destinations that Page and Moy Marketing offer are shown below.

New destinations

- North Pole by icebreaker – board the most powerful icebreaker in the world, see polar bears roaming across frozen wastes and stand on the North Pole all before returning to Arctic Russia.
- South Pole by air – from Chile down to the Antarctic camp at Patriot Hills – the starting point for many famous expeditions.
- Climb Mt Kilimanjaro – spend five days reaching the roof of Africa
- Greenland – an island out of this world where the sun never sets. Activities include a sail amongst the icebergs and a helicopter ride over a glacier.
- Ecuador and the Galapagos islands – Indian culture in Quito, then set sail for the Galapagos islands aboard a first class motor yacht.
- Heli-hiking – in the Canadian Rockies (a helicopter drops you on a mountain, you walk all day, then it picks you up).

Source: Motivation Matters – Page and Moy Marketing.

The company has been very careful to make these new destinations safe and to avoid unnecessary risks through careful planning. Organizations from the information technology sector have been particularly attracted to these new challenging programmes to broaden the horizons of their staff. The company predicts that the desire to have a 'once in a lifetime experience' will continue to be a popular trend in the incentive travel market.

Examples of incentive and conference travel organized by Page and Moy Marketing

Some examples of events that have been organized by the company are shown below.

AT&T Capital

AT&T Capital needed a flexible, self-contained 'environment' for seventy-two hours of group presentations, open forum discussions, customer service training and team-building. The lead-time was short and the brief specific: a venue close to an international airport (but not too close to a major city), accommodation for 200, a core event them, all staging, audiovisual (AV) and speaker support, nine breakout rooms, a totally interactive team-building 'activity' and two themed gala dinners; all within six weeks.

The concept of 'Connect' was first developed, and then applied across all areas of staging, audio and lighting, speaker support materials, print and video.

A key team-building activity was designed around a bespoke interactive computer game, in which delegates were given mental, physical and business-related challenges.

Connect also took into account the fact that several of the delegates only spoke English as a second language. Simultaneous translation in three languages was available at main business sessions, and the two gala dinners were themed around the universal language of music – a 1970s GlamRock night (featuring The Brothers of Perpetual Excitement and a lot of glitter) and a Blues Brothers night, ensuring something for everyone.

We'd like our first pan-European staff conference to be informal and fun . . . we've got 178 delegates, from twelve countries, and we want to bring them together as a team.

Galileo

Galileo, the world's leading travel technology and distribution company, asked Page and Moy Market-ing to handle the event management logistics for their worldwide conference. Entitled 'The Galileo International Automation Conference'; the event was designed to position Galileo as 'the travel agents' partner in a changing world'.

GALILEO - Your Partner in a Changing World

Madrid was eventually selected for the three-day event, which included plenary sessions, business seminars and workshops. An exhibition was set up to allow delegates access to the industry's leading airlines, hotel chains, car hire companies and other suppliers.

Pre-event planning consisted of invitations, registration and the collection of delegate fees. Once registered, each participant received colour-coded luggage tags, a smart-card badge and joining instructions.

On site, a total of 1600 people arrived from over fifty countries, travelling in a fleet of thirty-seven coaches and staying in ten different hotels. Logistics were simplified by the use of an electronic badging system which made it possible to track people, leave messages, broadcast which seminars still had space and record who attended which presentation.

Some of the highlights of the social programme included a dinner at the Palacio del Negralego, and an exclusive performance of the West End musical *Buddy* – the original cast having flown in specially for the occasion.

We want to persuade travel agents worldwide that we are their vital business partner in this fast changing world.

Rolls-Royce

Rolls-Royce Motor Cars Limited wanted an incentive to motivate their Dealer Principals worldwide. So just what do you offer the people who have been everywhere and done everything!

The answer has to be something that they cannot buy for themselves – and so the Paris to Monte Carlo rally was conceived. Page and Moy Marketing put together the initial launch brochure and a series of bulletins and teasers to be dispatched worldwide to keep the challenge in the forefront of everyone's minds.

The Rolls-Royce International Rally attracted winners worldwide, all of whom were met in Paris and transferred to the Hotel Crillon. After a night's stay and full briefing, competitors took to their Rolls-Royce and Bentley motor cars to follow a prearranged route (overnighting in Relais et Chateaux properties) via Reims, Gilly les Citeaux, Annecy, Chateau-Arnoux, finally arriving at the Hotel de Paris in Monte Carlo.

Page and Moy Marketing were responsible for:

- initial concept and all print and production
- venue selection and inspections
- production of a route book including alternative routes
- individual joining instructions for each couple
- route questionnaire
- advance and back-up cars
- all travel logistics including incoming/outgoing flights worldwide, transportation of cars, hotel bookings, food and beverages.

How do we motivate those people who have everything!

Source: Page and Moy Marketing literature.

It can be seen from these examples that the company is responsible for organizing a large amount of travel, tourism and hospitality services on behalf of clients. It also arranges back-up services such as multimedia presentations and marketing communication services.

Conclusions

Page and Moy Marketing is an example of a large UK-based incentive and marketing service agency that helps organizations in their development of specialist events. Incentive travel forms an important part of business travel.

Discussion points and essay questions

1 Discuss the advantages that a specialist agency can offer a large corporate client in their design and organization of incentive travel.
2 Suggest reasons for the fact that large companies are increasingly offering travel rather than cash, as an incentive.
3 The interest in adventure tourism has been a trend in both mainstream tourism and incentive travel. Critically evaluate the changes in consumer behaviour and the tourism sector that have brought about this development.
4 Page and Moy Marketing is an example of an intermediary in the business travel market. Evaluate the role that intermediaries play in the development of business tourism.

The authors would like to thank Mr Kevin Rogers of Page and Moy Marketing Limited for his help in the writing of this case study.

16 The role of trade fairs in meetings and incentive travel marketing

In a sector where personal selling plays such a vital role in marketing, it is not surprising that trade fairs make a very important contribution to the marketing of services and facilities in the meetings and incentive travel sectors.

This case study covers two major trade fairs in Europe. *International Confex* takes place in London and is the UK's leading event for the meetings industry. In 2000 there were 1300 exhibitors divided into four sectors as follows:

- UK destinations, venues, and incentive travel
- overseas destinations, venues, and incentive travel
- corporate hospitality events
- event support services.

Approximately 9000 buyers were expected to visit the event.

A seminar programme covering topics of interest to professionals takes place in parallel to the exhibition itself. Topics at International Confex in 1999 included:

- risk management
- the role of the Internet in conference management
- chartering award
- planning global meetings
- booking speakers
- public and press relations
- staff motivation
- quality standards.

These seminars are usually presented by companies with a commercial interest in the product, service or issue in question.

Exhibitors use the exhibitions to announce major developments, or launch new products and services. In 1999 these included, for example:

- the development of the £10 million Bath Spa Project in Bath, UK
- the new 'London Eye' was being promoted, for the first time, as a product launch venue
- the creation of Conference Devon in the UK to private conference venues in the country

- the availability of the Royal Yacht *Britannia* as a unique venue, in its moorings in Scotland
- the opening of the new IMAX cinema at the Bournemouth International Centre in the UK
- the newly built conference centre in Linz, Austria
- a £6 million refurbishment of the Sheraton Brussels Hotel, Belgium
- plans by the Le Meridien Hotel in Limassol, Cyprus, to build a conference hall with a capacity of 1000
- a $48 million renovation of the Prague Congress Centre in the Czech Republic
- the £50 million refurbishment of the Palais de Congrés de Paris in France
- the new 8000 capacity International Congress Centre in Munich, Germany
- the building of a 2500 capacity conference centre at the Sofitel Copsis Hotel, in Rhodes, Greece
- the launch of two new ships with meeting room facilities by the Silversea Cruise Company
- the announcement that Dubai now offers over 200 luxury hotel properties with 19 000 rooms
- the Sol Media hotel chain promoted the opening of its new properties in Europe and the Caribbean
- the building of a new congress centre in Cape Town, South Africa
- the building of new conference hotels in Thailand
- the construction of a new £440 m convention centre in Boston, USA.

EIBTM is the major European trade fair for the incentive travel sector. In 2000 it took place in Geneva, and attracted nearly 2900 exhibitors from 100 countries.

EIBTM has a supporting seminar programme which is not on the same scale as that of International Confex. The exhibitors at EIBTM represented a broad range of players within the incentive travel sector. This is illustrated by the variety of advertisements contained in the official show guide published as a supplement in *Conference and Incentive Travel* in May 2000.

These were as follows:

Destinations	*Hotels and resorts*
Iceland	Club Med
Zurich	Concorde Hotels
Hong Kong	Carnoustie, Scotland
Vienna	Crowne Plaza Hotels International
Aruba	Le Meridien, Limassol, Cyprus
Switzerland	Coral Bay, Paphos, Cyprus
Seattle	Radisson SAS
Ireland	Moncrieff Dalm, Scotland
Monaco	Aeneas Hotel, Cyprus
	Hilton Malta
	Scottish & Newcastle Hotels, UK

Conference and exhibition venues	*Cruise lines*
Barbican Centre, London	Royal Caribbean
Hillingdon, London	Intern

Alexandra Palace, London
SECC, Glasgow
Hayles Conference Centres
International Conference, UK
New Connaught Rooms, London
Wembley, London

Airlines and airports	*Other organizations*
Dubai Airport	Corporate
Thai International Airways	Incentive Travel and Meetings Association

Both exhibitions are 'business-to-business' exhibitions in that the visitors are all business people – rather than the general public – selling goods and services to each other.

While exhibiting at such shows is very expensive, running often to tens of thousands of pounds, it is clearly reviewed as an effective method of selling by business tourism organizations.

Discussion points and essay questions

1 Why are trade fairs an important part of marketing in the business tourism sector?
2 What factors do you think define the success or future of a trade fair for both exhibitors and visitors?

17   Hilton – services for the business traveller

Introduction to the company

Hilton International CO was acquired by Hilton Group plc for $1 billion in October 1987. Hilton Group is one of the UK's top 100 companies listed on the London Stock Exchange, with a market value of approximately £4 billion. The company was formerly known as Ladbroke Group plc and this name was changed in 1999.

The group had a turnover of £1901.8 million and an operating profit of £254 million in 1999. The company has continually added to their portfolio of hotels, by acquisition of individual hotels and chains, new development and extensions.

On the 13 January 1997, the group formed a worldwide alliance with Hilton Hotels Corporation, the owner of the Hilton name within the USA. This alliance has meant that Hilton Hotel Corporation (HHC) and Hilton International (HI) are co-operating on sales and market loyalty programmes, central reservation systems and other services.

A merger between the group and Stakis plc was agreed on the 26 March 1999.

Hilton currently splits their operations into four geographic areas: Europe, Africa and the Middle East; the Americas; Asia Pacific; and the UK. The group is managed by an executive board and four Area Presidents.

Hilton International has a major strategic aim: to expand globally with their first-class hotels, convention centre and serviced apartments in city centre locations. They are also keen to expand their operations at international airports, particularly to focus on the business traveller. (See Table 17.1.)

A very important part of the expansion plans is the rebranding exercise that has been carried out since the strategic marketing alliance between Hilton Hotel Corporation and Hilton International CO. Since the alliance it has been necessary to eliminate confusion by creating a single worldwide focus on quality and service.

Alliance achievements to date

- Development of a single brand positioning to serve as a framework for Hilton marketing activity worldwide.
- Launch of single logo for worldwide application on Hilton signage and collateral.
- Development of a new hotel naming architecture that will make it easier for guests to identify Hilton properties worldwide.

Table 17.1   Hilton International growth plans, 2000 onwards

Hotels	Open date	No. of rooms
1 Hilton Tobago, Tobago	Q3, 2000	200
2 Hilton Dalian, China	Q3, 2000	375
3 Hilton Dubai Jumeirah	Q3, 2000	394
4 Hilton Mauritius Resort	Q3, 2000	205
5 Hilton Budapest WestEnd, Hungary	Q3, 2000	232
6 Hilton Seremban, Malaysia	Q4, 2000	348
7 Hilton Auckland, New Zealand	Q4, 2000	202
8 Hilton Melbourne Airport, Australia	Q4, 2000	280
9 Hilton Sofia, Bulgaria	Q4, 2000	246
10 Hilton Jeddah, Saudi Arabia	Q4, 2000	350
11 Hilton London Paddington, London UK	Q1, 2001	355
12 Hilton Chongqing, China	Q2, 2001	420
13 Hilton Buenos Aires Residences, Argentina	Q1, 2001	200
14 Hilton London Trafalgar Square	Q1, 2001	131
15 Hilton Shenyang, China	Q1, 2001	380
16 Hilton Copenhagen Airport, Denmark	Q1, 2001	358
17 Hilton Adana SA, Turkey	Q1, 2001	320
18 Hilton Bolshoi Moscow, Russia	Q2, 2001	218
19 Hilton Dreamland Golf Resort, 6 October City, Cairo	Q2, 2001	200
20 Hilton Royal Residences Jeddah, Saudi Arabia	Q4, 2001	112
21 Hilton Mactan Island Resort & Towers, Cebu, Philippines	Q4, 2001	360
22 Hilton Ain El Sokhna, Egypt [second phase]	Q4, 2001	175
23 Hilton Kuwait Resort and Marina, Kuwait	Q4, 2001	294
24 Hilton Marsa, Alam Coral Beach Resort, Egypt	Q1, 2002	294
25 Hilton Jerusalem 2, Israel	Q2, 2002	300
26 Hilton Xiamen, China	Q3, 2002	370
27 Hilton Beirut, Lebanon	Q3, 2002	485
28 Hilton Kuala Lumpur Sentral	2002	500
29 Hilton Manchester	2002	345
31 AIC Hilton Lagos Airport, Nigeria	2002	300
		8949

Source: Hilton International.

- Selection of a jointly managed and funded advertising agency Bozell World-wide, who have created the brand's first worldwide advertising campaign, 'It happens at the Hilton'.
- Global integration of the sales force, now called Hilton Sales World-wide. US and Mexico offices are now direct by HHC; offices throughout the rest of the world are directed by HI.
- The International launch of Hilton HHonors, Hilton's frequent-guest programme. Since its launch in January 1997, almost three million new members have enrolled worldwide and more than fifteen new partners, including Air France, LatinPass, Japan

Airlines, Lan Chile and Varig, have joined the programme bringing the total number of travel partners to over thirty.
- Development of a new worldwide central reservations system (CRS) by the jointly owned Hilton Reservations World-wide (HRW).
- Inclusion of all Hilton properties on www.hilton.com
- Establishment of a global network and system for public relations support (*source*: Hilton International).

Hilton Hotels Corporation and Hilton International CO, a subsidiary of Hilton Group plc, have a worldwide alliance to market the Hilton brand, the world's best known hotel brand. Both companies are recognized as leaders in the hospitality industry.

Global brand identity and global advertising

The group unveiled a new global brand identity in 1998 following the forming of the alliance. This development was seen as a very important move to help in the Hilton business strategy of aggressive expansion plans. The global branding exercise resulted in a new symbolic logo which the business and leisure traveller can recognize on a worldwide basis. The new logo features a bold blue 'H' which is encircled to symbolize the strength and innovative style of the brand. The development of the new logo was accompanied by the launch of a new global advertising campaign in October 1998. This campaign featured a new strapline 'It happens at the Hilton'. A press campaign focused on real-life 'happenings' in Hilton hotels rather than on hotel products and services. The whole campaign was developed to have universal appeal.

A $10 million press and poster campaign was placed in Pan-European, Pan-Asian, UK, German, Australian, Canadian and US titles in an attempt to get across the idea of universal appeal of the Hilton brand. Poster sites were selected at international airports so that international business travellers would begin to recognize the new brand identity. The group also placed advertisements in the international business press and it was expected that an average of over 75 per cent of international business travellers would see these campaigns.

Hilton International and the business traveller

> '*Where the business traveller goes, Hilton will be there*'
> (David Jarvis, former Chief Executive of Hilton International).

Hilton International has focused on offering the business traveller a high-quality service. The company has developed a full range of services that cater to the changing needs of the business traveller. These services include the provision of Towers and Executive Floors where the customer can upgrade to a higher standard of accommodation. The Hilton hotels also have fully staffed business centres, video-conferencing facilities and, in many rooms, generous in-room workspaces and lighting with data points for laptop computers. A full range of the services on offer to the business traveller is shown in Table 17.2.

Table 17.2 Services for the business traveller at Hilton International

Service	Name	Benefits
Booking/reservation	Hilton Reservations World-wide	Fully integrated, user friendly, in-depth information, sales prompts, guest recognition
Internet service	www.hilton.com	Access to: ● Hilton Value Rates ● Destination Guides ● Interactive Mapping ● CEO Software ● Floor Plans for meetings/function ● Snap! Online – Access to thirteen channels ● Press Room ● Hilton Trade Track Poll ● Hilton.com.Membership ● Hilton Group Value Data ● Group Reservation ● Hilton HHonors®
Reward programme	Hilton HHonors®	Reward programme for frequent travellers
Meeting service	Hilton Meetings	Launched March 2000 Upgrading of facilities and services
Business facilities	Hilton International Executive Floor	Exclusive area in the hotel for business traveller

Source: Hilton International.

Hilton International has been relying more on their central reservation systems and online booking systems for the development of the business market. The Hilton HHonors guest reward programme tries to keep a loyal customer base by offering customers a range of benefits.

Hilton International launched a new meeting product, Hilton Meetings, to try to ensure consistency of services on offer to the business traveller who is organizing a meeting or event. The delivery of a consistent service is considered to be one of the most important features for meeting organizers and delegates. 'We're working in a £2 billion marketplace and need to provide customers with a contemporary environment and a flexible range of services. With the launch of Hilton Meetings we plan to stay ahead of our competition and retain our number on position' (Rachel Wright, Brand Manager, Hilton Meetings).

Hilton International have also created Executive Floors to help the business traveller relax. This service was a new concept when it was launched in 1993 and it is now available in more than sixty hotels in over thirty countries worldwide. Hilton Hotels Corporation in the USA offers a similar service – Hilton Towers.

Table 17.3 Executive Floor and Clubroom specifications

The Executive Floor	*Clubroom*
A place to work: Two telephones Alarm clock/radio Desk and chair Desk level plug sockets and PC data points Reading lamp Personal safe	PC adapter plugs available at check in All day complimentary beverages, snacks and canapés Books and games Business support services Complimentary breakfast Designated non-smoking area Lounge area Selection of local and international newspapers and magazines
A place to relax: Choice of local and international satellite channels including English language stations (plus CNN) Bathrobe and slippers Choice of permanent non-smoking rooms Comfortable armchairs Complimentary tea- and coffee-making facilities Ice bucket Iron and ironing board Large bottle of complimentary mineral water Radio music channels Tissues on dressing table	
Bathroom facilities: Bathmat Bath-sheet size towels Face cloths Hairdryer Range of additional amenities including shampoo, soap, shower cap, moisturizer, tissues, cotton wool	
Other services: Morning delivery of complimentary local or international newspaper Dedicated check-in/check-out on Executive Floor Dedicated Executive Floor Manager	

Source: Hilton International.

The Executive Floor's upgraded rooms have been created in line with the international business traveller's top three priorities which are to get a good night's sleep, to have the opportunity to freshen up and, in equal third place, the chance to work, relax and eat (research carried out for Hilton by Emphasis Research and Partner Tanner in 1998). The full range of services that are on offer on the Executive Floor are shown in Table 17.3.

Hilton International considers itself to be at the leading edge in the provision of services for business travellers. The company has won many awards for their business services. These include the awards listed in Table 17.4.

Table 17.4 Hilton International awards – UK

Executive Travel	1997 Best Airport Hotel World-wide (Bronze) for the Zurich Kloten Airport Hilton
	1997 Best Airport Hotel in the UK (Silver) for the London Gatwick Airport Hilton
	1997 Hotel With The Best Restaurant (Bronze) for The Langham Hilton, London
	1997 Best Hotel Group in the UK (Bronze) for both Hilton International and Hilton National
	1997 Best Hotel Group In Europe (Silver) for Hilton International
	1997 Best Hotel Group in the Middle East (Bronze) *for Hilton International*
	1997 Best Hotel Group in Asia/Pacific (Bronze) for Hilton International
	1997 Hotel Group with the Best Loyalty Programme for Hilton Honors
Travel Weekly	1999 Best Worldwide Hotel Group for Hilton the sixth consecutive year
Travel Industry Globe Awards	1999 Best US Hotel Group for Hilton
Business Traveller	1997 Best Chain in the UK (Silver) for Hilton International
	1997 Best International Hotel Chain in Continental Europe (Bronze) for Hilton International
	1997 Best International Hotel Chain in the Middle East (Bronze) for Hilton International 2000 Best UK Business Hotel Chain
Trade Travel Gazette	1997 Top European Hotel Group (Silver) for Hilton International
Travel Bulletin	1997, 1998 and 1999 Top International Hotel Chain for Hilton International
Business Travel World	1997 Best Business Hotel Group in Western Europe
National Sales Awards 1999	Best Use of Technology in Selling

Source: Hilton International.

Conclusions

Hilton International will continue to undergo an aggressive growth strategy on an international basis. A major part of this growth strategy will be in the provision of hotel services for the business traveller. The company will benefit from the recently developed corporate logo and global advertising campaign to get a consistent message across to all customers. The development of new services and the continuing upgrading of hotel facilities will also form an important part of this strategy.

Discussion points and essay questions

1 Discuss the way that the marketing alliance between Hilton Hotel Corporation and Hilton International CO can help in the development of corporate business.
2 Discuss the way in which the provision of the Executive Floor encourages repeat purchase from business travellers.
3 Critically analyse the benefits of a major hotel group, such as Hilton International having a universal brand identity and global advertising campaign to expand their corporate business. Are there any disadvantages associated with this approach?
4 'Central to the success of Hilton Meetings will be the dedicated meeting specialists at each hotel' (Rachel Wright, Brand Manager, Hilton Meeting). Critically evaluate the benefits of the Hilton Meeting Service to the conference or events organizer.

The authors would like to thank Julia Clark and Nicola McDowall of Hilton International for their help with the writing of this case study.

18 Historic Conference Centres of Europe

The Historic Conference Centres of Europe is a network of conference centres that are based in historic buildings in Europe. A list of the members of the network is shown below:

Austria	*Grazer Congress Convention Center, Graz* The nineteenth-century building houses a Beethoven memorial Hofburg Congress Center & Redoutensale, Vienna The halls and staterooms are of the former Hapsburg imperial palace
Belgium	*Flanders Congress and Concert Centre, Antwerp* This is a historic building near to the centre of Antwerp
Finland	*Paasitorni Conference Centre, Helsinki* An outstanding example of art nouveau architecture
France	*The Pope's Palace International Congress Centre, Avignon* The Congress Centre occupies two wings of the medieval Pope's Palace
Germany	*Congress Center, Mannheim-Rosengarten* A historic building in the centre of a business and cultural centre *Das Kurhaus, Wiesbaden* The main landmark of the elegant spa city of Weisbaden *Historiche Stadthalle am Johannisberg-Wuppertal* *Music and Conference Centre* An architectural jewel of the late nineteenth century
Ireland	*Dublin Castle Conference Centre* A magnificent eighteenth-century Georgian quadrangle of buildings
Malta	*Mediterranean Conference Centre, Valletta*

Portugal	*Palácio da Bolsa Porto* A national monument that is classified as World Heritage by UNESCO
Spain	*The Conference and Exhibition Centre of Córdoba* The centre is located in the former San Sebastian Hospital built between 1512 and 1516
Sweden	*Norra Latin City Conference Centre, Stockholm* A former school built in the Florentine Renaissance
The Netherlands	*Beurs von Berlage, Amsterdam* Amsterdam's former stock exchange
United Kingdom	*The Café Royal, London* The Café Royal was established in 1865 by a Parisian wine merchant

Source: Historic Conference Centres of Europe marketing literature.

The aim of the network is to open up historic centres as commercial ventures and to encourage tourism of the cities in which they are situated. The marketing strategy focuses on the American and European markets to develop more international business. This strategy particularly focuses on the encouragement of US organizations to hold their meetings in Europe. The basic idea of the network is shown below.

The basic idea

- There are numerous conference centres in historic buildings equipped with state-of-the-art convention technology in historic city centres.
- As an organized group, one of the alliance's duties is to make this fact evident to the market.
- The alliance does not only aim at commercializing its historic heritage in a better and more effective way, but also aims at distinguishing its member centres from modern conference facilities.
- The alliance will focus on business development (association market/corporate market), backed up by the advantage of exchange of know-how and networking of information and offers the possibility that meetings can rotate among the member centres.
- Consequently, destinations which are not well known in the market and whose position in the market is not so strong due to less potential will get a greater chance to acquire business.

Source: Historic Conference Centres of Europe marketing literature.

The development of the network is of particular advantage to areas of Europe that need development and injections of money, such as Dublin or Porto. The joint marketing of these centres means that an increase in conference tourism is encouraged and money is spent in the local economies.

The group is organized from a permanent head office in Graz, Austria. This office manages all the marketing, advertising and public relations work associated with the network. The office commissions high-quality promotional material and organizes sales promotions activities such as presentations, workshops and shows. A common budget is agreed by all the members of the network and this budget is controlled and administered by the head office in Graz. The Steering Committee of the alliance consists of five representatives of member centres, rotating each year.

The alliance currently has fifteen members, but it is planned to increase this to twenty to twenty-five in the next period. Details of previous activities and planned activities are shown below.

Previous activities

- Participation and presentation at EIBTM show 1997, 1998, 1999 and 2000 in Geneva, press conference, promotion and direct mail campaigns.
- Production of promotion material.
- Production of a stand to establish a homepage on the Internet.
- Workshops, receptions, presentations, study tours.

Planned activities

- Workshops, presentations and study tours.
- Presentations in cities such as Brussels, Washington, London, Paris, etc.
- Direct mailings.
- Participation at international shows such as EIBTM, ASAE, ESAE, IT+ME, MPI, etc.
- Permanent representatives in the USA to increase efficiency and to fulfil the requirements of the market

---

The Historic Conference Centres of Europe has won awards for extraordinary concepts and creative realization of promotional material. The alliance won the 1999 PRIMA Awards, an international competition recognized by the American Society of Association Executives (ASAE). The alliance won first place for a marketing campaign which was judged as having 'beautiful presentation, sound strategy and execution and good use of a unique selling proposition'. The promotional material developed by the alliance has been recognized as being outstanding in the way in which it shows the unique character of the historic buildings.

Conclusions

The Historic Conference Centres of Europe is a joint marketing venture and a very exclusive club. The buildings have to be at least 100 years old and offer superior service, management standards and state-of-the-art convention technology. The centres must be situated in cities that are known for their rich cultural and architectural heritage.

These rules of membership has meant that the alliance has been very successful at attracting European and American business into these major centres.

Discussion points and essay questions

1 Discuss the benefits that an alliance can offer to an individual conference centre that wants to market itself in overseas markets.
2 Evaluate the different methods of promotion that an alliance such as the Historic Conference Centres of Europe can use to promote the members.
3 Critically evaluate the benefits that a rich cultural and architectural heritage can offer a city that wants to develop business tourism.
4 The development of a historic building as a conference venue will depend on the balance between tradition and state-of-the-art technology. Evaluate the ways in which the manager of a historic conference centre can achieve this balance.

The authors would like to thank Ingrid Behugel von Flammerdinghe of Historic Conferences of Europe for her help with the writing of this case study.

19 Business services and loyalty programmes offered by major hotel groups

The major hotel groups have a large part of their revenue originating from business clients. The hotel industry is consolidating and there have been a number of recent major takeovers. This has meant that these large hotel groups that have to compete very aggressively for business. This case study looks at the type of marketing activities that the large hotel companies have undertaken to try to gain loyal business customers in the highly competitive market.

The importance of business service for major hotel groups

Business travel originating from individuals and conference- and incentive-related business contributes a major source of the revenue for large hotel chains. Conference and incentive travel forms a major part of this business and it is very important for the large hotel groups to continue to develop the market. This means that the hotel groups have to offer the right facilities and work with the right intermediaries to develop this business.

Conference and incentive business

The main industrial sectors that hold conference and incentive travel events are pharmaceuticals, banking, insurance, telecommunications, information technology and the automotive industry. The conference and incentive business is generally buoyant, although certain important sources of business such as the insurance and information technology sectors have shown a recent decline in sales. The division of conference and incentive travel varies according to the hotel group, and Internet booking has become an important part of the business. A large part of the conference and incentive business is booked via an agency. A recent survey of the major hotel groups revealed information about the conference and incentive travel business of the major hotel groups. The results of this survey are shown in Table 19.1.

Table 19.1 The conference and incentive travel business of major hotel groups

Ranking in 2000 (1999)	Name of chain	Number of hotels	Percentage of conference-related bookings	Percentage of incentive-related bookings	Percentage of groups booked through agencies	Dedicated conference booking service	Web site
1 (-)[1]	Accor	3500	n/a	n/a	80	Yes 020 8237 8820	www.accorhotel.com
2 (1)	Bass Hotels and Resorts	2700	80	20	80	Yes 0800 897121	www.basshotels.com
3 (2)	Marriott International	2000	70	30	70	Yes 020 7591 1036	www.marriott.com
4 (3)	Starwood Hotels and Resorts	750	80	20	90	Yes 020 7290 7171	www.starwood.com
5 (-)[1]	Choice Hotels Europe	540	85	15	75	Yes 0500 616263	www.choicehotelseurope.com
6 (4)	Hilton International[2]	445	80	20	70	Yes 0800 856 8100	www.hilton.com
7 (-)[1]	Golden Tulip Hotels[3]	406	n/a	n/a	n/a	n/a	www.goldentulip.com
8 (6)	The Forte Hotel Group	400	n/a	n/a	n/a	Yes 0345 383940	www.forte-hotels.com
9 (5)	Sol Melia	250	66	34	60	Yes 020 7388 7080	www.solmelia.com
10 (7)	Hyatt Hotels and Resorts	195	70	30	25	Yes 020 8335 1234	www.hyatt.com
11 (9)	Radisson SAS Hotels and Resorts	126	66	34	n/a	Yes 00 32 2702 9200	ww.radissonsas.com
12 (10)	Regal Hotel Group	99	84	16	65	Yes 0845 300 2030	www.corushotels.com
13 (11)	Moat House	95	86	14	n/a	Yes 0500 712713	www.moathousehotels.com
14 (12)	Concorde Hotels International	72	75	25	70	Yes 0800 181591	www.concorde-hotels.com
15 (14)	Millennium Hotels and Resorts	57	66	34	75	Yes 0845 302 0002	www.stay.with-us.com
16 (-)[1]	Movenpick Hotels and Resorts	41	80	20	n/a	n/a	www.movenpick-hotels.com
17 (17)	Maritim	40	87.5	12.5	45	Yes 020 8545 6910	www.maritim.com
18 (18)[4]	Fairmont Hotels and Resorts	37	43	57	80	Yes 020 7389 1126	www.fairmont.com
18 (15)	Shangri-La Hotels and Resorts	37	57	43	2	No	www.shangri-la.com
20 (-)[1]	De Vere Hotels and Leisure	30	79	21	70	Yes 0870 240 0101	www.devereonline.com
20 (19)	Kempinski Hotels and Resorts	30	75	25	n/a	Yes 020 8307 7693	www.kempinski.com
22 (-)[1]	Orient Express Hotels	22	50	50	n/a	No	www.orient-expresshotels.com
23 (23)	Corinthia Hotels International	19	87.5	22.5	99	Yes 020 8943 4194	www.corinthia.com
23 (24)	Pan Pacific Hotels and Resorts	19	60	40	n/a	Yes 020 7323 2133	www.panpac.com
25 (28)	Hanover International	14	n/a	n/a	n/a	Yes 0345 444123	www.hanover-international.com
26 (26)	Marco Polo	7	50	50	20	No	www.marcopolohotels.com

Notes: 1. Not ranked in 1999.
2. Hilton International acquires Stakis Hotel in March 1999.
3. Current information incomplete due to ongoing takeover by W H Hotels.
4. Formerly Canadian Pacific Hotels.

Source: Conference and Incentive Travel (July/August 2000).

Table 19.2 Leading hotel chains of the world: priority clubs and business services

Hotel chain	Number of hotels	Brands	Business services	Conference services	Priority club	Web site
Accor	3500	• Sofitel • Novotel • Mercure • Ibis Hotels • Formule 1 • Etap • Jardins	Business travel programme – dedicated business advice/booking	Company solutions – helping companies to book and arrange conference/meetings	• The Accor Corporate Card • The Sofitel Exclusive Card • The Novotel World-wide Card • The Club Mercure Card • The Ibis Card • The Formule 1 Card • The Accor Asia Pacific Advantage Card	www.accorhotel.com
Bass Hotels and Resorts	2700	• Holiday Inn World-wide® • Holiday Inn Express® • Inter-Continental Hotels and Resorts® • Staybridge Suits® • Crowne Plaza Hotels®	Business travel services and bookings	Bass Hotels and Resorts meeting site	• Priority Club World-wide® • Six Continents Club®	www.basshotels.com
Marriott	2000	• Marriott • Courtyard • Fairfield Inn • Residence Inn • Spring Hill Suites • Town Place Suite • Renaissance Partners • The Ritz-Carlton • Ramada	Marriott event planner Marriott Satellite Video-Conferencing Network	Marriott's meeting planner Partner with eighteen airlines Marriott Conference Centers	Marriott Rewards, including Elite Membership bringing special rewards	www.marriott.com
Starwood Hotels and Resorts	750	• Westin • Sheraton • Four Points • St Regis • The Luxury Collection • Starwood	Business services vary according to hotels	Conference booking services	Starwood Preferred Guest[SM] • preferred guest • gold preferred guest • platinum preferred guest	www.starwood.com
Choice Hotels Europe	540	• Comfort • Quality • Clarion • Sleep Inn • Rodeway Inn • EconoLodge • Mainstay Suite	Choice club card Full range of business services	Dedicated conference service	Favoured Guest Card	www.choicehotelseurope.com

Company	No.	Brands	Business services	Conference services	Loyalty programmes	Website
Hilton International	445	• Hilton® • Doubletree® • Embassy Suites® • Hampton Inn® • Harrison Conference Centre® • Hilton Garden Inn® • Homewood Suites by Hilton® • Red Lion Hotels and Inns® • Conrad International®	Dedicated business service	Dedicated conference service	Hilton HHonors® Hilton Grand Vacations Club®	www.hilton.com
The Forte Group (Granada)	400	Le Meridien Hotels and Resorts Forte Posthouse Hotels Forte Heritage Hotels The Grosvenor House London	Corporate privilege service gives privileged rates to corporate clients Partnership with eighteen airlines	Dedicated conference service	MOMENTS.COM global reward and recognition programme	www.forte-hotels.com
Sol Meliá	250	Sol Meliá	Central reservation and dedicated business service	Dedicated conference service	Club Amigos MAS Loyalty Programme	www.solmelia.com
Hyatt Hotels and Resorts	195	Hyatt	Hyatt Certificates™ – incentive and promotion certificate Online booking service	Dedicated conference service Hyatt Meeting Connection™ Hyatt Meeting Concierge™		
Radisson Hotels World-wide (part of CarlsonHotels World-wide)	126	Radisson: • Radisson Bed and Breakfast Breakaway℠ • Family Magic® • Senior Breaks℠	Global reservations Business class service Radisson World-wide Hospitality Programme	Dedicated conference booking service Radisson Meeting Solution℠ E-scapes by Radisson℠	Radisson Gold Reward℠ Customized email service	www.radissonsas.com

Source: Conference and Incentive Travel (July/August 2000) and authors' own research.

It is interesting to note that in the majority of cases, conference-related bookings form the major part of the total conference and incentive business. Some of the hotels rely much more on agencies to book their conference and incentive business than others.

The use of an agency is particularly noticeable for the larger hotel groups such as Accor, Bass Hotels and Resorts, and Starwood Hotels and Resorts. Most of the major hotel groups have developed web sites and conference booking services with dedicated telephone numbers to help their business clients. The hotels also rely heavily on the national tourist organizations to generate conference and incentive travel in the various countries in which the hotels are located. This is particularly important for larger conferences that bring people together from across the world and which are planned and organized a long time in advance.

Large hotel groups offer the business client the comfort of a familiar and reliable brand to try and gain loyalty from corporate clients. The small chains rely more heavily on developing high levels of specialist and personalized service to encourage repeat purchases from their business clients. Many hotel chains have found that the development of an integrated business and conference service with a priority club and web site has been very successful in the development of the conference and incentive market. The business services priority clubs offered by major hotel chains across the world are shown in Table 19.2.

It can be seen that the major hotel chains have developed increasingly sophisticated services and promotional techniques to develop the business and conference market. The Accor group has developed a specialist set of promotional tools and services for each of its brands, whereas other hotel chains such as Bass Hotels and Resorts have concentrated on an integrated set of tools and services across the whole range. The development of a specialist business and conference service is of particular importance for the larger hotel chains, and this needs to be integrated with the priority club.

Customer loyalty schemes in the hotel sector

An important aspect of the development of corporate and business travel for the larger hotel chains has been the development of priority clubs aimed at the individual business customer or, more importantly, the corporate client. The airlines were the first companies in the travel industry to introduce frequent-flyer programmes, and hotel groups quickly followed with their own schemes. Many of the upmarket hotel chains appeared very similar in appearance and facilities. The loyalty scheme tries to encourage loyal customers who recognize the special nature of particular brands. Successful loyalty marketing relies on a sophisticated mix of rewards, recognition and relationship marketing. Many of the leading hotel groups have developed very sophisticated mixes of customer loyalty schemes aimed particularly at the loyal business traveller. An outline of the loyalty schemes on offer is shown in Table 19.3.

It can be seen from Table 19.3 that the hotel groups are developing loyalty schemes to differentiate themselves from their competitors. Certain hotels such as Inter-Continental Hotels and Resorts, and Kempinski Hotels and Resorts have developed loyalty systems that offer benefits to customers during their stay. Other hotel chains such as Accor and Hilton offer sophisticated reward systems that are tied up with their business partners such as airlines, and car hire firms. Table 19.3 shows that many of the schemes are becoming similar in nature, if not in detail, and the hotel chains are having to develop increasingly sophisticated and far-reaching schemes to keep ahead of the competition.

There have been recent examples of the use of extremely aggressive marketing techniques to gain customer loyalty using loyalty schemes. Evidence suggests that most of the major hotel chains have a major objective to increase the membership of their loyalty programmes. The basis of this competition depends on the operator. Bass Hotels and Resorts competes by offering a large volume of hotels, whereas Carlson Hospitality World-wide (Radisson) has integrated their hotel loyalty scheme with their other hospitality and leisure brands. Starwood Hotels and Resorts competes on the basis of the flexibility and inclusiveness of their loyalty schemes.

'All of our research shows that a loyal customer is an extremely profitable customer. If we can increase loyalty by even a small margin, we can increase profitability by a very large margin' (Curtis Nelson, CEO, Carlson Hospitality World-wide, 1999). This quote illustrates the importance of hotel loyalty schemes in the aggressive hotel marketing business.

New trends

Mergers and acquisitions in the hotel sector have already changed the nature of competition in the business sector. There has been a growth in global hotel companies and it has become easier to brand hotels across national boundaries. This has meant that the business customer can be encouraged to be loyal on a global, rather than purely national level.

The increasing reliance on technology is also bringing about fundamental changes in this market. Booking on the Internet and communicating by e-mail is having a major effect on the booking and organization of conference and incentive travel, for example. The installation of technological systems such as e-mail in rooms and high-speed Internet access in hotel properties is also having a major effect on business customers.

The introduction of satellite video-conferencing by companies such as Marriott is allowing companies to use much more sophisticated technological systems for their conferences and meetings. The irony is that it is this technology that could undermine the future of business travel.

Table 19.3 Hotel loyalty schemes

Hotel group	Name of scheme	Benefits of scheme
Accor	• The Sofitel Exclusive Club 450 FF to join • The Novotel World-wide Card • The Club Mercure Card Spend 12 nights or more in Mercure • The Ibis Card • The Formule 1 Card 100 FF to join or free	Various benefits according to the card including: • Reductions on room rate • Free room nights • Added services/VIP treatment • Discounts • Special menus
Bass Hotels and Resorts	Priority Club World-wide® Six Continents Club® Free membership (Approximately 6 million members)	Ten points per US dollar spent on non-discounted rooms Partnership with twenty-four airlines and car hire firms Free stays, upgrades, express check-in, express checkout, late checkout, Family stays
Marriott	Marriott Rewards Free membership	Ten points per US dollar spent at Marriott Partnerships with nineteen airlines and car hire firms Free stays, free car rental, free Eurostar travel, free cruise or golf packages, free theatre tickets, free leisure vouchers, free theme park entry
Starwood Hotels and Resorts	Starwood Preferred Guest Free membership	Two points per US dollar spent on room rates Partnership airline and car hire firms Free stays, room upgrades, free room service, gift vouchers
Choice Hotels	Favoured Guest Card £15 to join	10% of accommodation bookings discounts with Budget hire car Spouse or partner stay free when sharing a room Room upgrade where available Express check in and check out Free newspaper
Hilton International	Hilton HHonours® Free membership (Approximately 6 million members)	Ten points per dollar spent at business rates 500 points per stay non business rates 250 points for travel partner Partnership with thirty two airlines and hire car firms Free stays room discounts, late check out, free newspaper, free use of health facilities

Company	Programme	Benefits
The Forte Group	MOMENTS.COM Free membership	One point for each £2 spent Free nights Promotional offers Discounts on business services
Sol Meliá	Club Amigos (Travel agent loyalty) MaS Loyalty Programme Free membership	Benefits including free stays, etc. for travel agents Distinguished guest services, free hotel stays
Hyatt Hotels and Resorts	Hyatt Golf Passport® Free membership (Approximately 2 million members)	Five points per US dollar 300 bonus points for using airline or business partners Partnership with ten airlines and car hire firm Free stays room discounts, express check in and check out, late checkout, free newspaper, free use of health facilities
Radisson Hotels World-wide	Radisson Gold Rewards ^{SM} Free membership	Points can be used at Radisson hotels, TGI Friday's, Italiann's restaurant, Country Inns and Suites by Carlson, McI World Com and Sky Mall
Marco Polo Hotels	The Tai Pan Club Must stay more than ten nights in a twelve-month period or spend $2000 or more on rooms and services (Approximately 10 000 members)	Express check-in and checkout Late checkouts, free morning coffee and newspaper, free days for spouse, discounts on services and business centre
Oberoi Hotels and Resorts	Oberoi Plus $30 fee (Approximately 750 members in Europe)	Upgrade to superior rooms, spouses can stay for free, occasional gifts
Kempinski Hotels and Resorts	Private Concierge Free	Priority check-in and checkout Guaranteed rate to corporate customers Free access to health facilities
Inter-Continental Hotels and Resorts	Six Continents Club Joining free of $100 renewable annually $35 (Approximately 100 000 members)	Free two-night weekend on joining Room upgrades Dedicated check-in desks Late checkout

Sources: Conférence and Incentive Travel (July/August 2000); *Business Traveller* (January 2000).

Conclusion

The development of sophisticated business services and loyalty programmes has been critical for the major hotel groups in an increasingly global and competitive market. The key objective of the major hotel chains is to gain loyal business customers, and the companies use an increasingly sophisticated range of distributors and promotional methods to achieve this goal.

Discussion points and essay questions

1 Discuss the likely effects that consolidation of the hotel industry will have on the provision of hotel business services in hotel chains.
2 Critically analyse the influence of technology on the business services on offer in hotels.
3 'If we can increase loyalty by even a small margin, we can increase profitability by a very large margin' (Curtis Nelson, CEO, Carlton Hospitality World-wide). Discuss the implications of this statement in relation to the marketing programme of large hotel groups.

20 The business class products of airlines

Airlines rely heavily on business people, who tend to pay higher prices for their air tickets than leisure travellers. However, these passengers are experienced air travellers who expect a range of extra services related to their needs in return for the higher fares they pay.

While not exclusively for business travellers, airlines have developed 'business class' services to meet the needs of this vitally important market segment. Since the first business class services developed in the late 1970s, these services have become ever more sophisticated. At first they focused on the flight itself but now business class passengers also enjoy a range of services on the ground too.

The business class product may now include:

- advance seat selection
- telephone check-in
- dedicated check-in desks
- extra baggage allowance
- use of a special lounge with newspapers, computer access, television and complimentary refreshments
- priority boarding
- separate cabin
- seats with extra legroom, width and angle of recline
- higher quality cabin décor
- enhanced in-flight entertainment
- higher quality food and drink
- a better cabin-crew:passenger ratio
- complimentary amenity kits
- in-flight, at-seat telephones
- at-seat – PC connections
- priority baggage collection at the destination
- frequent-flyer reward programmes.

However, there are substantial variations in the product between different airlines. If we consider legroom and seat pitch, to use the technical term, then a survey of long-haul business class services, published by *Business Traveller* magazine in 1999 showed significant differences between different carriers, as can be seen from Table 20.1.

Table 20.1   Seat pitch in business class on long-haul services by selected airlines, 1999

Airline	Aircraft	Seat pitch, centimetres	Seat pitch, inches
Aer Lingus	A330	132.0	52
Air China	B747–400	102.0	40
Air India	B747–400	96.5	38
Bangladesh	DC10	89.0	35
Garuda	B747–400	157.0	62
Lot Polish Airlines	B767–300	142.0	56
Swissair	A330	122.0	48
United	B767–300	122.0	48

Source: *Business Traveller* (May 1999).

There were also differences in seat pitch between different types of aircraft within the same airline. For example, 'Olympian', the business class product of Olympic Airways, of Greece, offered 150 centimetres/60 inches of seat pitch on its A340 aircraft, but only 104 centimeters/42 inches on its B747 aircraft (*Business Traveller*, May 1999).

The business class market is very competitive on most routes and business travellers often look to specialist magazines for consumer advice. *Business Traveller* is one such magazine. It carries out consumer surveys on business class flights and publishes the results. Its survey divides a business class flight into five sections, namely:

- first impressions (check-in)
- boarding
- seat comfort
- the flight (meals, drinks, service)
- arrival (baggage reclaim).

Each flight can score a maximum of five points for each category, thus gaining a potential maximum score of twenty-five. While not scientific, these surveys are still widely read by business travellers. In May 1999, *Business Traveller* published a survey of the long-haul business class services of a range of airlines. The results are shown in Table 20.2.

The authors have examined eight advertisements for business class services contained in the May 1999 issue of *Business Traveller* in terms of the percentage of the copy dedicated to different aspects of the airline business class product. The results are contained in Table 20.3.

In this competitive market, airlines are constantly seeking new ways of differentiating their business class product from that of their competitors.

At the same time airlines are constantly trying to make their frequent-flyer programmes more attractive by adding high-profile hotels, car hire companies and retailers to the networks, for example. However, some of these 'brand loyalty' schemes are proving less effective than hoped by the airlines as travellers shop around and join a number of such schemes.

In Europe, there is also growing competition on short-haul routes from the 'no-frills' carriers such as easyJet, Go, and Ryanair. Some companies are willing to sacrifice the 'luxuries' of business class travel to save on their travel bills.

Table 20.2 *Business Traveller* flight check of selected long-haul business class services, 1999

Airline	Route	First impressions (out of 5)	Boarding (out of 5)	Seat comfort (out of 5)	The flight (out of 5)	Arrival (out of 5)	Total (out of 25)
Aer Lingus	Chicago–London	4	5	4	4	5	22
Air New Zealand	London–Auckland	4	5	4	4	3	20
Air Zimbabwe	London–Harare	3	2	3	3	3	14
British Airways	New York–London	3	3	3	4	3	16
Canadian Airlines	London–Toronto	4	5	5	5	5	24
Cathay Pacific	London–Hong Kong	5	4	4	4	5	22
Continental Airlines	London–Newark	5	4	4	4	4	21
Malaysia Airlines	Kuala-Lumpur–London	4	2	3	2	4	15
Qatar Airways	London–Doha	4	5	5	5	4	23

Source: *Business Traveller* (May 1999).

Table 20.3 The proportion of text dedicated to different aspects of the business class product in selected advertisements in *Business Traveller*, May 1999

Airline	Seat comfort and flight	Food and drink (%)	On-board facilities (%)	Level of service (%)	Frequent-flyer programme (%)	Other (%)
United	25					75 (Size of network, quality of cabin crew)
Finnair					40	60 (Range of connections from Helsinki)
Iberia	35	20	25			20 (General/promotional text)
Delta	25					75 (General improvements to business class)
Qantas	20	10	10	15	45	(Included statements designed to show that passengers were consulted to produce the new business class product)
All Nippon Airlines			5	50		45 (Large photograph of two stewardesses)
Canadian Airlines	40	50	5			5 (availability of laptop PC access at seat)
Lot Polish Airlines	5	5		10	80	(Size of route network, on-ground services, and frequent flyer programme – two-page editorial – only one section on business class service specifically)

Source: *Business Traveller* (May 1999).

The business class market looks set to continue to be very competitive, with airlines having to be ever more innovative to justify the large price differentiation between business class and economy air travel.

Discussion points and essay questions

1 What are the advantages and disadvantages for airlines of offering a business class service?
2 How might airlines differentiate their business class product from that of their competitors in the future?

---

21 Frequent-flyer programmes – Lufthansa and Air France

Airlines are keen to encourage brand loyalty, particularly among business travellers who make regular trips. Their main weapon in the battles to attract such travellers is the frequent-flyer programme. These schemes are becoming ever more complex and important to customers and travellers. In this case study we will examine two European airline frequent-flyer programmes.

'Miles and More' – Lufthansa, Germany

This revamped programme offers rewards for those who fly frequently with the airline. The further you fly the more miles you receive, and the more expensive the ticket the more benefits you receive.

For example in 2000, an economy class ticket from Frankfurt to New York earned the traveller 3851 miles each way. Business class journeys on the same route received 7162 miles each way. A return business class fare would, therefore, earn 14 324 miles for the traveller. In mid-2000, this latter number of miles would be enough to earn the traveller a return upgrade from economy to business class between Frankfurt and Munich or a one-way upgrade to business class from Munich to Moscow or Frankfurt to Istanbul. Two such business class return flights from Frankfurt to New York would earn the traveller a free return economy ticket from Hamburg to Munich or from Karachi to Dubai.

However, members of the programme cannot only earn miles and spend miles on Lufthansa flights, but also on the services of other members of the Star Alliance – airlines which in 2000 included Air Canada, SAS, Thai International, United Airlines and Varig. Miles can also be earned and redeemed in 2000 with sixteen other airline partners.

Miles are also available and redeemable with Lufthansa partners in different sectors of the tourism industry, including, in 2000:

- four car hire companies
- fifteen hotel chains.

Miles can also be used for:

- trips in a vintage JU 52 aircraft
- using a Lufthansa pilot simulator

- tickets to Disneyland® Paris
- a day of driver training at BMW
- hot-air balloon rides.

Three classes of card are available, offering different levels of benefits, namely:

- Miles and More Card
- Frequent Traveller Card
- Senator Card.

'Frequence Plus' – Air France, France

Under the Air France card, in 2000–1, members could earn miles by flying with Air France or twelve of its partner airlines. They could also earn miles through booking a hire car with one of six companies, staying at properties owned by nine major hotel chains, using one of four telephone companies, paying bills with American Express cards or even sending flowers via Teléflora.

Let us see how a traveller might benefit from this scheme.

In August 2000 a traveller from the UK flew on a business trip to San Francisco, in L'Espace, the equivalent of business class, from London, via Paris. In doing this he or she will have earned 19 710 miles. The traveller's accommodation for four nights in San Francisco in a Sheraton hotel earned another 500 points. He or she hired a Hertz car for one day and earned another 400 miles. Our traveller changed 5000 francs into dollars at Paris with CCF Charge, earning another 500 miles. At the end of the trip our traveller has accumulated enough miles for any one of the following:

- a return economy class ticket from London to Toulouse
- a return economy class ticket on any domestic route within Mexico
- an Indian Airlines return economy class ticket on a domestic route within India
- a free night's accommodation at a Le Meridien Hotel
- a free weekend in an apartment for four or five persons in the off-peak season with Pierre et Vaccances
- a free driving lesson in a Porsche 911.

However, there are problems with frequent-flyer programmes for each of the stakeholders:

1 The airline often does not achieve brand loyalty with these schemes because travellers join more than one. Airlines therefore have to compete, expensively, with each other's frequent-flyer programme
2 The business traveller or consumer often finds these schemes complicated and gets annoyed by the numerous conditions that surround a lot of the 'free' rewards
3 The customers or employers become annoyed that they pay the bills but the traveller, their employee, gains the benefits.

Nevertheless, these schemes are expanding and are being linked to those of other sectors including hotels, car hire, leisure activities, and so on.

Even if they wanted to, airlines would probably now find it virtually impossible to abandon such schemes, which consumers have now come to expect. In the increasingly deregulated and competitive world of the airlines such incentives for travellers are likely to be with us for a long time to come.

Discussion points and essay questions

1 Discuss the costs and benefits of frequent-flyer programmes for airlines.
2 Discuss the factors which may make one airline's frequent-flyer programme more attractive to a traveller than another.

22 Airports and business travellers – Singapore Changi airport

For frequent business travellers, airports are a necessary evil. A good airport can bring extra business to a city and its locally based carriers. For example, the efficiency of Schipol, Amsterdam, makes it a popular place for UK travellers to transfer on to flights to destinations that are further afield. This brings extra passengers to the Dutch airline, KLM, and extra revenue to the airport authorities through, for example, retail sales and food and drink sales.

One of the best airports in the world for business travellers is Changi airport in Singapore. Many business travellers choose their itinerary, deliberately, to allow them to transfer flights or even stop over in Singapore. This is good for Singapore Airlines and for the airport authorities. But why is Singapore such a good airport for the business traveller?

First, it is clean, modern and airy with a relaxed but safe atmosphere. For transit passengers, the journey between flights is very efficient and stress free. If the passenger needs to change terminals for their next flight they can use the automated 'skytrain' which makes the journey in around one minute.

If the passenger has a few hours to spare in Singapore, they can take a free bus tour of the city and be back in time for their onward flight.

The airport has a range of facilities which the business traveller appreciates, including:

- a relatively inexpensive transit hotel where the traveller can rest between flights in a hotel room, with a shower, television and a wake-up call service
- a fitness centre with a gym and sauna
- various types of massage are available
- an excellent business centre offering a full range of services
- a wide variety of outlets offering all kinds of food and drink for travellers
- excellent shopping facilities in both terminals
- staff are available who speak a wide variety of international languages.

Singapore is regularly voted the best airport in the world by business travellers, some twenty years after it was first opened.

Discussion points and essay questions

1 Discuss what you consider to be probably the three most important factors which influence whether or not a business traveller will enjoy using a particular airport.
2 Select an airport with which you are familiar or which you can visit. Evaluate its strengths and weaknesses from the point of view of a business traveller.

23 The British Universities Accommodation Consortium*

The British Universities Accommodation Consortium (BUAC) is a marketing consortium that represents sixty-eight member universities across the UK. It helps the organizers of meetings and conferences to choose the correct university for their particular needs.

The conference and meeting business at universities in the UK

British universities provide a very important part of the country's contribution to the conference and meeting market, which is estimated to be worth £4–5 billion a year. The British Conference Market Trends Survey supported by the British Tourist Authority and the BUAC indicated that British universities now host more than 30 000 conferences a year. The use of universities as conference and meeting venues has been largely due to increase in levels of service and technology standards.

These universities have improved their accommodation for meetings and conferences, and often now have state-of-the-art technological systems that match the facilities on offer at major hotels. Many of the universities have invested heavily in high-quality residential accommodation. Some of the universities have even built dedicated year-round residential conference and training centres, and employed internationally recognized chefs to lead the banqueting teams.

BUAC

Details of the sixty-eight universities which are members of BUAC, and their locations, are shown in Figure 23.1.

BUAC is managed by Carole Foreman, the Executive Director, who is assisted by a small staff team. The BUAC central office is located in new purpose-built accommodation at the University of Nottingham's parkland campus. The BUAC Central Office assists international conference and events managers in their planning and organization processes. The office helps in the early stages of searching for an appropriate venue. Member universities then offer organizers their personal attention to help the event run as smoothly and efficiently as possible. The universities provide a detailed price quotation and organizers can arrange to inspect the chosen venue before confirmation of booking. A summary of the services on offer at British universities that are handled by BUAC are shown below.

---

* In January 2001 BUAC merged with Connect Venues, a similar organization promoting the facilities of academic venues. The new organization, VENUEMASTERS, has attracted 99 university and college venues based throughout the UK into its initial membership. VENUEMASTERS will continue to promote venues in the academic sector and offer a venue finding service to event organizers.

Location Map & List of Members

Our extensive choice of locations have the added benefit of excellent communication links with the rest of the country by road and rail and in most cases ample on-site parking.

1	ABERYSTWYTH	18	DERBY	
2	ASTON • Birmingham	19	DUNDEE	
3	BANGOR	20	DURHAM	
4	BATH	21	EAST ANGLIA • Norwich	
5	BELFAST • Queen's	22	EDINBURGH	
6	BIRMINGHAM	23	ESSEX • Colchester	
7	BRADFORD	24	EXETER	
8	BRISTOL	25	GLAMORGAN	
9	BRUNEL • Uxbridge	26	GLASGOW	
10	CAMBRIDGE • Conference Cambridge	27	KEELE	
11	CAMBRIDGE • Churchill	28	KENT • Canterbury	
12	CAMBRIDGE • Fitzwilliam	29	LANCASTER	
13	CAMBRIDGE • Robinson	30	LEEDS	
14	CAMBRIDGE • St John's	31	LEICESTER	
15	CAMBRIDGE Anglia Polytechnic University	32	LIVERPOOL	
16	CARDIFF	33	LIVERPOOL • John Moores	
17	CIRENCESTER Royal Agricultural College	34	LONDON • East London	
		35	LONDON • Greenwich	

36	LONDON • Kingston	52	OXFORD • Conference Oxford
37	LONDON • Middlesex	53	PORTSMOUTH
38	LONDON • North London	54	PRESTON • Central Lancashire
39	LONDON • Goldsmiths	55	READING
40	LONDON • Imperial	56	ST ANDREWS
41	LONDON • King's	57	SALFORD • Greater Manchester
42	LONDON Queen Mary/Westfield	58	SCARBOROUGH
43	LONDON • Royal Holloway	59	SHEFFIELD
44	LONDON • School of Economics	60	STIRLING
45	LOUGHBOROUGH	61	STRATHCLYDE
46	MANCHESTER	62	SURREY • Guildford
47	MANCHESTER Business School	63	SUSSEX • Brighton
48	MANCHESTER • U.M.I.S.T.	64	SWANSEA
49	NEWCASTLE	65	ULSTER
50	NEWPORT • Shropshire Harper Adams University College	66	WARWICK • Coventry
51	NOTTINGHAM	67	WYE • Ashford, Kent
		68	YORK

Figure 23.1 BUAC location map and list of members
Source: BUAC marketing literature.

Conferences, training, meetings, groups and exhibitions at British universities

'BUAC members lead the market with the most diverse choice of facilities at the most competitive prices.'

'BUAC is firmly established as the first choice of countless companies and professional organisations ... many of whom re-book on an annual basis.'

'The high standards and the value for money offered by British universities attract newcomers every year, who add to the ever-growing list of satisfied BUAC customers.'

Nationwide choice

'Whatever the event or gathering BUAC will have a venue to suit':

- over sixty highly individual venues throughout the UK – both traditional and modern
- locations include major city centres, towns, coastal sites and rural areas.

First-class facilities

'As befits centres of excellence in learning, British universities offer high standards in purpose-built meeting and study facilities':

- large, tiered lecture theatres; seminar rooms for plenary and syndicate sessions
- meeting rooms with adjacent space for display areas
- video-conferencing facilities
- audiovisual aids with technical support
- television and film studios
- language laboratories
- computer workshops.

Accommodation

'The comfortable, modestly priced accommodation offered by British universities will ease the pressure on any budget':

- full-board, self-catering or bed and breakfast options
- choice of single study bedrooms, twin rooms or family rooms
- thousands of new rooms, many *en suite*, being built every year.

'Whether your gathering is for a handful or for hundreds, most British universities can provide a self-contained centre where your delegates can meet, eat, socialise and sleep.'

Catering

'Fast turnaround for large numbers . . . an intimate lunch for a few . . . or a silver service banquet for hundreds . . . a British university will have something to suit your taste':

- waitress service restaurants
- formal dining rooms
- self-service cafeterias
- coffee bars.

For all events, professional chefs are on hand to arrange theme dinners and banquets. Many universities now offer comprehensive selections of wines to complement a meal.

Leisure facilities

'Combine business with pleasure at a British university by taking advantage of the sports and leisure facilities':

- bars and lounges
- television and games rooms
- indoor and outdoor sports facilities including squash, badminton and tennis courts
- sports pitches and athletic tracks
- indoor swimming pools and fitness centres.

Conference team

'At every British university you can rely upon the professional support of a dedicated conference team. Committed to meeting your needs before and during your event, your team members will do all they can to make your event a success':

- conference co-ordination
- sports and outdoor programmes
- spouse programmes
- team-building events
- group activities and excursions
- party events
- banquets with after-dinner speakers.

Year-round facilities

'Many universities now offer year-round facilities. Often custom-built, these centres provide high standards of accommodation coupled with the most modern exhibition and conference facilities.'

'Most universities also offer year-round non-residential facilities for day meetings, training courses, product launches, social events, and banquets.'

'Easy access by road, rail and air with ample on-site parking at the majority of venues are added bonuses.'

Group accommodation

'University accommodation is ideally suited for group visits. The range and style of accommodation available is extensive with catering options to satisfy budgets both large and small. The sports and leisure facilities will be at the group's disposal and special activities such as sports evenings or outings can often be arranged for larger groups. Whether a holiday or business group you can make full use of the amenities on and around the campus such as banks, shops, launderettes and cafeterias.'

Residential courses

'For a totally different style of break you should try a British University Activity and Study Holiday. These specialised residential courses, encompassing sport, leisure and study are now available at many universities.'

Source: *British University Venues*, BUAC (1999).

Organizations that have used BUAC and British university accommodation for conferences and meetings

A large range of organizations from the UK use BUAC to help to arrange their conferences and events using university accommodation. Some examples of these organizations are shown below.

The reasons for UK-based organizations using BUAC and university accommodation for their conferences and events

'We have very specific requirements which certainly some universities can meet' said Freya Levy, events co-ordinator with the *Environment Council* which is an independent charity dedicated to enhancing and protecting Britain's environment through building awareness, dialogue and effective solutions.

'Comfortable and affordable meeting and residential accommodation are a high priority – along with a lot of wall space! Our courses usually involve a maximum of 20 delegates for between one and six days, and feature training in stakeholder dialogue and environmental facilitation techniques. The format includes extensive use of flip charts and delegates' contributions made on big sheets of paper mounted round the walls.

We make regular use, for example, of Wast Hills House, a country-house style residential conference centre which has just become part of Birmingham University's Conference Park. Some of the Council's events involve up to 150 participants – which makes solving the wall-space demands a bit trickier. The BUAC Venue Search service is very helpful, as is their *Annual Guide to British University Venues*', she added.

'BUAC members certainly offer facilities that interest us', said Roger Llewellyn, conference manager with the *Royal College of Psychiatrists*. 'And the BUAC Show is always a helpful way to make contact with pre-researched members and venues. I had three or four locations in mind for events taking place over the next couple of years – and I was able to see them all at the show.'

'Our events involve anything from 80 to 500 delegates – sometimes even more. In an ideal world we need destinations that will motivate overseas participants, as well as UK delegates, to take the time and undertake the cost, to attend. That means attractive towns and cities with our business and residential accommodation within very easy reach. Unfortunately, some university-based year-round centres are not located close enough to outside attractions, and other facilities are only available in vacation periods.

As with all medically associated meetings, there is a mushrooming demand for the very latest in communication and presentation technologies – PowerPoint facilities, for example, have made OHPs and similar projection systems, virtually redundant. The other big challenge is to match delegates' expectations of good-quality hotel-standard facilities and service standards, with low cost.'

The *Institute of Electrical Engineers* makes regular use of universities' cost-conscious accommodation and comprehensive technological capabilities for super-technical events involving anything from 100 delegates to 400, typically spanning two to five days.

'I have used the Venue Search in the past and found it very helpful,' said IEE conference executive Molly Corner. 'In the past year we have used York twice and Bath for one event – their respective conference teams gave us absolutely tremendous back-up.'

Source: News@buac

The use of British universities by international organizations is also an important part of the market and two examples of this are shown below.

Elderhostel – USA

An example of an overseas organization using universities as a conference site.

Elderhostel is a non-profit-making organization that helps adults over 55 and their partners gain an educational experience. The organization is based in Boston, USA, and in 1993, the organization established a base in Canterbury, UK. The Elderhostel's Programme Manager is based in Canterbury and she organizes all the programmes for the UK which are held in all sorts of venues but particularly in universities that are members of BUAC.

Elderhostel has used university venues over a number of years, including:

- Edinburgh University, Pollock Hall
- London School of Economics, Roseberg Hall
- University of Wales, Bangor, Friddoedd site
- Durham University
- York University
- Strathclyde University
- Stirling University
- Dundee University.

The organization use the universities to develop their schedules because they offer the benefits of everything being under one roof. The BUAC central referrals system and annual show allows Elderhostel staff to source new locations and sort out booking and organizational arrangements. Universities also offer Elderhostel a much more viable proposition compared to the cost at hotels. The use of different universities means that each programme that is developed is unique. Two examples of schedules that were based on universities are shown below:

Britain's Art and Culture

- Action-packed days in Edinburgh, Bangor in North Wales and at the London School of Economics.
- Lectures about Edinburgh's architecture, Scottish paining, the new Scottish Parliament, Celtic bards and harpers, life in Tudor-times Wales, and all about London's Museums.
- Trips to Stirling Castle, St Andrews' golf courses, Abbotsford House, Beaumaris and Bangor, Caernarfon Castle, Snowdonia, the British Museum in London – plus evenings packed with traditional entertainment.

Discovering Gardens

- Insights into how gardens and rural landscapes were created in medieval times, for the Italian Renaissance, and through the Victorian and Edwardian eras.
- Visits to Hampton Court, Sissinghurst Castle, Chipping Campden and the Cotswolds, Painswick Village and Gloucester Docks, Bath and Blenheim Palace Gardens.
- And lots more.

Source: News@buac

AXA Group – France

An example of an overseas organization using a UK university as a conference base.

The AXA Group is a Paris-based company that employs 130 000 people in fifty countries worldwide. The company is a world leader in insurance and financial services.

The company wanted to hold an international network event for their executive managers and the event was held at the historic and atmospheric University of St Andrews on Scotland's Fife coast. The Summer School was organized to improve the understanding of a world in evolution and for the managers to reflect on what would become the key factors of performance in the future. These two themes were analysed by delegates who were accompanied by scientists, economists, philosophers, sociologists and managers.

A complex business programme involving parallel lecture sessions and workshops was accompanied by a social programme which included dinner at Prestonfield House hotel, golf, folk-singing, highland dancing, whisky tastings, organ recitals, walking tours, receptions and a traditional Scottish banquet.

Jean-Louis Viarguis, HR Manager with AXA Corporate Human Resources explained why he chose St Andrews as the location for this prestigious conference: 'For 1998 we were looking for an old university setting anywhere in Europe, outside France, and one which could offer accommodation and business facilities for 400 delegates. It was a deliberate decision to seek an ancient setting because we were working on the twenty-first century development of our company and wanted a challenging and interesting contrast to that theme. We also wanted to give the event a definite feeling of "going back to university", in order to enhance a sense of learning, communication and fun.

We needed to be close to an international airport because delegates were coming in from all over the world. We looked at universities in Germany, Belgium, Spain and other parts of both the UK and Ireland. In the end we chose St Andrews not just for its location and facilities, but for its excellent customer services. Nothing was too much trouble, everyone was just so keen to meet our requirements.'

The delegates also enjoyed the academic setting of the university and despite the rain, the conference proved to be very successful with delegates leaving in an enlightened frame of mind.

Source: News@buac

Promotion of BUAC

BUAC carries out extensive promotion activity to help the member universities to grow their conference and events business. This promotional activity includes:

- A yearly guide to British University Venues.
- The BUAC Show held annually in London during October. This allows organizers to review all the facilities on offer from all member organizations of BUAC.

- News@buac – a review of recent conferences held at British universities and general news items published and sent to a mailing list four times a year.
- www.buac.co.uk – a web site that shows all the latest news on availability and special offers.

Conclusions

BUAC has been very successful as a marketing consortium in developing the business of conference and events at British universities. This business has grown alongside the development of the facilities and services at the universities. Universities now provide a very important source of accommodation and events originating from the UK and internationally.

Discussion points and essay questions

1 Discuss the advantages that a British university can offer to a conference and event organizer.
2 Discuss the advantages that the marketing consortium (BUAC) offers its member universities in the development of their conference and events business.
3 Critically analyse the contribution that a marketing consortium can offer in the conference and events business.

The authors would like to thank Carole Forman, Executive Director of BUAC, for her help with the writing of this case study.

24 Disneyland® Paris Business Solutions

Disneyland® Paris resort has been developing as a major European theme park over the past decade. The resort was developed with the idea that visitors to the theme park would stay on site after visiting the theme park, at one of the hotels that were built to accompany the theme park development. It had always been the objective of the Disneyland® Paris management that they would develop business and incentive travel within the resort to improve occupancy and secure financial stability.

The Disneyland® Paris Business Solutions division was established in 1996 with the aim of developing this business for the company. This case study reviews the facilities on offer at the Disneyland® Paris resort and looks at the type of client that is using these facilities.

Disneyland® Paris: an ideal location for a business conference

The Disneyland® Paris resort has an ideal location for the development of the business conference market. Disneyland® Paris was designed to be in a central location in Europe and with visitors coming to the resort from all over Europe and beyond.

The Disneyland® Paris Convention Centre is very well served for transport in Europe. The resort can easily be reached by plane, train or car. Roissy Charles-de-Gaulle and Orly international airports are close by. Rail links from Disneyland® Paris Marne-le-Vallée station are excellent and the RER service links the resort to Paris centre in thirty minutes. TGV services also link the Marne-le-Vallée station to main cities in France and other major destinations across Europe. The station also has direct links to the cities of London and Brussels via the Eurostar service that was launched in 1996.

The facilities of Disneyland® Paris for business conferences

The Disneyland® Paris resort is ideally placed for the development of business and incentive clients. The resort has seven themed hotels with a total of 5700 rooms including the Disneyland® Hotel, the art-deco style Hotel New York and the New England themed Hotel Newport Bay Club (Figure 24.1). Business clients of Disneyland® Paris can therefore choose their preferred hotel and conference centre, and can even theme and brand their own event.

Figure 24.1   Hotel New York® and Newport Bay Club®

A detailed review of the facilities on offer at Disneyland® Paris for the business client are shown below.

Key facts and figures: Disneyland® Paris Business Solutions

1 Two convention centres with 10 500 m²/112 900 sq. ft of meeting space – ninety-five meeting rooms for 10 to 2500 delegates – comprising the Hotel New York® Convention Center and the Newport Bay Club® Convention Center:
   (a) Hotel New York® Convention Center has 5000m²/53 760 sq. ft total floor area; two plenary rooms/ballrooms (1600 m²/17 200 sq. ft and 2000 m²/21 520 sq. ft); fifty-five meeting rooms.
   (b) Newport Bay Club® Convention Center has 5500m²/59 140 sq. ft total floor area; 1 plenary room/ballroom (1800 m²/19 355 sq. ft); twenty-nine meeting rooms; one exhibition hall (3000 m²/32 260 sq. ft).
   Four meeting rooms are also available at the Disneyland® Hotel and six at the Sequoia Lodge®.
2 Special events for 10 to 15 000 delegates. Private events in the theme park, themed evening in the park, gala dinners and shows in the ballrooms of the two convention centres or in the Disney® Village.
3 Seven themed hotels with 5700 rooms:
   (a) Disneyland® Hotel (496 rooms, 18 suites)
   (b) Hotel New York® (563 rooms, 27 suites)

(c) Newport Bay Club® (1093 rooms, 13 suites)

(d) Sequoia Lodge® (1011 rooms, 14 suites)

(e) Hotel Cheyenne® (1000 rooms)

(f) Hotel Santa Fe® (1000 rooms)

(g) Davy Crockett Ranch® (498 bungalows)

4 Disneyland® Paris Business Solutions: dedicated to corporate events. A 240-strong, multilingual team is entirely dedicated to conferences and incentives.

The hotels and restaurants combined with those available in the Disney® Village and the theme park offer business clients more than fifty different places to eat and each restaurant can be chosen for its style of cuisine and for the required timing.

The Hotel New York and Newport Bay Club Convention Centers have been designed to host meetings and events of every size from 20 to 2500 participants. Both conference centres have approximately 5000 sq. m of fully modular space including a large reception hall and the latest in audiovisual and telecommunications technology. The venue can offer everything from multi-image presentations to global satellite links in conjunction with their official partner, France Telecom.

A conference with a large number of delegates can be housed in the large number of syndicate rooms that are available on the site. Specialist requirements for particular clients are also accommodated at the site. One example of this was the recent IBM conference that required a large exhibition site. The outdoor rink in front of Hotel New York was drained for this event. Flooring was laid and a large marquee was erected to house the in-house exhibition.

The advantages of the Disneyland® Paris resort

There are many advantages to using the Disneyland® Paris resort for business conferences and incentive events. These advantages have been summarized by the company and are shown below:

Conference and incentive business at Disneyland® Paris: the advantages

- A superb location at the heart of Europe, 20 miles east of Paris.
- Easily reached by air, train – including Eurostar – or by car.
- A unique mix of conference space, hotel accommodation and leisure facilities
- 5700-room hotel capacity.
- Tailor-made conference and corporate events.
- Multilingual professional staff.
- A key contact working with the client from the design stage through to the actual event.
- Unrivalled facilities and services.
- A spectacular portfolio of gala evenings, shows and entertainment.

Source: Disneyland® Paris Business Solutions

This list shows that there are many advantages for the business travel organizer of using the Disneyland® Paris resort. One of the key advantages for the resort is that it provides a world-class convention location where business can be mixed with leisure. The resort offers recreational activity for everyone. There is a twenty-seven hole championship golf course, floodlit tennis courts, indoor and outdoor swimming pools, ice skating, fitness centres and saunas, steam baths and exercise machines, beauty salons, and the rides and attractions of the theme park itself. This offers the client the possibility to play golf on one occasion and then experience the thrills of the theme park rides, such as Space Mountain on another occasion.

Group entertainment events are very popular with corporate customers and can range from 'Big Band' style gala dinners to competitive treasure hunts that foster teamwork. Large groups can enjoy the benefits of special exclusive evenings in the park with any of the five themed lands being for the client's exclusive use during the programme.

The business at Disneyland® Paris from launch to the present day

The conference and incentive business has created substantial business for the Disneyland® Paris resort since its launch. Figures for 1998 show that Disneyland® Paris has become one of the top conference destinations in Europe. In 1998, more than 1400 events took place at the resort ranging from 10 to 3000 delegates in size and this resulted in 165 000 room nights. The UK has become the strongest European market for conventions at Disneyland® Paris, after the local French market.

This increase in business was strongly linked to the opening of a new conference centre at the Newport Bay Club® in October 1997 which doubled the resort's capacity for conferences. The growth in the UK market has been a particular strength in the total development of European business. Reina Herschdorfer, the Director of Convention and Incentive Sales UK at the time, summarizes the reasons for this development:

> Disneyland Paris® is often in the unique position of being the only non-UK destination to be considered as a conference venue as it is seen as an extension of the UK rather than an overseas destination. The Newport Bay Club® has also proved to be a huge success for our market, partly due to the New England theming, but also the excellent conference facilities available.

The growth of business from the UK has been a particular feature of the total increase in sales. Scrutiny of the clients for events held at Disneyland® Paris over recent years (Table 24.1) also show that there have been many important clients from other countries.

Organization of the business conference

The Disneyland® Paris Business Solutions operation is managed from an on-site office in Paris. There is a director here who has overall control of the business and manages three members of a closely knit team. The business in the UK is developed from a UK office

Table 24.1   Disneyland® Paris Business Solutions' clients, 1998–9

7–14 July 1998	Gillette – a meeting of Gillette's distributors and clients to coincide with the World Club
21 July–4 August 1998	A meeting of European distributors of John Deere, the German-based company that manufactures agricultural equipment and supplies
24–27 August 1998	CYCLEUROPE.*SA* – a meeting of distributors and retailers
24–27 August 1998	Sales seminar for the sales force of Cassenne pharmaceutical laboratories
19–26 September 1998	IBM Transaction and Messaging – technical talks, exhibition and cocktail party
10–17 October 1998	Planet Tivoli (Tivoli System) – a major annual event bringing together customers and partners
16–17 October 1998	European Food Summit – symposium and discussion on the subject 'Food, health, well being', bringing together decision-makers from the food industry, the retail sector, the pharmaceuticals and cosmetics industries
25–27 October 1998	European Security Forum – annual convention of members of the association
27–28 November 1998	Annual Buuygues Group Managers' Meeting
5 December 1998	Annual Skippers Meeting and Press Conferences
6–10 December 1998	PriceWaterhouseCooper – Legal and Tax Departments Conference
7–10 January 1999	Nycomed–Amersham–Imaging Europe – International Region Sales Conference 1999
19–20 January 1999	Volkswagen France – the new 'Beetle' launch for Volkswagen dealers
4–8 February 1999	Business Centre Regus – company annual meeting
11–12 March 1999	The Treasurers' Forum 1999 – International company treasurers conference
21–24 March 1999	FNSAGA. Federation Nationale des Syndicats d'Agents Generaux d'Assurance – national conference and annual general meeting
26–29 May 1999	Bochringer Ingelheim – pharmaceuticals company. Worldwide meeting.

Source: Disneyland® Paris Business Solutions

managed by a director who has an assistant who helps with day-to-day activities. The management structure of the organization is shown in Figure 25.2.

The management of a particular conference or event on behalf of a client is managed by one individual manager from the team who is appointed following the contracted agreement. He or she oversees the business and negotiates with the client concerning plans, special requirements, etc. The manager also offers additional services to the client as required, shown below.

On-site office:

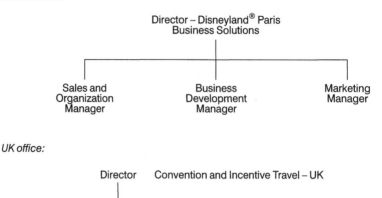

UK office:

Director   Convention and Incentive Travel – UK

Assistant   Convention and Incentive Travel – UK

Figure 24.2   The management structure of the Disneyland® Paris Business Solutions staff

---

Additional services that are offered to Disneyland® Paris business clients

Incentives

A range of incentives are on offer to clients. These include:

- a stay at Disneyland Paris
- gift certificates
- passports to the theme park
- group rates
- gifts.

Entertainment

A range of entertainments are on offer to the conference organizer. These include:

- treasure hunts
- happy hours
- exclusive use of part of the theme park
- dinner shows
- gala evenings
- Disney® Village events
- sport leisure and relaxation event
- trips to Paris.

Source: Disneyland® Paris Business Solutions

Promotion of Disneyland® Paris Business Solutions

The business is promoted in a number of ways to their clients and potential clients. These methods include:

- a full rage of brochures and printed material explaining different aspects of the products
- a specially designed CD-ROM that shows prospective clients the range of products and services on offer
- a Disneyland® Paris Business Solutions newsletter that is produced every month and sent out to existing/potential clients
- direct promotion with individual clients and incentive houses
- a web site – www.dlpbusiness.com

The web site, launched in January 1999, gives business clients everything they need to know about planning a conference at Disneyland® Paris. The site was specifically designed with the conference planner in mind and includes comprehensive information about the convention centres at both hotels.

The web site also outlines all the resort hotels, the various shows on offer and entertainment incentive products, as well as maps, function-room layouts, capacities, technical services, etc. A news page features the latest offers and new services. The service also allows a client to check for availability, rates and brochures.

Conclusions

Disneyland® Paris has been very effective at developing business trade for their theme park operation. The development of this business has been particularly focused on the UK, although clients have come from all over Europe. The development of this business has allowed the company to boost capacity in their hotels and make contribution to overall improvement in financial performance.

Discussion points and essay questions

1. Discuss the ways in which the development of conference and incentive travel can help in the overall strategy of a visitor attraction such as Disneyland® Paris.
2. Discuss the ways in which the Disneyland® Paris Business Solution promotes itself to potential clients. Evaluate the importance of the different methods of promotion that are used.
3. Disneyland® Paris has the advantage of being able to offer business clients the opportunity to combine business and leisure during the same event. Critically evaluate the reasons why this feature is particularly important for the development of conference and incentive business.

The authors would like to thank Carlo Olejniczak, Marketing Manager, Disneyland® Paris Business Solutions for help with the writing of this case study.

25 LEGOLAND® Windsor (UK)

LEGOLAND® Windsor is a theme park situated in the south of England, which was opened in 1996 by the LEGO Group. The primary business of the theme park is to entertain families with young children, and the majority of people who visit the park are there for leisure. The company has, however, developed a corporate business. Corporate clients spend, on average, more at the park but the management recognize that this business must not interfere with the general running of the park. The park is graced by an elegant house, St Leonard's Mansion, which forms the centrepiece for the development of the corporate leisure and hospitality business. LEGOLAND® does not have any accommodation on site, although the company can arrange overnight accommodation for corporate visitors either in Windsor or the surrounding area.

Historical background to the LEGO® Group

Ole Kirk Christiansen founded the LEGO® Group in Billund, Denmark in the 1930s. He had the idea that he could make learning for children both fun and educational, and started the business by developing wooden toys that fitted together. He devised the name LEGO® from two Danish words 'Leg Godt' which means play well. It was also discovered later that 'lego' in Latin means 'I put together' or 'I assemble'.

A very interesting development of the company was when his son, Godtfred Kirk Christiansen, decided to convert the wooden toys into plastic injection moulded versions in 1947, and the modern LEGO® bricks were launched in 1949, sold under the name 'Automatic Building Bricks'.

The development of the LEGO® Group has been rapid over the past forty years, and it is now a leading name in the international toy industry. LEGO® toys are now sold in more than 60 000 shops in 138 countries and there are five product programmes (brands) – LEGO PRIMO®, LEGO DUPLO®, LEGO SYSTEM®, LEGO TECHNIC® and LEGO DACTA®. The LEGO® Group continues to be innovative in its developments and is constantly producing new ideas, new methods of building and new ideas of learning.

The LEGO® Group is an international company, but it is still owned by the original Danish family. The group has fundamental respect for children and has the motto 'Only the best is good enough'. It was a natural extension of the LEGO® toy business for the group to expand into the theme park business where children and adults could have an educational but fun experience.

LEGOLAND® parks

A brief history of the LEGOLAND® parks is shown below.

LEGOLAND® parks: the story so far

1968	LEGOLAND® opens in Billund – 6 million bricks – over 600 000 visitors in first season.
1970	Billy Smart circus family opens the Windsor Safari Park.
1977–88	Windsor Safari Park changes ownership several times.
1989	The LEGO® Group – research begins for developing other LEGOLAND® Parks – over 1000 sites considered.
1990	LEGOLAND® Billund – over 1 million guests.
1992	Windsor Safari Park goes into receivership. The 150-acre site near Windsor to be location of first new LEGOLAND® park outside Denmark.
1992–3	New homes secured for all the safari park animals. LEGOLAND® Windsor – planning, design, site preparation plus model design and construction begins.
1993	LEGOLAND® Billund – 1 284 828 guests.
1994	Construction begins – services, foundations and infrastructure.
1995	Big Ben placed in Miniland – one year to go. Buildings, rides, attractions all become established. LEGOLAND® Billund – now 43 million bricks – over 1.3 million guests.
1996	Final installations, final touches, recruitment of LEGOLAND® team.
March 1996	Grand opening of LEGOLAND® Windsor – 25 million bricks. First season – over 1.4 million guests.
1999	Projected opening of first park in the USA – LEGOLAND® Carlsbad, near San Diego, California.

Source: Legoland® Windsor, *Souvenir Guidebook*.

It can be seen from this history that the group developed the first LEGOLAND® Park in their home country, Denmark. LEGOLAND® Windsor was the second park to be opened, closely followed by the third park in San Diego, California. A fourth park, LEGOLAND® Germany, situated in Günzberg is also on schedule to open to the public in June 2002.

The land for LEGOLAND® Windsor was purchased when the Windsor Safari Park went into liquidation in 1992. The park is set within a park and borders the Crown Estate owned by the Royal Family. The park is also home to St Leonard's Mansion, an elegant house that was built in the 1700s. This house has had an interesting history and has gradually been upgraded since the 1700s. The American auto manufacturer Horace Dodge upgraded the house with a majestic façade and lavish interiors. Joseph Kennedy and his family lived in the house from 1937 to 1940 while he was acting as ambassador to the UK. The Windsor Safari Park company occupied the house from 1969 to 1992, and the house and surrounding park was purchased in 1993 by the LEGO® Group.

LEGOLAND® Windsor today

LEGOLAND® Windsor is aimed at families with children aged 2–12. The park is divided into five main areas. The *Imagination Centre* allows children to build LEGO® models and try them out. *Miniland* is an area where twelve scenes from Europe have been recreated using 20 million LEGO® bricks. *Duplo® Garden* is aimed at younger children and has animated models that the children can operate. *LEGO® Traffic* is sponsored by Vauxhall® and allows children [and adults] to drive motorized cars. *My Town* is a town that has been created using the LEGO® town play themes. *Wild Woods* incorporates a number of rides particularly aimed at older children. *Creation Centre* incorporates 'Racers' new for 2001 and also enables guests to see the LEGO® model makers in action.

There are a range of catering outlets dotted around the park. These include *The Hill Top Café* that offers a range of freshly prepared drinks and food. *Papa Mole's Ice Cream and Coffee Shop*, *Pasta Patch* that offers fresh pasta and *Harbourside Restaurant* that offers baked potatoes, stir fry, salads, pastas and cakes.

Corporate events at LEGOLAND® Windsor

The educational theme of the LEGOLAND® park and the presence of St Leonard's Mansion, has allowed the sales management team at the park to develop corporate events. The park provides a new and exciting venue for family-oriented corporate events: company fun days, themed evenings, client hospitality and team-building programmes, and association days. The park has employed a corporate sales manager to develop this business and corporate sales have developed as a result.

Details of the corporate events on offer are shown below.

Exercise your imagination

Meetings and conferences

The Mansion House offers two meeting rooms: the JFK Drawing Room for up to 120 guests and the Boardroom for twelve. Meetings can also be arranged at certain times of the year in the theatres within the park.

Corporate hospitality and fun days

The JFK Drawing Room and adjoining terrace are ideal for entertaining a maximum of 300 guests with a barbecue or informal buffet. The attractions of the park and the JFK Drawing Room make an ideal combination for company fun days and corporate hospitality. The Picnic Grove and My Town Marquee are alternative areas for entertaining – both are right in the heart of the park.

Themed dinners

Areas of the park can be used privately after it closes for themed dinners which include the rides and attractions as part of the entertainment. Themes include the Cowboy Adventure Barbecue, starting with a ride on the log flume, and Medieval Merry Makers Evening, complete with the Dragon Roller Coaster. The park also lends itself to a range of other themes and ideas.

Team-building and motivation

LEGOLAND® Windsor is an inspirational place for team-building activities including workshops using LEGO® DACTA and LEGO® MINDSTORMS. With over 150 acres of park there is also plenty of space for outdoor pursuits.

Company magazine voucher promotions

Vouchers organized alongside text and pictures in company magazines can include a money-off promotion giving discounts on the gate on arrival at the park.

It can be seen that the park offers a range of corporate activities, from serious meetings and conferences in the JFK Drawing Room to fun events incorporating some of the activities in the park. Two examples of the special evening themed meal package – the Cowboy Adventure Barbecue and the Medieval Merry Makers Evening are shown below.

LEGOLAND® Windsor evening themed meal packages

Medieval Merry Makers Evening

Follow in the footsteps of St George and pursue the dreaded Dragon into the LEGOLAND® Castle, then join the fun in the medieval courtyard with the King and the Royal Court followed by feasting at the Knight's Table – beware the Dragon may strike at any time!

As a Medieval Merry Maker for the night, your evening includes:

- exclusive use of the Castleland section of the park throughout the evening, including use of the Dragon Ride
- the King and Royal Costumed Characters to assist you with your merry-making!
- a themed medieval meal served at the Knight's Table
- a gift from the King to remind you of your merry-making!

Menu:

- Castle Garden Rich Broth
- The King's Feast of Spit Roasted Meats or the Queen's Vegetarian Delicacy with fresh seasonal vegetables from the Castle Kitchens
- Damsel's Desserts
- Dragon Fired Roasted Coffee.

Cowboy Adventure Barbecue

It's hoe down time in the Wild Woods, enjoy the fun of panning for gold in the Gold Wash, get a little wet on the Pirate Falls and have a spin with the Spider.

As a Cowboy for the night, your evening includes:

- exclusive use of the Wild Woods section of the park throughout the evening, including use of the Pirate Falls Log Flume, Spinning Spider and the Gold Wash where guests can pan for gold
- Costumed Characters and additional entertainment to ensure that all guests 'Go Wild in the West'
- a themed barbecue meal served from the Crossed Ribs restaurant.

Menu:

- tantalizing Western Broth – *to get any Cowboy or girl off to a yee-har start*
- meat and vegetarian selection from the Cowboy's Grill accompanied by Crossed Ribs Salad Selection with either Jacket or Baked Sweet Potatoes – *a real taste of the west*
- choice of Classic American Pies – *a sweet tasty end*
- strong Western Coffee.

Source: LEGOLAND® Windsor.

The LEGOLAND® Windsor park also offers corporate clients the opportunity to have the exclusive use of the park and catering can be arranged to suit the particular event.

LEGOLAND® Windsor has also developed a series of team-building icebreakers, incentives and computer workshops that can be built into a corporate visit to the park. Details of these are shown below.

LEGOLAND® Windsor team-building, icebreakers, incentives and computer workshops

LEGOLAND® Windsor is an inspirational place to host a meeting, seminar or conference, and during your time using the facilities, you should take advantage of the endless activities available for icebreakers, team-building and incentives.

All activities can be tailored to your individual needs to assist in several areas, from delegates just having fun, to practical assessments of delegates' achievements with the various activities available.

We don't believe we have covered every idea – so if there is something in particular you would like us to investigate, please ask!

Team-building and icebreakers
Mosaic Magic
Approx. time guide 10–20 mins.
Equipment: LEGO® board and various LEGO® tiles. Each tile has a coloured shape stamped on it. Fully portable for use in meeting rooms and workshops.
Aim: To form a pattern with the tiles so that no two patterns or colours are connected.

Logical Logos

Approx. time guide 20–30 mins.
Equipment: Buckets of LEGO®. Fully portable for use in meeting rooms and workshops.
Aim: To build your company logo out of LEGO®.

Explain and Build

Approx. time guide 10–15 mins.
Equipment: Several LEGO® bricks to make a small model. Fully portable for use in meeting rooms and workshops.
Aim: Secretly to build a model with the given number of bricks, then describe your model to a partner without them seeing your model, so they can build a copy.

Get Moving

Approx. time guide 25 mins.
Equipment: LEGO® bricks and Speed Ramp Race Track. Dedicated freestyle workshop exercise.
Aim: Delegates have to construct vehicles from the LEGO® DACTA kits. The models are constructed and then raced on the speed ramp. Delegates then get an opportunity to improve their vehicles for the second race. Points are scored based on the average score from both races.

Tall Towers

Approx. time guide 25 mins.
Equipment: LEGO® DUPLO bricks and Earthquake Simulator Boards. Dedicated freestyle workshop exercise.
Aim: Delegates have to construct towers from the DUPLO bricks. The objective is to build the tallest, strongest and cheapest tower that can withstand the Earthquake Simulator Boards. Points are scored based on the number of bricks used and the length of time the tower stands.

Miniland Quiz

Approx. time guide 20–40 mins.
Equipment: Pen, questions paper and Miniland!
Aim: Miniland is an area of the park built from 20 million LEGO® bricks. The quiz is centred on the European sights including Brussels, Amsterdam, Paris and London. The quiz is designed to make delegates look at the model-making in more detail.

Treasure Trail

Approx. time guide 60 mins.
Equipment: Pen and questions paper.
Aim: The quiz is designed for guests to get to see the whole park by following clues and answering questions.

Pan for Gold

Equipment: Gold Pan and the Gold Wash in the park.

Aim: As part of LEGOLAND® Windsor one of the attractions is a series of streams filled with gold nuggets. Guests have to pan for the gold in traditional Western style with a metal pan. Once they have collected enough gold, the gold is weighed and if guests have panned enough nuggets they can exchange the gold for a medallion.

Incentives

Miniland

Miniland is at the heart of LEGOLAND® Windsor and is made of over 20 million LEGO® bricks. Many European countries are represented in Miniland, including Belgium, Italy, Germany, Netherlands, France, Sweden and Denmark, plus several areas of the UK including Edinburgh Castle, Cornwall, Stonehenge, Leeds Castle, Brighton and London. If you are launching an incentive to one of these areas then why not bring your team to LEGOLAND® to launch the incentive and host your 'kick off' meeting. A team photograph around Sacré Coeur is an excellent way to get your team rolling to earn their incentive to Paris.

The Dragon and the Pirate Falls

These are two of the main rides at LEGOLAND® Windsor and both offer team photo opportunities at critical points around the ride – an excellent, fun way to get your team together.

Prices for the activities above are available on request and are based on number of delegates attending, time of year and other areas of the park being used

Computer workshop activities

MINDSTORMS®

Approx. time guide 25 mins.

The newest LEGO® product launches LEGO® into the next century. LEGOLAND® Windsor is home to one of only three Mindstorms centres in the world. The objective of MINDSTORMS is to follow a computer program to build a LEGO® robot.

This is a challenging, mental exercise that is also a race against your opponents.

LEGO® DACT

Approx. time guide 25 mins.

This LEGO® product also incorporates the use of electronics. Delegates are faced with the task of constructing a LEGO® electronic device following a computer program. The real test comes when your equipment is tested. All models built can be applied to equipment used in every industry, such as gears and lifting mechanisms.

Source: LEGOLAND® marketing literature.

The educational nature of the park allows this type of development for corporate business.

Organization and accommodation

The corporate sales team at LEGOLAND® Windsor will help clients to develop their own corporate events and incentives. The park does not have accommodation on site and corporate guests have to arrange their own accommodation in Windsor or the surrounding area. The sales team has developed a specially designed brochure of accommodation in co-operation with the Southern Tourist Board. This provides clients with a list of quality-assured accommodation within easy reach of LEGOLAND® Windsor.

The brochure gives information about the Royal Windsor Information Centre that offers a seven-day accommodation hotline.

Promotion of the LEGOLAND® Windsor corporate business

The corporate business is marketed by way of exhibitions, advertisements and three regional salespeople who, with the travel trade, associations and charities, seek to educate businesses about the LEGOLAND® Corporate Experience. Once the business has been won, the details of the particular event are discussed and an operations team makes sure that the event meets the client's expectations on the day.

Conclusions

LEGOLAND® Windsor is a very successful theme park that has managed to develop a substantial leisure business for families and children. It has continued to develop other sources of business alongside the leisure business. Corporate hospitality is one part of this business development. Sales to the corporate trade have continued to grow substantially and the park management has been able to capitalize on the educational and fun themes of the different parts of the LEGOLAND® Windsor Park. Co-operation with the Southern Tourist Board allows the park to recommend suitable accommodation for clients who want to stay overnight. The sales team envisages that the financial contribution from corporate business will continue to grow in the future.

Discussion points and essay questions

1 Discuss the benefits that LEGOLAND® Windsor offers the client for the organization of corporate leisure and hospitality events.
2 Discuss the effect that a lack of accommodation on the LEGOLAND® Windsor site could have on the development of corporate leisure and

hospitality events. Outline ways in which the park has tried to overcome this problem.

3 The organizers of corporate leisure and hospitality events are increasingly looking for new and exciting venues. Critically analyse the particular benefits that a theme park such as LEGOLAND® Windsor can offer the corporate market.

4 'Corporate guests do on average spend more while they are here, but we are limited in the amount of business we can do, and it must never interfere with the general running of the park' (Zoe Hill, Sales Executive, LEGOLAND® Windsor). Critically analyse this statement and suggest ways in which the management team at LEGOLAND® Windsor can effectively harmonize leisure and corporate business at the Park.

The authors would like to thank David Marshall, Head of Sales, for the help that he gave with the writing of this case study.

26 Amsterdam RAI International Exhibition and Congress Centre

Amsterdam RAI is an international group that is involved in the design and development of international exhibitions and congresses. The company was originally founded in Holland, but has increasingly developed international business. The International Exhibition and Congress Centre in Amsterdam is seen as a major strategic development by the Amsterdam region. The hosting of large conferences and exhibitions brings substantial numbers of visitors to the Amsterdam region every year and this has a multiplier effect on the local economy.

The company also develops exhibitions and conferences in Maastricht, Holland, and other international venues.

A brief history of Amsterdam RAI

Amsterdam RAI dates back to 1893 when H. W. Buyer, a bicycle manufacturer, proposed that the Bicycle Industry Association should organize a bicycle exhibition. The first exhibition took place in Amsterdam in 1895. In 1900 the name of the association was lengthened to include the letter 'A' for automobile because there were a growing number of motor cars that needed an exhibition site. The RAI obtained its own building in 1922 which was used for the next forty years. The exhibition business flourished and the exhibition centre was extended twice in 1925 and 1928 to provide an exhibition area of 13 000 sq. m. There was an increase in the amount of exhibitions after the Second World War and business grew rapidly.

There were two shows held for commercial vehicles and private cars in 1950, and the growth in trade forced the RAI to look for a much larger building that would accommodate this increase in business.

The board of the RAI realized that the cost of the exhibition centre would far exceed their financial resources so they started negotiation with Amsterdam's municipal authority to secure funding.

It was important that the finance obtained should not impose a financial burden on the RAI's operations in the future, and to avoid this a limited partnership was established in which RAI was the managing partner and Amsterdam the sleeping partner. The local authority at the same time expressed the wish that the exhibition facilities be combined with a conference centre.

The new RAI building was opened in 1961 and a separate private company was established to manage the building. The private company is also responsible for running the congress centre and the RAI restaurant. This combination of exhibition halls and conference centres is one of the main reasons that the RAI has proved so successful at organizing trade fairs and conferences.

There have been major developments from the 1960s onwards, culminating in the building of a new exhibition hall of 12 000 sq. m being added in 1990.

Amsterdam as a European and international venue

Amsterdam has been developed as a major destination for the movement of cargo and people across the European continent. The central position of Amsterdam and the development of an excellent transport infrastructure has meant that Amsterdam has a favourable location and unrivalled infrastructure for the development of the conference and exhibition business. Amsterdam Schipol airport is one of Europe's major gateways with eighty-five airlines serving 219 cities and ninety-four countries worldwide. The airport is 6 miles (10 km) or eight minutes by train from the Amsterdam RAI. The same rail service links up with the European rail network and the city is accessible by road. Amsterdam is a small city that is well served by public transport systems and hotels.

The marketing literature of Amsterdam RAI shows how the city is placed for hosting conference and exhibitions.

> *Allow yourself to be charmed and captivated by the special ambience that Amsterdam has to offer. Enjoy strolling along the canals and delightful little streets with its countless monuments from the 17th century. There are at least fifty museums to discover. Enjoy the cafe society so unique to Amsterdam with welcoming terraces. When your business is wrapped up for the day, dine in an intimate little restaurant, and then get ready to explore the city's exhilarating nightlife.*
>
> *This cosmopolitan, colourful city has something for everyone. Ideal for mixing business with pleasure. Speaking foreign language comes easily for its hospitable citizens. The Dutch capital has always been a thriving commercial, scientific and industrial centre. Welcoming international congress and exhibition groups is an important industry, in which the Amsterdam RAI International Exhibition and Congress Centre plays a major part.*
>
> *By every criterion the Amsterdam RAI is the foremost venue for business visitors and congress participants. As one of the world's leading, best-equipped exhibition and congress centres, the RAI draws 2.5 million visitors each year to international and national congresses, trade fairs, exhibitions and conferences. This includes commercial, scientific, and political events.*
>
> *The Amsterdam RAI: it's all there for you and your visitors: 'Always the ideal business climate'. (Amsterdam RAI marketing literature)*

Amsterdam is also able to offer a series of historic and interesting venues that can be used as part of the programme for conference. Details of these venues are given below.

Rijksmuseum

'If you choose the Rijksmuseum, your reception will have something of a royal aura, since it will beheld amidst one of the world's finest collections of old masters and other works of art. After a brief tour of the museum and dinner in front of Rembrandt's painting, *The Night Watch*, you will appreciate why this is such an exclusive venue.'

Van Goghmuseum

'Vincent Van Gogh, the master of light. Since this museum opened in 1971 it has been extremely popular with visitors to Amsterdam. The central reception hall is therefore the ideal place to express the art of hospitality. A dinner, buffet or reception staged among the many splendid works of art, will be a real happening.'

Muiderslot

'The past once again comes to life at this historic castle. No matter what form your evening takes, the Muiderslot guarantees a perfect setting. The rooms such as the Knights Room, even the kitchen itself, appeal to the imagination of every guest. In this way you ensure that your reception has a special atmosphere. The atmosphere of a place where tradition and style go hand in hand.'

Concertgebouw

'For over a century the renowned acoustics of the Concertgebouw (concert hall) have ensured that it has witnessed the performance of the finest music. The feeling of genius permeates every corner of the building. Guests feel privileged to be in such unique surroundings. The ideal backdrop for every reception, dinner or party.'

PartyTheatre Festige

'At this theatre venue your guests will never cease to be surprised. All the senses are indulged. Theatre means emotion, fantasy, imagination. This is the ideal venue for a business presentation or a lively party. If you want to be sure that your guests will have an unforgettable evening, this is the place to be.'

Geelvinck Hinloopen House

'You arrive by a spacious canal boat at one of the finest seventeenth century mansions situated beside the splendid Prinsengracht canal. Your guests can first enjoy a leisurely aperitif in the splendid classical garden and then dine in one of the stately rooms decorated in the style of the times. A princely reception in all senses of the word.'

Salon Cristofori

'The splendid piano showroom of the world-famous Bösendorfers. Two rooms in this marvellous seventeenth century warehouse are at your disposal. The intimate Vienna Salon for small groups of guests, and the delightful Concertzaal, where you can host receptions and dinners for around 120 guests against a background of piano recitals.'

Beurs van Berlage

'Designed by one of the best known Dutch architects of this century, Hendrik Petrus Berlage. The rooms provide scope for receptions of anywhere between 20 and 2,000 guests. For stylish dinners, product presentations and swinging parties.'

Amsterdam ArenA

'The Amsterdam ArenA is one of Europe's largest multifunctional stadiums. There can be few people who have never heard of Ajax's home ground. But this unique venue provides much more. It has the ideal ambience for business-to-business events and meetings. And on the gastronomic front you can arrange for first-rate meals to be provided by Amsterdam ArenA Culinair, a subsidiary of Amsterdam RAI. Everything down to the smallest detail is arranged for you. The Amsterdam ArenA is a real happening for you and for your guests.'

MECC Maastricht

'The Maastricht Exhibition and Congress Centre in the south of the Netherlands hosts hundreds of conferences, exhibitions, and other events each year. And all of them are organised by the true professionals and take place in a perfect setting. You can choose from 2 auditoriums, 24 meeting rooms, an Expo Foyer and two exhibition halls. And your guests can be put up in excellent hotels.'

Source: Amsterdam RAI.

The role of the RAI International Exhibition and Congress Centre in the local economy

The development of the RAI International Exhibition and Congress Centre has formed an integral part of the Southern Axis Master Plan of the Municipality of Amsterdam. The Southern Axis is the residential and office district around the southern section of the orbital motorway (the A10) in Amsterdam. The area is located near to Schipol airport and Amsterdam city centre, and this is the reason why it is popular with international companies. The organizations that have helped with the development of this area include Vrije University, the World Trade Centre, the RAI, ING Bank and ABN Amro. The master plan has been drawn up to safeguard the proper development of the area in the long term. There are also plans to improve communications, with the introduction of a North/South Metroline.

The current Amsterdam RAI business

Amsterdam RAI has its head office in Amsterdam, Holland. The company also has venues in Amsterdam and Maastricht, Holland, and offices in major international cities. Details of the operations of the company are shown below.

Amsterdam RAI: worldwide offices

Head Office: Amsterdam RAI.
Venues: Amsterdam RAI; MECC (Maastricht Exhibition and Congress Centre).
Offices: Turret RAI in the UK; Düsseldorf RAI in Germany; Singapore RAI in Singapore; RAI – South Africa in South Africa; Bangkok RAI in Thailand; Boston RAI in the USA; Dubai RAI in Dubai; Paris RAI in France.

Source : Amsterdam RAI annual accounts.

The main business of the Amsterdam RAI company is summarized below.

The main business of the Amsterdam RAI company

1 Exhibitions and Trade Fairs division.
2 Publication of trade journals.
3 Marketing communication services.
4 Rental and facility services.
5 Catering.

Source: Amsterdam RAI annual accounts.

The consolidated turnover of the RAI Group rose by 12.3 per cent in 1998 to reach 396.1 million guilders. The shares of turnover abroad represented 11.6 per cent of these figures and was reduced largely due to the economic crisis in Asia.

The distribution of the turnover is shown in Table 26.1.

Table 26.1   Distribution of turnover, 1997 and 1998 (percentage)

	1998	*%*	*1997*	*%*	*% change*
Exhibitions and trade fairs	159.4	40.2	148.5	42.1	7.3
Publications of trade journals	29.2	7.4	30.4	8.6	−3.9
Marketing communication services	56.8	14.3	46.6	13.2	22.2
Rental and facility services	61.7	15.6	49.3	14.0	25.2
Catering	64.1	16.2	60.7	17.2	5.6
Other activities	24.9	6.3	17.1	4.9	45.6
Total	396.1	100	352.6	100	12.3
The Netherlands	350.0	88.4	300.2	85.1	16.6
Abroad	6.1	11.6	52.4	14.9	−12.0

It can be seen from Table 26.1 that a large proportion of the turnover comes from the exhibitions and trade fairs. Other activities, such as catering, rental and facility services generate substantial revenues in their own right. The Amsterdam RAI company is managed by a supervisory board and management team that has responsibility for the operations and financial management role.

Supervisory board and management of Amsterdam RAI

This comprises:

- Chairman of the Supervisory Board
- Members of the Supervisory Board (6)
- Managing Director
- Director of Trade Fairs and Exhibitions
- Director of Exhibitions and Congress Facilities
- Director of International Operations
- Director of Strategy and Communications
- Deputy Managing Directors (4).

The supervisory board considers that international development is critical for the growth of the business. The company was very disappointed when the Dutch Monopolies and Mergers Board blocked a proposed merger between the RAI Group and Royal Dutch Jaarbeurs in 1999. This veto according to A. A. L. Mirken, Managing Director of the Group, has affected the two companies involved but also undermined the position of the Netherlands as a leading centre of exhibitions and trade fairs.

The Amsterdam RAI International Exhibition and Congress Centre

The Amsterdam RAI hosts more than fifty major events each year ranging across international congresses, trade fairs, and exhibitions and meetings. The complex is now 87 000 sq. m in size and is one of Europe's most important venues for international events. The complex has twenty-two congress rooms, with seating capacity for up to 1750 people, and eleven exhibition halls.

The Amsterdam RAI is professionally equipped and staffed to meet the needs of international meetings. A summary of the facilities, and a site plan (Figure 26.1), show the range of facilities on offer.

The facilities and services that are on offer at Amsterdam RAI Exhibition and Congress Centre

1 Auditorium centre – full range of rooms with a capacity of 32–1176 people.
2 Forum centre – full range of rooms with a capacity of 80–709 people.
3 Exhibition halls – eleven halls of various sizes.
4 Restaurants – five self-service and two 'a la carte'

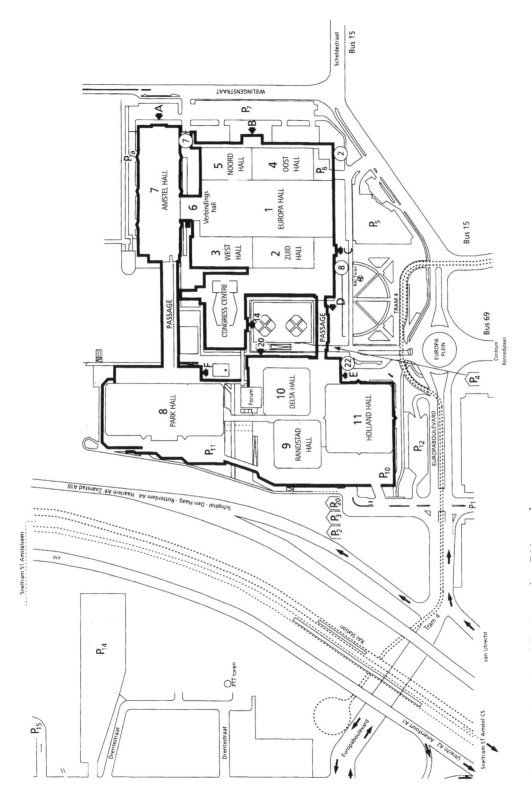

Figure 26.1   Site plan of the Amsterdam RAI complex

5 Services:
   (a) organization
   (b) presentation technology
   (c) event catering
   (d) marketing communications
   (e) RAI Hotel Service
   (f) RAI Hostess Service.

The Amsterdam RAI International Exhibition and Congress Centre offers a wide range of facilities and services, including exhibition halls and conference rooms available for hire.

The centre also offers clients a full range of services that will help the organizers of a particular event. These services include *organization*. Maco concept will develop comprehensive concepts for all events. Amsterdam RAI will organize exhibitions and events on behalf of clients. Eurocongress will organize a conference for associations, businesses and the public sector. Amsterdam RAI also has a department which specializes in organizing special events such as fashion shows or product demonstrations.

Presentation technology can be arranged for clients by the Audiovisual Conference Service (ACS) of the RAI. This organization will design audiovisual presentations and suggest the appropriate use of technology.

Event catering is organized by Amsterdam RAI Catering Services. They organize catering for the conference organizers and attendees, the general public and for the exhibitors. They offer anything from basic catering to specialist services such as sculpting company logos in icing sugar, ice sculptures and speciality confectionery.

Amsterdam RAI offers a *marketing communication* service to clients. A'D'M'P is a full-service advertising consultancy. RAIWORLD is a multimedia organization that can help exhibitors and conference organizers with their marketing communications plan.

The *RAI Hotel Service* arranges for and guarantees hotel accommodation in the vicinity of the RAI, in the centre of Amsterdam and at the airport. It can supply the organizer with information about the available hotels and offer booking advice. The RAI Hotel Service offers its services free because it is the largest buyer of hotels in Amsterdam. It can also arrange reduced room rates for conference and exhibition organizers.

The *RAI Hostess Service* helps clients with their hosting of exhibitions and events. The organization has a large team of hosts and hostesses who are available at all times and speak many foreign languages. They can help with the welcoming of guests or in the smooth running of the conference or event.

Looking to the future

Amsterdam RAI is very keen to develop their international business further. At the same time, the company is keen to continue as a major contributor to the development of the Amsterdam area, and to the Netherlands, as a major European conference and exhibition venue.

Discussion points and essay questions

1 Discuss the main facilities and services that contribute to the success of the Amsterdam RAI exhibition and congress centre.
2 Evaluate the importance of Amsterdam RAI offering both exhibition and conference facilities on one site to the success of the organization.
3 Evaluate the contribution that a major exhibition and conference centre can give to the development of business tourism in a particular country.
4 'Our real strength lies in the way we inspire people' (Amsterdam RAI). Critically analyse this statement in relation to the successful organization of successful exhibitions and conferences.

The authors would like to thank Maurits Van der Sluis for the help that he gave with the writing of this chapter.

27 Business tourism in Hong Kong – City of Life

Background

Hong Kong is made up of three distinct geographic areas: Hong Kong island, the Kowloon peninsula, and the New Territories and outlying islands. Hong Kong lies at the centre of Asia and is the region's top single destination with around seventy airlines connecting it to more than 120 cities around the world. The city became a special administrative region of China after the official handover ceremony on 1 July 1997 by the British government.

The city has continued to develop as the Asian business centre, and has attracted organizations and people from all over the world. The opening of the new Hong Kong

International airport in July 1998 has helped with this continued development. Hong Kong has become very attractive as a destination for clients, conferences, exhibitions and incentive packages. This has meant that Hong Kong has grown in importance over the last few years, despite the recession which has hit the Asian economies during the late 1990s. Some key facts about Hong Kong are shown below.

Key facts about Hong Kong

Visitors from most countries do not require visas for periods ranging from one week to six months. Check with any Chinese consulate or embassy or the Hong Kong Tourist Association's (HKTA's) web site: www.hkta.org

- The HK dollar is pegged to the US dollar at about US$1 = HK$7.7.
- English remains an official language; English signage is maintained.
- Hong Kong is one of the safest cities in the world. The Hong Kong Police still patrol the streets and maintain order as they did under British sovereignty.
- Hong Kong has a sophisticated health care system and no inoculations are required for visitors.
- Most shops and markets are open seven days a week. Late-night shopping is common.
- Hong Kong's subtropical climate has distinct seasons. Temperatures range from 25°C to 31°C in summer to 10°C to 20°C in winter.
- The time zone is eight hours ahead of Greenwich Mean Time; thirteen hours ahead of US Eastern Standard Time.

Source: HKTA.

The city

The city of Hong Kong provides unforgettable sights and experiences. The city is extended every year as new land is reclaimed from the sea and new apartment blocks, offices, and convention and exhibition centres are built. The city bursts with dynamism and explodes with energy. The city has over 2000 years of history and culture, but it is also one of the world's most modern cities. There are many cultural sights to see, including monasteries, temples and baronial houses. The city offers a wide choice of cuisine and there is an incredible number of restaurants. Hong Kong also has a wide range of festivals including the Chinese New Year festival, which includes colourful parades and fantastic firework displays over the wonderful Hong Kong harbour. The historic Star Ferries still cross the from Hong Kong island to Kowloon, which is one of the most spectacular ferry crossings in the world. The Hong Kong Tramways double-decker trams still cross the city and provide an inside look at the city's bustling street life and crowded markets.

British colonial heritage is apparent in Hong Kong City and Hong Kong's oldest surviving colonial building is now the museum of Tea Ware. The official residence of the twenty-five governors of Hong Kong until 1997, Government House, is also a spectacular sight. Visitors can also enjoy exciting race action at the Happy Valley or Sha Tin racecourses. They can also shop in one of the most exciting shopping cities in the world, where stylish de luxe malls and boutiques go hand in hand with exciting day and night markets.

Away from the bustling city, Hong Kong is also surprisingly green, and there are many opportunities to make exciting and informative trips to the countryside, beaches, mountains and parks. Repulse Bay has a popular beach for swimming and the visitor can reach tranquil green outlying islands using the frequent ferry services. Lantau Island offers well-marked trails and trekking paths.

Hong Kong offers a whole city of contrasts. Business executives in suits go hand in hand with local citizens in traditional costumes. Property developers consult feng shui experts to ensure that the elements are balanced in their architectural designs. World-renowned groups have built hotels on prime sites of land. This means that Hong Kong is an ideal centre for business meetings, conferences and incentive travel.

Tourism statistics for Hong Kong

The pattern of visitor arrivals to Hong Kong is shown in Table 27.1.

It can be seen from Table 27.1 that there was a general increase of all visitors to Hong Kong from all regions of the world up to 1996. Since 1996, there has been a general decline in visitor numbers, particularly from the North Asia and South Asia regions. This has been largely due to the recession that hit the Asian region during this period. Table 28.1 also reveals that there has been an upturn in visitors from China and Taiwan to Hong Kong during 1998.

The downturn in visitors to Hong Kong since 1996 has meant that many tourism businesses, including hotels, have been experiencing financial pressures due to declining numbers and falling occupancy rates. The development of business tourism and other sources of income have been a major challenge for the Hong Kong tourism sector.

Conventions, exhibitions and corporate events in Hong Kong

One of the major ways of promoting business travel to Hong Kong has been to develop the convention, events, and corporate events in Hong Kong. Table 27.2 shows the number of events that have happened in Hong Kong from 1989 to 1999.

It can be seen from Table 27.2 that there has been a fluctuating demand for HKTA events during the 1989–9 period. The exhibition and trade show market has been fairly stable although the events are increasing in attendance numbers. Incentive travel and corporate meetings business has also shown a general decline during the same period. The total numbers attending conferences exhibitions and corporate events in Hong Kong does represent, however, a significant proportion of total visitor numbers. The business brings substantial revenue to the Hong Kong economy.

Table 27.1 A summary of visitor arrival statistics to Hong Kong, 1989–9

Country/territory of residence	1989	% growth	1990	% growth	1991	% growth	1992	% growth	1993	% growth
The Americas	812 920	−14.6	807 692	−0.6	822 397	+1.8	924 253	+12.4	1 008 313	+9.1
Europe, Africa and the Middle East	782 539	−8.4	816 093	+4.3	879 840	+7.8	1 036 973	+17.9	1 164 923	+12.3
Australia, NZ and South Pacific	311 088	+1.4	311 763	+0.2	284 965	−8.6	309 302	+8.5	318 241	+2.9
North Asia	1 343 184	+0.1	1 516 421	+12.9	1 444 429	−4.7	1 520 681	+5.3	1 505 983	−1.0
South and South East Asia	835 923	−7.1	988 967	+18.3	1 150 165	+16.3	1 383 343	+20.3	1 374 513	−0.6
Taiwan	1 132 904	+3.6	1 344 641	+18.7	1 298 039	−3.5	1 640 032	+26.3	1 777 310	+8.4
All others	35 535	+0.6	40 897	+15.1	40 516	−0.9	46 938	+15.9	55 238	+17.7
Subtotal	5 254 093	−4.2	5 826 474	+10.9	5 920 351	+1.6	6 861 522	+15.9	7 204 522	+5.0
Mainland China	730 408	+6.8	754 376	+3.3	875 062	+16.0	1 149 002	+31.3	1 732 978	+50.8
Total	5 984 501	−3.0	6 580 850	+10.0	6 795 413	+3.3	8 010 524	+17.9	8 937 500	+11.6

Country/territory of residence	1994	% growth	1995	% growth	1996	% growth	1997	% growth	1998	% growth
The Americas	1 026 409	+1.8	986 342	−3.9	973 132	−1.3	1 043 787	+7.3	1 029 405	−1.4
Europe, Africa and the Middle East	1 245 134	+6.9	1 249 915	+0.4	1 278 174	+2.3	1 176 187	−8.0	1 040 842	−11.5
Australia, NZ and South Pacific	322 195	+1.2	335 867	+4.2	381 901	+13.7	354 730	−7.1	332 541	−6.3
North Asia	1 723 024	+14.4	2 044 264	+18.6	2 779 439	+36.0	1 726 526	−37.9	1 124 833	−34.8
South and South East Asia	1 337 066	−2.7	1 419 699	+6.2	1 616 007	+13.8	1 498 465	−7.3	1 195 491	−20.2
Taiwan	1 665 330	−6.3	1 761 111	+5.8	1 821 279	+3.4	1 782 580	−2.1	1 812 684	+1.7
All others	68 320	+23.7	159 551	+133.5	541 619	+239.5	526 858	−2.7	441 523	−16.2
Subtotal	7 387 478	+2.5	7 956 749	+7.7	9 391 551	+18.0	8 109 133	−13.7	6 977 269	−14.0
Mainland China	1 943 678	+12.2	2 243 245	+15.4	2 311 184	+3.0	2 297 128	−0.6	2 597 442	+13.1
Total	9 331 156	+4.4	10 199 994	+9.3	11 702 735	+14.7	10 406 261	−11.1	9 574 711	−8.0

Source: HKTA.

Table 27.2 Statistics on conventions, exhibitions and corporate events, 1989–9

Year	Associations		Exhibitions and trade shows		IT		CM	
	Events	Pax	Events	Pax	Events	Pax	Events	Pax
1989	221	30 439	96	85 329	–	–	–	–
1990	195	24 602	77	97 051	–	–	–	–
1991	245	42 127	57	94 851	–	–	–	–
1992	257	64 311	58	111 119	–	–	–	–
1993	301	65 627	47	137 071	–	–	–	–
1994	182	36 575	59	170 998	996	79 879	289	11 955
1995	268	69 009	63	170 010	1493	89 562	351	13 497
1996	294	57 042	59	176 771	2270	100 698	407	21 471
1997	291	76 651	64	193 086	1225	69 817	593	26 988
1998	176	35 926	57	174 815	831	56 816	245	19 008
1999	180	44 700	56	200 000	900	58 000	260	19 760

Notes: Figures for IT (incentive travel) and CM (corporate meetings) are probably only a percentage of the total market; it is almost impossible to gather 100% of data.
'–' denotes figures not available.

Source: HKTA.

The HKTA offices

The HKTA was set up in 1957 to develop tourism business in Hong Kong. The HKTA had a budget of HK$530 million in 1998 of which HK$261 million was used for marketing activity. The HKTA has offices across the world:

- Head Office – Hong Kong (www.hkta.org).
- Asia – Beijing; Tokyo; Osaka; Seoul; Singapore; Taipei.
- Australia and New Zealand – Sydney; Auckland.
- Europe, Africa and the Middle East – London; Paris; Frankfurt; Rome; Barcelona; Johannesburg.
- The Americas – Los Angeles; New York; Chicago; Toronto.

The HKTA is the official government-sponsored body that represents the tourism industry in Hong Kong. The organization offers visitors to Hong Kong a wide range of services including leaflets and information. Its web site has up-to-date information about news in Hong Kong, seasonal promotions and festivals, and general information about Hong Kong.

The Hong Kong Convention and Incentive Travel Bureau

The Hong Kong Convention and Incentive Bureau (HKCITB) is a specialist division of the HKTA. It was established to advise and help international and regional event planners. The objectives of the organization are not just about promoting Hong Kong as a destination. It also ensures that all events in Hong Kong are professionally organized by working with and supporting organizers throughout the planning and delivery of the event. The HKCITB has offices throughout the world. The services that it offers are shown below.

Services that the HKCITB office offers

Brings your international events to Hong Kong by:

- researching and retaining information on professional bodies in a wide range of countries
- putting you in touch with your counterparts in Hong Kong or overseas
- preparing written proposals and audiovisual materials for presenting your invitation.

Plans your events every step of the way by:

- identifying suitable venues for meetings and incentive events, and recommending various accommodation choices for participants
- co-ordinating inspections of Hong Kong facilities by decision-makers
- participating on conference organizing committees.

Organizes an unforgettable event for your delegates and incentive partners by:

- offering innovative and creative ideas on social programmes, team-building exercises and providing contacts for tours, special events and theme parties
- recommending pre/post-conference tour options
- sourcing service suppliers such as airlines, conference organizing companies and destination management companies.

Promotes your events to generate good attendance by:

- providing shell posters and flyers for overprinting your own promotional messages
- supplying audiovisual materials for presenting Hong Kong to potential participants
- assisting in worldwide promotion.

Ensures your events run smoothly in Hong Kong by;

- advising on the invitation of local dignitaries for officiating at opening and closing ceremonies
- advising on customs and immigration procedures to facilitate the entry of participants and exhibits
- supplying tourist literature, including maps and guidebooks, for participants upon their arrival.

Source: Venues HK: The Official Convention Exhibitions and Incentive Travel Facilities Guide, HKCITB.

The HKCITB's office in London is one example of the bureau but it has a presence worldwide in all the offices of the HKTA. The bureaux were established in the 1970s to develop the specialist conference and incentive travel to Hong Kong.

The London bureau has a director who leads two teams of staff. One of the teams works on conventions and the other team works on incentive travel. The bureau provides impartial and practical advice to convention planners. It can help to plan an event from the earliest proposal stage to the conclusion of the event. The bureau also provides a complete range of reference material for the planning of events in Hong Kong.

Spotlight on Hong Kong – into the millennium

Spotlight on Hong Kong – into the millennium, was launched by the HKTA in 1996. It was an umbrella-marketing programme that proactively identified, invited and worked alongside event organizers to promote top-quality international events in Hong Kong. Target events were categorized under different headings:

- Sport
- Art and cultural entertainments
- Festivals and conventions
- Trade fairs
- Exhibitions.

Table 27.3   Conferences in Hong Kong, 2001 onwards

2001		
Mar	International Conference on Construction	400
15–18 May	International Hospital Federation 2001 Congress	2 000
18–20 May	8th District Annual Toastmasters Convention	800
3–6 Jun	54th World Newspaper Congress	1 300
	8th World Editors Forum Conference Info Services Expo 2001	
1–4 Jul	8th International Congress on Sound and Vibration	800
Jul	2nd International Pacific Rim Conference on Crime and Public Policies	100
Jul	Hong Kong Medical Forum 2001	500
Aug	The 5th International Chinese Statistical Association International Conference	200
5–9 Oct	2001 Annual Conference of the Asian Securities Analysts Federation	300
Oct	11th East Asian Actuarial Conference	500
5–8 Nov	10th International Conference of Drug Regulatory Authorities	450
5–8 Nov	12th World Productivity Congress	2 000
14–18 Nov	6th Congress of Asian Society of Hepato-Biliary-Pancreatic Surgery	600
Nov	13th World Federation of the Deaf RS A/P Representative Meeting	130
Dec	2001 Eddie Wang International Surgical Symposium	200
	Comite Int'l d'Esthetique of de Cosmetologic General Assembly	500
	World Association for Psychosocial Rehabilitation Regional Meeting	
2002		
Jun	19th Asian Association of Convention and Visitor Bureaux Annual Conference	60
Jul	Hong Kong Medical Forum 2002	500
10–13 Nov	World Congress of Accountants	6 000
Dec	Eddie Wang International Surgical Symposium	200
	International Psychogeriatric Association Regional Meeting	600
2003		
19–23 Feb	International Cardiac Pacing & Electrophysiology Society World Symposium	3 000
Jul	Hong Kong Medical Forum 2003	500
Dec	Eddie Wang International Surgical Symposium	200
2004		
Jul	Hong Kong Medical Forum 2004	500
Nov	Eddie Wang International Surgical Symposium	200
2004	Asia Pacific Dental Congress	2000
2005		
27 Jun–1 Jul	Lions Clubs International Convention 2005	30 000
Jul	Hong Kong Medical Forum 2005	500
Dec	Eddie Wang International Surgical Symposium	200
2006		
Jul	Hong Kong Medical Forum 2006	500
Dec	Eddie Wang International Surgical Symposium	200

Source: HKTA.

The campaign has been used to build on Hong Kong's reputation as the event capital of Asia, to focus attention on Hong Kong and to attract more visitors to Hong Kong. The work that has been carried out promoting Hong Kong has meant that there are many conferences already planned for many years to come. A summary of these is shown in Table 27.3.

The HKTA has recently developed a new promotion – The Hong Kong Value plus promotion that provides special hotel and venue discounts. This offers 50 per cent discount off regular prices in over forty hotels in Hong Kong and up to 40 per cent discount in two major convention centres.

The HKTA has also developed an interactive web site – www.hkta.org/cit/index.htm – which provides comprehensive information on venues, special activities, themed parties, future conferences and exhibitions, and specialist services provided by the HKTA.

Conclusions

Hong Kong has been developed as a major hub for business in Asia. This has helped the city develop as a major tourism venue for both leisure and business travellers. The recession of the late 1990s, however, meant that hospitality and tourism businesses in Hong Kong had to be much more effective in capturing different sources of income. The HKTA plays a major part in the development of new initiatives and business tourism is seen as a major part of this initiative. The organization has a long-term strategy to keep Hong Kong as a major business tourism venue in the new millennium.

Discussion points and essay questions

1 Discuss the ways in which the development of business tourism can contribute to the overall tourism strategy of a city such as Hong Kong.
2 Discuss the role that the worldwide offices of the HKTA will have in developing business tourism in Hong Kong.
3 'Hong Kong is compact yet diverse, providing a good opportunity to discover both its urban heart and unexpected rural beauty in a single day' (HKTA). Evaluate the factors that are required to make a city appropriate as a business tourism venue.
4 The conference business can provide a major source of income for a hotel faced with a period of recession. Outline the ways in which a hotel could attempt to build a profitable conference business. Discuss the ways in which they would balance the demands of this conference business with their leisure business.

The authors would like to thank Patricia Conibear, Manager – Conventions, Exhibitions and Corporate Events, HKTA, London (1999), for her assistance with this case study and Sharon Wood, Manager – Europe Conventions, Exhibitions and Corporate Events.

28 Switzerland Convention and Incentive Bureau (SCIB)

Switzerland is a major European tourist destination. The country has developed a number of high-profile initiatives to help the development of tourism to the country. The Switzerland Convention and Incentive Bureau is one example of these initiatives. This enables the country to generate repeat sales in a highly competitive market.

Switzerland – the destination

Tourism is an important source of revenue for Switzerland. Switzerland is in an ideal location in the centre of Europe to generate tourism. It has beautiful and historic centres that help in the development of a substantial tourism business. Business tourism in Switzerland accounts for 10–15 per cent of the total number of bed nights, resulting in between 7 and 10 million bed nights per year. Business tourism contributes about 1.6 to 1.7 million Swiss francs per year, which represents about 8 per cent of the country's total tourism revenues. The worldwide business of tourism based on meetings, congresses and conferences is on the increase and it is planned that Switzerland will benefit from this increase.

Switzerland is centrally situated in Europe and this makes it an ideal location as a congress and incentive destination. Swissair and Crossair both operate excellent airline links to over 500 international destinations and there are excellent motorway and rail services across Europe, making Switzerland very accessible. The country itself is an excellent location for business and incentive travel. There are beautiful and historic cities and towns surrounded by beautiful mountains, lakes, seemingly eternal icefields and a wonderful natural environment. The country also has the reputation of offering Swiss hospitality throughout the hotels that join together to form the Swiss Hotels Association.

Switzerland at a glance

- Magnificent panoramas.
- Quality and service.
- Reassuringly safe.
- Cultural diversity.
- Multilingual.
- Short travelling distances.
- Traditional standing.

Source: Switzerland Convention and Incentive Bureau.

The country also offers some beautiful and interesting locations in which to hold business conventions and meetings.

Switzerland – some memorable locations

Fribourg
The superb old town is the example par excellence of medieval European architecture. Numerous festivals, concerts, theatres, shows and sporting events confirm that the town is right up to date.

Davos
Highest town in Europe and the largest Alpine resort. Its special atmosphere and limitless leisure possibilities tempt you to come here for meetings, seminars, sports, relaxation and enjoyment – and return.

Lugano
Swiss town with Mediterranean flair idyllically situated on Lake Lugano. Attractions for visitors are the traffic-free historical town centre, superb buildings in the Lombard style and exclusive museums.

Lausanne
On Lake Geneva, surrounded by vineyards, lies the Olympic capital, with none of the hustle and bustle of large city life. Historic sights, the Olympic Museum, markets, wines, culture and sheer *joie de vivre*.

Grindelwald
No other Alpine resort can match the imposing panorama of Eiger, Mönch and Jungfrau as seen from this glacier village. The local chairlifts and gondolas are Europe's longest and beat all records.

Leysin
Leysin is like a south-facing balcony with superb views of Lake Geneva, the Rhone plain and Mont Blanc. Nestling amidst a nature reserve this typical mountain village offers an authentic background for sports, culture and folklore.

Geneva
World Metropolis with famous views of Mont Blanc displaying French *savoir-vivre*, cultural delights and lively nightlife. In addition, this United Nations city has all the advantages of a holiday resort.

Pontresina
Every corner oozes traditional Engadine charm. The artist Salvador Dali visited Pontresina with his paintings, and here hospitality is also elevated to an art form.

Basel

The three-countries town, famous for its architecture, museums and fairs, and the centuries-old influences by Celts, Romans, Germans, and Huguenots.

St Gallen

Today still, famous fashion houses use materials from this nineteenth-century centre of the textile industry. Guests enjoy the area's diversity by visiting the picturesque Old Town, the famous abbey library, Lake Constance or the quaint Appenzell villages.

Montreux

The 'Pearl of the Swiss Riviera' lies at the foothills of the Alps on Lake Geneva. Its beauty and mild climate are legendary. It is famous all over the world for its festivals and the Chillon Castle, Switzerland's most photographed building.

Crans-Montana

This high sunny south-facing plateau in the heart of the Alps hosts the annual European Masters Golf Tournament. Crans-Montana is not only known for its green meadows, but also for its year-round skiing area.

St Moritz

One of the world's most famous holiday resorts and Switzerland's unique Olympic venue. Celebrate with us on 322 days of sunshine each year, the exclusive ambience and bubbly champagne climate.

Berne

Not Switzerland's largest town, but its capital. Six kilometres (4 miles) of arcades ensure no one gets wet when browsing in the medieval setting of Europe's longest covered shopping arcade.

Flims

The mild sunny high-altitude climate, combined with pure natural beauty, makes one forget everyday worries. Flims shares the famous White Arena with the neighbouring resorts of Laax and Falera.

Engelberg

The symbol of Engelberg, Mount Titlis (3239 m. or 10 600 ft above sea level) is by no means the only highlight offered by this outstanding visitor's paradise. Do not forget your camera!

Gstaad

For many people this resort represents the essence of chic. Exclusive boutiques and international tennis tournaments can be found here alongside the local cheesery or the alphorn maker's workshop

Luzern

The mighty gateway to the South in a superb setting on Lake Lucerne, framed by the mountain giants of Pilatus and Rigi, with vistas into the snow-covered Alps.

Interlaken

Interlaken means 'between the lakes' and crystal-clear waters are to be found both left and right of the town. Do not miss a journey up to the highest railway station in the Alps, the famous Jungfraujoch at the 'Top of Europe'.

Zurich

Switzerland's downtown Zurich, with museums, galleries, operas and theatres, picturesque Old Town, exclusive shops, highly rated gastronomy – in short, a world city.

Source: Switzerland Convention and Incentive Bureau.

Switzerland offers many world-renowned events and festivals and has museums and architectural sights that range from the classical to avant-garde. The country holds many traditional events that audiences can often take part in, and this is very attractive to conference organizers. The cuisine of Switzerland is rich in regional specialities and local wines can act as an excellent accompaniment to these dishes.

Switzerland Tourism

Switzerland Tourism (ST) is the official destination marketing organization for the country. The role of ST is to stimulate demand both at home and abroad, and it is keen to promote the country as being both traditional and trendy. The organization develops and evaluates clients' needs according to their country of origin. A prime responsibility of the organization is to collaborate with touristic and non-touristic partners to enable Switzerland to offer excellent packages for all clients. It relies heavily on electronic systems, international agencies and representatives to develop the Swiss tourism business. There are worldwide offices that help in this development.

Switzerland Tourism worldwide

- Switzerland – Zurich
- Great Britain and Ireland – London
- Austria and East Europe – Vienna
- Italy – Milan, Rome
- Japan and Asia – Tokyo
- France – Paris
- Benelux – Amsterdam
- Germany – Frankfurt, Düsseldorf, Berlin, Hamburg, Munich
- North America and Canada – New York, Los Angeles, Toronto
- South-East Asia – Hong Kong
- Korea – Seoul

Source: Switzerland Convention and Incentive Bureau.

Switzerland Tourism also relies on many organizations to help with the development of tourism to the country.

These organizations can offer transport to and from Switzerland, and excellent venues in which to hold business conferences and meetings. The specialist organizations offer services such as the planning and organization of business meetings and conferences, and specialist events such as medical and technical conferences. Media and audiovisual effects can also be planned and arranged by these specialist services. All of these services are co-ordinated by ST. The organization has set up the *Switzerland Convention and Incentive Bureau*, which has particular responsibility for helping clients with organization and planning business conferences and meetings in Switzerland, with representatives in Great Britain, France, Benelux, Scandinavia and North Africa, and the head office in Zurich, Switzerland.

The Switzerland Convention and Incentive Bureau

The members are:

Central Switzerland	**Montreux**
Graubünden	**Pontresina**
Lake Geneva Region	**St. Gallen-Lake Constance**
Varais	**St. Moritz**
Basel	**Zermatt**
Bern	**Zürich**
Crans-Montana	**AKM Congress Service**
Davos	**Hotels of Switzerland**
Engelberg	**LTI TOURS Ltd**
Flims Laax Falera	**MCI Travel Switzerland**
Fribourg	**Spectrum Events AG**
Geneva	**Welcome Swiss**
Interlaken	**Crossair**
Lausanne	**Swissair**
Lugano	**Swiss Travel System**
Luzern	**Europcar**

Promotion by the Switzerland Convention and Incentive Bureau

Promotion of Switzerland as a business location is carried out by the Switzerland Convention and Incentive Bureau. This organization uses different techniques and different organizations to carry out this promotional activity. The offices of the Switzerland Tourism Organization are an important source of help and advice for conference and meeting organizers. The following services are offered free of charge and without obligation:

- Assistance with site inspections
- Detailed information

- Unbiased advice
- Contact addresses and submission of quotes.

The organization produces a detailed guide to promote Switzerland as a business venue. This is – *Switzerland – where the world meets*. Extracts from this guide for the city of Geneva show the detail that this promotional guide give to clients who are deciding whether to locate their event in Switzerland. This level of detail is critical for conference and meeting organizers.

Geneva

Geneva, city of peace. This World Metropolis is the birthplace of the International Red Cross and houses approximately 200 international government and independent organizations as well as the European headquarters of the United Nations. Apart from its humanitarian role, Geneva is also renowned for its culture, congresses and fairs. The natural beauties of its surroundings, with views of Mont Blanc, the French *savoir-vivre* and the relaxed atmosphere of this town have fascinated people for more than 2000 years. In the Old Town, visitors can witness Geneva's rich past. The town's symbol is the 140 metres/ 460 ft. high giant fountain at the edge of the lakes spraying a white veil over the harbour.

Getting there

By air: International Airport Geneva is 10 minutes by car from the town centre.
By rail: direct rail connection airport–town centre 6 minutes.
By car: connected directly to the national and international motorway system.

Incentive infrastructure

Geneva offers a unique combination of international flair, Swiss efficiency and French charm. Its superb location on Lake Geneva, surrounded by vineyards, the Jura mountains and the close-by Alpine range promise unique excursions and impressions. First-class hotels, diverse gastronomy, interesting entertainment possibilities plus numerous cultural offerings will make your stay an unforgettable experience.

Congress infrastructure

Geneva, a small-scale town (170 000 inhabitants only), is regularly placed among the five most important World Conference cities. Modern fairs and congress infrastructure with a great variety of conference rooms, more than 100 hotels in all price categories and numerous possibilities for exceptional leisure events, guarantee complete success for your next event.

Activities, leisure programmes and sights

Sightseeing tour including Geneva's 2000 years of history and the surrounding area; visit to Montreux and Chillon Castle; visit to Lausanne and Gruyères; excursion to Chamonix and Mont Blanc; gala evening at the Opera House; dine around in the Old Town with its 2000-year-old history and more than forty restaurants, seemingly waiting just for you; lake-cruise by paddle-steamer; medieval dinner in a castle, numerous sports and much more.

Hotel capacity

- deluxe (five star): 3520 beds, 2185 rooms
- first class (four star): 4520 beds, 2690 rooms
- upper middle class (three star): 3125 beds, 1750 rooms
- others: 3100 beds, 1810 rooms
- total: 14 265 beds, 8435 rooms.

References

- World Aids Conference (12 000 participants)
- ISOC Internet Kongress (4000 participants)
- World Corporate Games (3000 participants)
- Telecom Symposium (100 000 visitors)
- ESPEN (2500 participants)
- IFRA, Congress and exhibition of Newspaper Technology (10 000 participants)
- Shelter USA (800 participants)
- Shaklee USA (1500 participants).

Address

Geneva Tourism, World Trade Centre
Route de l'aéroport 10
PO Box 598, CH-1215 Geneva 15
Phone: +41 (0)22 929 70 00
Fax: +41 (0)22 929 70 11
E-mail: info@geneva-tourism.ch
Internet: http://www.geneva-tourism.ch

Example of types of activities available in Geneva

Programme/activity/ excursion	Description	Duration	Participants (max.)
Wine-tasting in the Genevese countryside	Journey through Geneva country with stop at a winery whose owner will proudly show his wine cellar and acquaint you with the various Genevese wines.	3 hrs	–
Cruise to Yvoire	Lake-cruise to medieval village of Yvoire, situated on the French side of Lake Geneva. Visit to handicraft boutiques and art galleries, lunch.	7 hrs	–
Three countries tour	Along Lake Geneva, across the Great St Bernard Pass into the Italian Aosta valley. Italian lunch, through the Mont Blanc tunnel to Chamonix, French stronghold of alpinism, and return to Geneva.	10 hrs	–
River rafting	From the French border straight into the centre of Geneva, an eventful journey on the river Arve for one and half hours.	3 hrs	–
Mountain-biking	A few hours of physical effort in clear mountain air on Geneva's doorstep, followed by a fondue dinner in a chalet on the Jura mountain heights.	5–8 hrs	40
Arthur's Club	An evening charged with atmosphere, on a theme to be decided, in one of Europe's largest discos.	3–10 hrs	1500
Cruise with orchestra/ dancing	Cocktail, buffet or elegant dinner with entertainment, with a choice of historic sailing dinghies, motor launches or paddle-steamers.	2–5 hrs	35–1000

Source: Switzerland Convention and Incentive Bureau.

Example of venue capacity information available

Venue	Largest room	Area (m²)	Capacity (concert)	Seminar	Banquet	Other rooms (no.)	Capacity	Additional exhibition area (m²)	Hotel (rooms/beds)	Technical (simultaneous translation)	Installations (projection equipment)	Installations Microphone
Arena	1	—	6500	—	—	—	—	—	—	—	—	—
PALEXPO	8	130–2200	100–2400	70–1500	100–200	18	10–15	90 000	—	x	x	x
CICG	4	320–1500	120–1800	120–95	40 + 30	9	16–50	500	—	x	x	x
CIP	2	114–326	100 + 300	45 + 185	—	6	18–125	200	—	0	0	x
Grand Casino	1	—	1371	—	220	1	1200	—	—	x	x	x
University	2	328 + 716	300 + 640	300 + 640	—	—	—	—	—	x	x	x
Festival Hall at Rhôex	3	215–485	240–910	159–268	240–500	—	—	—	—	—	x	x
Sports Centre at Vernets	1	2800	4200	—	—	2	10–50	—	—	0	0	0
La ferme du Vignoble	2	125 + 231	100 + 200	65 + 170	65 + 180	—	—	—	—	0	x	x
Arthur's	2	80–1800	—	—	80–1420	—	—	—	—	0	x	x
Forum Meyrin	5	110–250	266–434	—	600	5	12–24	150	—	—	—	x
Hotels												
Beau Rivage	7	21–330	15–250	20–120	12–350	—	—	—	97/166	0	x	x
Intercontinental	13	40–150	35–700	20–500	30–550	—	—	500	353/506	x	x	x
Noga Hilton	13	37–800	20–800	20–400	10–550	—	—	5000	410/580	x	x	x
Président Wilson	10	70–1500	70–1100	50–800	60–900	—	—	600	210/540	x	x	x
la Réserve	7	19–167	25–175	12–100	20–160	—	—	—	114/255	0	x	0
du Rhône	10	36–365	30–240	10–150	10–180	—	—	—	214/355	0	x	x
Mövenpick	15	16–609	22–800	20–350	20–500	—	—	1000	350/545	0	x	x
Holiday Inn	8	57–252	50–250	40–140	40–200	—	—	—	305/443	0	x	x
Penta	10	61–558	50–850	35–650	35–650	—	—	300	308/496	x	x	x
Warwick	7	20–244	10–260	20–140	20–220	—	—	—	169/332	0	0	x

Notes: a further 25 meeting rooms are available in hotels or elsewhere.
x = permanently installed, 0 = available on request.

Conclusions

Switzerland is a beautiful location for the development of business tourism. The Switzerland Conference and Incentive Bureau has been established by Switzerland Tourism to help with the development of this business on a world-wide basis.

Discussion points and essay questions

1 Discuss the reasons why the Switzerland Convention and Incentive Bureau has concentrated on a mix of traditional and avant-garde features of Switzerland to develop business tourism in the country.
2 Explore the reasons that conference and meeting organizers need very detailed promotional information before they decide on a country venue for an event.
3 Customer loyalty schemes have been used very effectively in the hotel sector to develop business tourism. Explore the value of a destination marketing organization such as Switzerland using such a scheme.
4 Critically evaluate the importance of a well developed and reliable infrastructure in the development of business tourism to a country. Illustrate your answer with a number of examples.

The authors would like to thank Roland Minder and Kimberly Jeker for their help with writing this case study.

29 Iceland

Iceland has developed as an important business tourism destination. The marketing of Iceland as a business tourism destination has been important because the country decided not to concentrate on mass tourism due to the affluent highly developed nature of the country.

The island decided to concentrate on different specialist forms of tourism including:

- business tourism
- off-peak season weekend breaks which increase occupancy when business travellers have gone
- stopover for people using the services of the state airline, Icelandair, between Europe and North America
- activity holidays such as riding, walking and nature watching.

Iceland has concentrated on the development of particular types of business tourism, including the development of conferences and incentive travel and product launches. The choice of these types of business tourism has been a reflection of the type of facilities on offer and the unique nature of the island. The growth of interest in adventure tourism as part of incentive travel programmes has also made Iceland attractive as a conference and incentive travel venue.

The Iceland Convention and Incentive Bureau which is an arm of the Iceland Tourist Board, has been important in dispelling some of the myths about Iceland as a business tourism venue. These include the idea that Iceland is cold and has snow all year round, that it is inaccessible and that there are no suitable hotels with appropriate business facilities. The Iceland Convention and Incentive Bureau has carried out extensive press and public relations activity to improve the image of Iceland.

Iceland as a conference and incentive travel venue

The product that Iceland offers as a travel venue includes a package of different items. These items include the destination itself, transport and hospitality services. These are shown in more detail below.

The items that contribute to Iceland being an ideal conference and incentive travel venue

Destinations

Reykjavik is the capital of Iceland and offers the only real destination on Iceland with suitable facilities. Travel programmes can incorporate the many beautiful areas of the island, as follows:

- The Myvatn area in Northern Iceland which has volcanic terrain.
- Hveragerdi, a village where natural steam heats greenhouses where fruit is grown.
- Thingvellir, the site of the world's first Parliament.
- An inland desert which is uninhabited.
- Sea cruises to see whales, dolphins and seals.
- Mountains where people can cross a glacier on foot.

Hospitality

- A range of hotels in Reykjavik, the capital, many of which are family owned. There are a number of small specialist hotels with 30–40 rooms.
- There is range of accommodation outside Reykjavik including small and medium-sized privately owned hotels, schools, guest houses, mountain refuges and farms.
- A full range of Icelandic food and international cuisine is available at a wide range of hotels and restaurants.

Conference venues

- A range of small- to medium-sized facilities in large hotels and purpose-built conference centres such as the Haskolabio Centre in the capital Reykjavik, which has five auditoria seating 1600 delegates.

Ground handlers and destination management companies

- There are a number of specialist organizations that arrange conference and incentive travel to Iceland.

Transport

- Direct flights to Iceland from Amsterdam, Baltimore, Barcelona, Copenhagen, the Faroe Islands, Frankfurt, Glasgow, Gothenburg, Greenland, London, Luxembourg, Milan, Munich, New York, Orlando, Oslo, Paris, Stockholm, Vienna, Washington and Zurich, with Icelandair.

Iceland is an expensive place to stay, and it is for this reason that the country has decided to concentrate on the least price-elastic aspect of business tourism, namely, incentive travel. It is important that Iceland offers unique incentive products to justify the high prices that it charges for hotels, meals and other services.

The high price of visiting Iceland means that many of the companies that visit the island for conferences and incentive travel originate in Nordic countries. A small business has developed in individual business trips that is largely based on the main economic activities of Iceland, namely, fishing, fish processing and generation of energy from natural sources.

Promotion

The Iceland Conference and Incentive Bureau uses a number of techniques to attract business tourists. These include:

- specialist promotional literature for event planners
- press and public relations activity
- sponsorship of travel industry awards
- familiarization visits for potential visitors
- advertisements in trade and press journals – for example, *Conference and Incentive Travel*
- web pages dedicated to Iceland.

Conclusions

Iceland is a good example of a country that has specialized in the development of business tourism linked to conference and incentive travel. The beautiful location and the increase of interest in outdoor and activity-based programmes in wild landscapes have made Iceland an exciting destination for conference and incentive planners. Small amounts of business tourism also originate from the economic activities of the island. Iceland has used the techniques of niche marketing to develop specialist business tourism.

Discussion points and essay questions

1 Discuss the reasons how Iceland has developed business tourism opportunities.
2 Discuss the features that make Iceland an ideal location for that adventurous incentive programme.
3 Critically evaluate the problems that Iceland has had in their development as a business tourism destination.

30 The marketing of Portugal as a business tourism destination

Most countries are increasingly involved in marketing themselves as business tourism destinations. Portugal is one such country and in January 2000 it sponsored a thirty-two page 'Portugal' supplement in the trade magazine, *Conference and Incentive Travel*. It was a combination of text, photographs and advertisements, and was sponsored by the Portuguese Trade and Tourism Office.

The supplement covered the whole of the country and was subdivided between the various regions as follows:

- Introduction to Portugal: seven pages
- Lisbon area: five pages
- Estoril: two pages
- Porto: two pages
- Algarve: two pages
- Madeira: three pages.

The rest of the space was taken up with advertisements for the following destinations and organizations:

- Portuguese Trade and Tourism Office, London
- Lisbon Visitor and Convention Bureau
- Sheraton Algarve Hotel
- Viva Travel, Madeira
- Alfa Hotel and Congress Centre, Lisbon
- Orient Express Hotels – Lisbon, Algarve, Madeira
- Dom Pedro Hotel, Lisbon
- Miltours Portugal
- British Airways
- Estoril and Sintra municipal tourism offices
- Porto
- Madeira Technopolo International Congress and Exhibition Centre
- Pestano Hotels and Resorts.

Among the promotional messages contained in the text were the following:

- 'Significant investment in high-tech facilities and a new professionalism is providing a magnet for event organizers.'
- 'The country benefited from massive investment in the run up to Expo '98 in Lisbon.'
- 'Enjoy a warm welcome and the convenience of daily 3-hour flights to Lisbon' [from the UK].
- 'Portugal has . . . creative and attentive destination management companies who make sure everything happens with consummate ease and seamless efficiency.'
- 'The Portuguese Tourist Office recognises that first-class back up is . . . essential. To this end, existing convention bureaux in Lisbon and Porto will be complemented by the creation of a dedicated bureau in the Algarve this year, to be followed by Estoril and Madeira'
- '[In Lisbon], the Expo '98 has left a legacy of first class conference and exhibition facilities, improved transport infrastructure, a range of new and upgraded skills and . . . a senses of confidence.'
- 'The pretty coastal town of Estoril provides the perfect escape from city life and is investing in new facilities to boost business.'
- 'Porto is all set to burst on to the conference scene as a result of major investment surrounding its selection as [European] City of Culture in 2001.'
- An Algarve for all seasons . . . There is plenty to see within a convenient distance and we make it easy for delegates to get to these places.'
- '[Madeira] is building hotels and improving its infrastructure to create a first class conference destination.'
- 'Despite its natural beauty, Madeira is only now establishing itself in the conference market.'

The supplement also features a number of other elements designed to attract business tourism, including the following:

- information on transport, mainly air travel, to Portugal
- case studies of action to demonstrate Portugal's commitment to environmentally friendly tourism
- examples of successful business tourism events that have been held in Portugal
- details of individual venues – capacities for example – in the destinations within Portugal
- ideas for sample conference social programmes in Lisbon, Estoril, and Madeira
- examples of unusual venues
- details of golf courses, a major attraction for some business tourists
- information on new hotels.

Stephanie Roberts published an article in May 2000 in *Conference and Incentive Travel*, also on the subject of Portugal. This article included four pages of text and five pages of advertisements. This article discussed the ways in which destination marketers in Portugal were trying to increase business tourism in the country.

Among other actions the Portuguese Trade and Tourism Office have sponsored familiarization visits to Portugal for selected buyers, in association with TAP Air Portugal. One such trip was to Lisbon.

As Roberts says:

> *Many of the agents had not been to the city for some years, and were pleasantly surprised by the developments, although there were a few aspects they felt could be improved.*
>
> *'First impressions are important' says Ryan, 'and I thought the city looked a bit tatty in parts. But to be fair, I do need to see more of it to form a final opinion'.*
>
> *Business Travel Team's Rolinson takes a different view. 'It's a shame there is still so much construction going on in the city, but when it's finished, it will be amazing,' she says. 'Yet I think what Lisbon suffers from is not having a heart – especially as we're so used to seeing city centres in Europe'.*
>
> *Like most capital cities, Lisbon does have its run-down areas, but it also offers the visitor a wealth of beautiful architecture and monuments, their styles influenced by the myriad of settlers in Portugal. 'For groups that are here for conferences, a city tour is imperative' says Banks Sadler project manager Emma Crichton.*

The article also quoted the views on Lisbon of a particularly influential buyer, Emma Crichton of Banks Sadler. She said:

> *Banks Sadler usually take one or two groups a year to Lisbon, although I personally have only taken one group there in 1998. The group stayed at both the Caesar Park hotel and the Estoril de Sol, although we only used the conference facilities at the Caesar Park.*
>
> *I found Lisbon to have a good range of hotel and conference facilities, particularly for medium-sized groups of 150 to 200. However, I thought that the Expo site was too large for this size of group. And even if we did take a group in the future, there is the problem of not having enough hotel facilities on site. That would involve having to transport delegates between the site and the city centre.*
>
> *Lisbon does have good venues for gala dinners, the Penha Longa Palace, for example, is beautiful and is an excellent size. Lisbon is easily accessible from the UK and its climate is generally good. A group need not only visit Lisbon, I would recommend they team it with a trip to Estoril's beaches and shopping in Cascais.*

Clearly, such activities can have negative as well as positive aspects but they are essential to influence the opinion of those who make major decisions on business tourism event destinations.

The article also stressed:

● the range of unusual incentive package ideas to be found in the Lisbon area
● the wide range of venues to be found elsewhere in the country, rather than just in Lisbon.

Another specialist, David Baker, Managing Director of David Baker Travel added that: 'Co-operation between venues in Lisbon and Estoril would enhance UK knowledge of the market. 'I don't think Lisbon grabs people immediately, although there is enough to do. If the city combines its promotion with coastal towns such as Estoril and historical areas such as Sintra, it would attract more business.'

The Portuguese Trade and Tourism Office also exhibits at major industry trade fairs. From this article it appears that while a good start has been made, there is still much to do in marketing Portugal as a business tourism destination.

Discussion points and essay questions

1 What factors might limit the beneficial impact which the promotional activities outlined in this case study might have on the marketing of Portugal as a business tourism destination?
2 If you were responsible for the marketing of Portugal as a business tourism destination, what action do you think you would need to take in response to the comments made by Emma Crichton?

Part Six
Glossary of Terms

Business travel and tourism is a distinctive field, or perhaps more accurately, set of fields, each with their own vocabulary or jargon.

At the same time there are differences in the terms used in different parts of the world, and wide use is made of acronyms.

Here is a brief glossary which, it is hoped, the reader who is unfamiliar with the industry, will find helpful. While it has a European flavour, the glossary does endeavour to be as international as possible.

A further, much larger glossary is provided, for the meetings industry at least, in the *IAPCO Meeting Terminology*, 4th edition, published by the International Association of Professional Congress Organizers.

Glossary of terms

AACVB – Asian Association of Convention and Visitor Bureaux.

ABPCO – Association of British Professional Conference Organizers.

ABTA – Association of British Travel Agents.

ACE – Association for Conferences and Events.

ACS – Audiovisual Conference Service.

AEO – Association of Exhibition Organizers.

AIIC – Association Internationale des Interprètes de Conférence.

AIPC – Association Internationale des Palais de Congrès.

ASAE – American Society of Association Executives.

ATOL – Air Travel Organizers' Licence.

ATLAS – Association of European Universities and Colleges which teach tourism and leisure.

AV – audiovisual.

BACD – British Association of Conference Destinations.

BECA – British Exhibition Contractors Association.

BITOA – British Incoming Tour Operators Association.

break-out sessions – An element of a conference programme where the delegates split into smaller groups, to discuss different issues, normally in separate rooms.

BTP – Business Tourism Partnership.

BUAC – British Universities Accommodation Consortium.

build-up – period of time during which exhibition stands and displays are erected, that may be a number of hours or more than one week.

business traveller – traveller whose sole or main reason for travelling is to attend an activity or event related to their employment.

c and i – conference and incentive.

CHA – Corporate Hospitality and Event Association.

CLC – Convention Liaison Council.

CM – corporate meetings.

CMM – Certificate in Meetings Management.

conference/congress/convention – generally taken to be a large-scale meeting, called a conference in the UK, congress in much of Europe and convention in the USA, although there are some differences between them, technically.

consumer – person who actually travels and uses business tourism services.

convention bureau – an organization responsible for marketing a city or area as a convention destination.

corporate hospitality – providing opportunities for business clients to enjoy leisure experiences for business purposes, for example, attending Wimbledon tennis championships as a guest of a company.

CPA – Critical Path Analysis.

CRS – Central Reservations System.

customer – person or organization who makes purchase decisions and pays the bill, but may not actually consume the business tourism services, for example, an employer.

delegate – a person attending a conference or meeting, although technically it is a voting representative at a meeting.

destination – a geographical location where an event takes place.

EFCT – European Federation of Conference Towns.

EIBTM – A major annual industry trade fair.

ESAE – European Society of Association Executives.

ESITO – Events Sector Industry Training Organization.

EVA – Exhibition Venues Association.

exhibition – an event where businesses try to promote their products or services directly to a target audience or audiences.

exhibition manual – manual that contains everything of interest to an exhibitor in relation to a specific exhibition.

fmcg – fast-moving consumer goods.

floor plan – layout plan of the floor space of an exhibition including the location and dimension of specific exhibition stands.

HHC – Hilton Hotel Corporation.

HI – Hilton International.

HKCITB – Hong Kong Convention and Incentive Travel Bureau.

HKTA – Hong Kong Tourist Association.

HRW – Hilton Reservations World-wide.

IACVB – International Association of Convention and Visitor Bureaux.

IAPCO – International Association of Professional Congress Organizers.

IATA – International Air Transport Association.

ICCA – International Congress and Convention Association.

incentive travel – the use of a leisure travel experience to reward or encourage good performance at work.

IT – incentive travel.

ITMA – Incentive Travel and Meetings Association.

JMIC – Joint Meetings Industry Council.

MECC – Maastricht Exhibition and Congress Centre.

meeting – a smaller event generally than a conference.

MIA – Meetings Industry Association.
MICE – meetings, incentives, conventions, exhibitions.
modular stands – an exhibition stand with walls and ceiling, furniture and displays.
MPI – Meeting Professionals International.

NTO – national tourist organization.
NVQ – National Vocational Qualification.

official contractor – contractor appointed by exhibition organizers to provide a specific service to exhibitors. In general these contractors have exclusive rights to supply these services; in other words, exhibitors can only purchase from them.

package deal stands – stands at exhibitions where the exhibitor provides a package that includes display space, walls, furniture and lighting.
participants – anyone taking part in an event as a consumer.
PC – personal computer.
PCMA – Professional Convention Management Association.
PCO – professional conference organizer.
PEST – political, economic, technological, social.
plenary session – part of a conference where all sectors are together in the same room.
pre-registration – events where participants are encouraged to register/buy tickets before the event.
presentation – a generally formal set-piece communication of ideas or information to an audience during an event.
product launch – event or show with sole purpose of introducing a new product or service to a target audience, or audiences.
programme – the schedule for events at a conference, training course, exhibition, incentive travel package or product launch.
public exhibition – exhibition where visitors are members of the general public.

road show – the same event being staged in a number of destinations or venues simultaneously or consecutively.
RTB – Regional Tourist Board.

seminar – short, generally small-scale meeting, often designed to provide information/ knowledge for the participants.
SEO – Society of Event Organizers.
shell scheme stand – basic stand construction erected by official contractors.
SITE – Society of Incentive Travel Executives.
SNCF – Société National de Chemins de Fer.
space-only site – rental space only at an exhibition where exhibitors have to construct their own stand, subject to the regulations of the organizers.
ST – Switzerland Tourism.

trade exhibition – exhibition at which businesses promote their products and services to other businesses.
trade show – exhibition of goods and services that is not open to the general public.

training course – event where the aim is to bring people together to impart information or develop new skills amongst the participants. Normally these are quite small-scale events.

UIA – Union of International Associations.

UNESCO – United Nations Educational, Scientific, and Cultural Organization.

VAT – value added tax.

venue – a building or site where an event takes place.

Visitor and Convention Bureau – see convention bureau.

VR – Virtual Reality.

WEFA/WITC –

WTO – World Tourism Organization.

Select bibliography

Until very recently academics rarely wrote about business travel and tourism. Even today there is a paucity of theoretical writing on the subject.

On the other hand, there are a growing number of professional journals in the field of business travel and tourism which are rich in detail on topical issues and operational matters.

The Internet is also becoming a useful source for those seeking data on business travel and tourism products, services and destinations.

This bibliography is designed to make the researcher aware of the full range of sources of ideas and data in this vital sector of tourism.

Alford, P. (1999) Database marketing in travel and tourism. *Travel and Tourism Analyst*, **1**, 87–104.

American Society of Association Executives (ASAE) (1997). *Meetings Outlook Survey 1998*. American Society of Association Executives and Meeting Professionals International.

American Express UK (1997). *UK Meetings Market Survey*. Amex Card Division.

Astroff, M. T. and Abbey, J. R. (1995). *Convention Sales and Services*. 4th edn. Waterbury Press.

British Association of Conference Destinations (BACD) (annual). *British Conference Destinations Directory*. BACD.

British Assocation of Conference Towns (BACT) (1996). *Findings for the UK Conference Industry*. BACT.

British Conference Market Trends Survey (1998). Annual Report.

Carey, T. (1997). *Crisis or Conference?* Industrial Society.

Chen, J. S. (2000). A comparison of information usage between business and travel users. *Journal of Hospitality and Leisure Marketing*, **7** (2), 65–76.

Costley, T. (2000). British conference market. *Insights*, January, B33–B45.

Cotterell, P. (1994). *Conferences: An Organiser's Guide*. Hodder and Stoughton.

Davidson, R. (1994). *Business Travel*. Addison Wesley Longman.

Department of Trade and Industry (DTI) (1997). *The Future of the British Exhibition Industry*. HMSO.

Dwyer, L. and Forsyth, P. (1997). Impacts and benefits of MICE tourism: a framework for analysis. *Tourism Economics*, **3** (1), 21–38.

European Federation of Conference Towns (EFCT) (1997). *A Report on Europe in 1996*. EFCT.

Fenich, G. G. (1992). Convention centre development: pros, cons, and unanswered questions. *International Journal of Hospitality Management,* **11** (3), 183–196.

Gartrell, R. B. (1991). Strategic partnerships for convention planning: the role of convention and visitor bureaux in convention management. *International Journal of Hospitality Management,* **10** (2), 157–165.

Gartrell, R. B. (1994). *Destination Marketing for Convention and Visitor Bureaux.* 2nd edn. Association of Convention and Visitor Bureaux and Kendall/Hunt.

Guerrier, Y. (1999). *Organisational Behaviour in Hotels and Restaurants: An International Perspective.* South Bank University.

Hensdill, C. (1999) The rewards wars. *Hotels,* April, 30–1.

Horner, S. and Swarbrooke, J. (1996). *Marketing Tourism, Hospitality, and Leisure in Europe.* International Thomson Business Press.

Insights (1999). September, A57–A64.

Ioamides, D. and Debbage, K. G. (eds) (2000). *The Economics of the Tourism Industry: A Supply-side Analysis.* Routledge, London.

Ladkin, A. and Spiller, J. (2000). The European exhibition market. *Travel and Tourism Intelligence* (2).

Lawson, F. (1982). *Conference and Convention Centres.* Routledge.

Leask, A. and Hood, G. L. (1999). *Unusual Venues for Conferences in the UK. International Association of Professional Congress International Meetings Market (1999–2000).* ICCA in conjunction with Association Meetings International.

Leong, M. U. and Chaplin, M. N. (1999). A corporate strategy for the hospitable environment for business travellers in Macau. Paper presented to the ATLAS Annual Conference, Munich, September.

Lilley, P. (1998) Hotel world. *Travel and Trade Gazette,* December, 34–5.

Maitland, I. (1996). *How to Organise a Conference.*

Marie, K. S., Kasavana, M. L. and Knutson, B. J. (2000). smart card = meet smart meeting planner. *Journal of Hospitality and Leisure Marketing,* **7** (2), 77–85.

Meetings Industry Association (MIA) (1998). *Steps to Success in the Meetings Industry.* MIA.

Convention Liaison Council and Joint Industry Council. (1993) *Meetings Industry Glossary.*

McCabe, V., Poole, B., Weeks, P. and Leiper, N. (2000). *The Business and Management of Conventions.* Southern Cross University, Australia.

Mistilis, N. and Dwyer, L. (1997). Capital cities and regions: economic impacts and challenges for development of the MICE industry in Australia. In *Tourism and Hospitality Research Conference: Building a Better Industry.* Bureau of Tourism Research.

Montgomery, R. J. and Strick, S. K. (1995). *Meetings, Conventions, and Expositions: An Introduction to the Industry.* Van Nostrand Reinhold.

Munro, D. (1994). Conference centres in the 21st century. In *Tourism: The State of the Art* (A. V. Seaton, ed.), John Wiley.

Muqbil, I. (1997). The Asian conferences, meetings, and incentives market. *Travel and Tourism Analyst* (2), 38–56.

NEC Group (1998). *National Exhibition Centre/NEC Arena.* NEC Group.

O'Brien, U. (1998). The European business travel market. *Travel and Tourism Analyst* (4), 37–54.

Pemble, A. (2000) Takeover time. *Conference and Incentive Travel,* (July/August) 25–35.

Penner, R. H. (1991). *Conference Centre Planning and Design*. Widney Library of Design.

Polikka, E. G. (ed.) (1997). *Professional Meeting Management*. 3rd edn. Professional Convention Management Association.

Ransley, J. and Ingram, H. (eds) (2000). *Developing Hospitality Properties and Facilities*. Butterworth-Heinemann, Oxford.

Rockett, G. and Smillie, G. (1994). The European conference and meetings market. Economist Intelligence Unit. *Travel and Tourism Analyst*, **4**.

Rogers, T. (1998). *Conferences: A Twenty-First Century Industry*. Addison Wesley Longman.

Seekings, D. (1996). *How to Organise Effective Conferences and Exhibitions*. 2nd edn. Kogan Page.

Shane, A. (1998). *The Business of Conferences in the Hospitality and Leisure Industries*. Butterworth-Heinemann, Oxford

Society of Incentive Travel Executives (SITE) (annual). *Incentive Travel Fact Book*. SITE.

Swarbrooke, J. (1999). Sustainable Tourism. *Management*. CAB International, Wallingford.

Swarbrooke, J. and Horner, S. (1999). *Consumer Behaviour in Tourism*. Butterworth-Heinemann, Oxford.

TW Tagungs-Wirtschaft (1992). Investment in conference centres up to the year 2000.

Venue: The Worldwide Guide to Conference and Incentive Travel Facilities (annual). Haymarket.

White, S. (1995). Battle of the UK destinations. *Conference and Incentive Travel*, September, 27–32.

World Tourism Organisation (1997). *Tourist Safety and Security*. 2nd edition. World Tourism Organisation, Madrid.

Yeoman, A. and Ingolds, A. (eds) (1999). *Yield Management: Strategies for the Service Industries*. Cassell.

Trade journals

Association Executive
Association Management
Association Manager
Association Meetings
Association Meetings International
Business Traveller
Conference and Exhibition Fact Finder
Conference and Incentive Travel
Congress Convenciones e Incentivos
Convene USA
Corporate Entertainer
Executive Travel
Expo News Magazine
Incentive Today
Incentive Travel & Corporate Meetings
Meetings Congress

Meetings Facilities Review
Meeting Planner International
Meetings and Incentive Travel
Meridian
Quality Travel Magazine
Successful Meetings
The Organiser
Travel GBI
TW Tagungs-Wirtschaft

Internet

An increasing amount of information on this sector is now to be found on the Internet relating to:

- professional organizers
- venues
- destinations
- professional bodies.

Index